068

Patterns in the mind

For Amy and Beth

Patterns in the mind
Language and human nature

RAY JACKENDOFF

 BasicBooks
A Division of HarperCollins*Publishers*

First published in 1993 by Harvester Wheatsheaf.

ISBN 0–465–05461–7

94 95 96 97   9 8 7 6 5 4 3 2 1

Contents

Preface vii

PART I **The fundamental arguments**
1 Finding our way into the problem:
   The nature/nurture issue 3
2 The argument for mental grammar 8
3 The argument for innate knowledge 21

PART II **The organization of mental grammar**
4 Overview 39
5 Phonological structure 53
6 Syntactic structure 66
7 American sign language 83

PART III **Evidence for the biological basis of language**
8 How children learn language 101
9 Language acquisition in unusual circumstances I 112
10 Language acquisition in unusual circumstances II 126
11 Language and the brain 141

PART IV **Mental capacities other than language**
12 The argument for the construction of experience 159
13 Music and vision 165
14 Language as a window on thought 184
15 Social organization 204

Further reading 223
Index 241

Preface

During the first part of this century, the predominant view of the human mind, especially among American psychologists, was that it is purely a product of its environment. According to this "behaviorist" view, babies come into the world knowing virtually nothing, and, guided by rewards and punishments inflicted by the environment, learn the complex associations that determine the patterns of their adult behavior. Moreover, the behaviorists contended, a truly scientific approach must eliminate all mystical talk of "minds" and "thoughts"; proper objectivity confines us to the description of behavior.

An important challenge to this view arose in the late 1950s, when the young MIT linguist Noam Chomsky published his little book *Syntactic Structures*, followed by a blistering critique of B.F. Skinner's behaviorist manifesto, *Verbal Behavior*. Chomsky demonstrated that human language behavior can be explained only in terms of complex principles operating in the speaker's mind, principles that cannot be acquired by the simple mechanisms of association posited by the behaviorists. In so doing, Chomsky consciously identified himself with a tradition of "rationalist" thought stretching back to Descartes, a tradition that in fact continued actively in European psychology throughout the behaviorist period in America.

Chomsky's work was one of the early landmarks of what came to be called the "cognitive revolution." Along with cognitive psychology and artificial intelligence, Chomskian generative linguistics breathed new vigor into the study of the mind, a vigor that continues unabated in today's cognitive science and neuroscience. The mind (or the "mind/brain," as it is often called) is now widely viewed as a complex information-processing device, a sort of biological computer, made up of numerous parts devoted to specialized tasks—a far cry from the simplistic behaviorist view. It has even become possible and fashionable to do research on those forbidden fruits, mental imagery and consciousness.

I've written this book because, despite the influence that generative linguistics has had on the study of the mind and brain, its leading ideas have not become generally accessible. Having spent a quarter of a century immersed in research based on these ideas, and nearly that long conveying them to undergraduate classes, I felt it worth trying to convey my fascination and that of my colleagues to a broader audience. Maybe it is only the self-centered presumption of a practitioner, but I love this material, and I have come to believe that it ought to be part of every educated individual's intellectual repertoire. The conceptual foundations of linguistics are every bit as exciting as those of evolution, genetics, cosmology, chaos theory, and quantum electrodynamics—and perhaps more so, for what they tell us about our innermost selves.

In laying out the book, I have drastically compressed the mass of intricacy that has become the linguist's stock in trade, while still trying to convey the flavor of current thinking. In selecting the material, I found to my delight that much recent research strikingly confirms and amplifies many of the classic hypotheses and analyses of twenty and twenty-five years ago. Thus, rather than describing the work in any sort of historical order, I have found it more interesting to give an overall picture of where things stand *now*, supported by the interweaving of older and newer results.

My goal is to offer the reader a few evenings of engagement with the ideas of modern linguistics, without a great investment in technical detail. It is my hope that it can be appreciated by interested laypeople and by professionals in related fields, and that it can also serve as supplementary reading for undergraduate courses in linguistics, cognitive science, psychology of language, and philosophy of mind.

* * *

It's a pleasure to be able to thank so many colleagues who helped with this project: Ben Bahan, Ursula Bellugi, Derek Bickerton, Daniel Büring, Noam Chomsky, Leda Cosmides, Susan Curtiss, Dan Dennett, Alan Fiske, Susan Goldin-Meadow, Roberta Golinkoff, Myrna Gopnik, Morris Halle, Katharina Hartmann, Gregory Hickok, Judy Kegl, Marcel Kinsbourne, Steve Kramer, Fred Lerdahl, Joan Maling, Elissa Newport, John Tooby, Denise Umans, Moira Yip, and Edgar Zurif. All of these have been generous with information and discussion in their areas of expertise, filling in gaps in my knowledge, firmly correcting my infelicities, and in many cases offering helpful advice on the presentation of the whole book. Just as important have been the comments and suggestions from nonprofessional readers: Steve Umans, David Aaron, George Yip, my father Nathaniel Jackendoff, my brother Sim Jackendoff, and especially my wife Elise, whose constant encouragement kept me feeling that the book was necessary. I should also thank my students over the years at Brandeis, who have helped me see what works and what doesn't, and whose enthusiasm about these ideas motivated me to write the book. Bob Bolick, former editor at Harvester Wheatsheaf, really got me going on the project and was everything I could want in an editor in terms of hard positive thinking about content, style, and readership; as the book took shape, Farrell Burnett took his place and has been equally inspirational. Whatever reservations any of these folks may have about the final product, I have none about my deep appreciation for their part in the enterprise.

A terminological caution

It is common in everyday speech to use the term "linguist" to refer to someone who speaks several languages. In this book, however, I have used the term "linguistics" in its standard professional sense, to refer to the study of the organization of language; a linguist is someone who examines the structure of one or more languages in an attempt to discover general principles. A linguist tends to know a lot *about* various languages and may or may not speak them. For someone who speaks a lot of languages, I prefer the terms "multilingual" or "polyglot".

PART I
The fundamental arguments

1 Finding our way into the problem: The nature/ nurture issue

Why are we the way we are? Are we born that way, or are we products of our environment? Or some mixture? These basic questions lie at the root of any inquiry into human nature.

These questions can be interpreted in various ways. Most often, I find, people tend to think of "the way we are" in terms of differences among individuals: one's "nature" is seen as an issue of metabolism or intelligence or personality. What makes one person fat and another skinny, one sociable and one shy, one good at math and another good at art? Could they have been different if they had been brought up differently? Which things about ourselves can we change, and which are we fated to live with?

Another frequent interpretation of "the way we are" is in terms of differences among groups. Could people differ in intelligence, social behavior, or moral qualities along lines of race or gender or culture? If such differences exist, are they products of heredity or the environment? Far too often, alleged hereditary differences among groups have been used to justify repression, then "supported" with pseudo-scientific evidence. For the moment, let me only observe that even if such differences should exist, they provide no grounds, scientific or moral, for wholesale repression.

The main issues of human nature I want to think about in this book, though, are at the level of the species: What makes human beings the way they are? How are we different from animals? How are we like other animals and different from computers?

In order to find out what *makes* us the way we are, it stands to reason that we have to look closely at the way we are. If we want to know the balance of responsibility between nature and nurture—and how much about ourselves we *can* change—it helps to have a better idea of what the combination of nature and nurture is responsible *for*. In this book, I want to use human language as a vehicle for examining "the way we are."

I have two reasons for choosing language as a focus. First, the possession of language has always been regarded as one of the major differences between us and the beasts, so it's important to find out just exactly what we've got and they haven't. (We'll see in the next chapter how human language differs from other animal communication.) Second, and to me more important, the modern study of language has uncovered complexities of the mind far beyond what anyone would have imagined thirty years ago—complexities that draw on evidence from, and have implications for, fields as disparate as neuroscience, child development, philosophy, and literary criticism. Consequently, understanding language offers the prospect of integrating biological and humanistic views of "the way we are."

How might we bring language to bear on questions of human nature? One natural way is to ask: How is human experience affected by the fact that we can all speak and understand a language? A number of answers come to mind pretty easily. Most obviously, by virtue of having language, we have access to history: our ancestors have conveyed to us, through either written documents or oral tradition, a record of what happened before we were born. Along with history, we get our culture's accumulation of technology, world views, and rituals—not to mention legal systems, propaganda, gossip, and jokes. Little of this, if any, could be transmitted without language.

Another thing that language does for us is make it possible to coordinate the actions of large numbers of people. A bird's alarm call can make a whole flock flee at once. But people can communicate more differentiated things such as: "When I give the signal, you people over there pull on your ropes, and you people here let go of your ropes, and you other guys over there push like crazy." This kind of directed and coordinated action is hard to imagine without language, and it's necessary in order to do things like erect large structures, a hallmark of advanced civilizations.

The advantage that language is perhaps most often said to confer on us is that it enables us to think. While there is a great deal of truth to this idea—language certainly is invaluable in helping us sharpen certain kinds of thoughts—we should be a little cautious about endorsing it entirely. For one thing, we probably don't want to deny the capability of thought to at least some animals. For another, not all *human* thought requires language. Did it take thought for Beethoven and Picasso to produce their masterpieces? (I think so.) Did it take *language*? (I don't think so.)

Whatever the precise relation of language and thought, though, it is undeniable that human existence is deeply affected by the ability to speak and understand language.

In this book, however, I want to ask a different question about the relation of language and human nature: *What does human nature have to be like to account for the fact that we can all speak and understand a language?* That is, I want to discuss not the *consequences* of having language but rather the *prerequisites* for language: What do we need in order to be able to talk?

It's hard to think up plausible answers to this question. Or rather, the answers that spring immediately to mind turn out to be less than persuasive. For instance, one possible answer is that we have language because we have bigger brains than (other) animals. Let's be a bit more careful, though. After all, there are other animals with big brains—elephants and whales have brains bigger than ours, and the brains of bottlenose dolphins are larger in proportion to body size than ours—but they don't have language (or if they do, it's nothing like human language).

It's natural to think that a big brain makes us more intelligent, and because we're more intelligent we've figured out how to talk. But in what ways does a big brain make us smarter? As we'll see, it's not so obvious how being smart in and of itself makes talking possible.

In fact, there is a basic difficulty with an explanation that relies just on brain size. For now, it can be stated like this: you can't always get an entirely new function out of a device just by adding more of the same parts. To take a crude example, you can't get your car to fly by adding more cylinders to the engine, or more speeds to the transmission, or more wheels or bigger windows. Its existing function of carrying you along the road comfortably may be improved in some way, but the damn thing still only travels on the ground. To get it to fly, you need some sort of structural innovation like wings or a helicopter rotor. A major theme of this book is that the same is true of the brain and language: expanding a monkey's brain to the size of ours would still not enable it to talk. Beyond size, there has to be some difference in the way our brains are put together.

For the moment, the main thing is to appreciate how hard a problem this is. The fact that we can talk (and cats can't) seems so obvious that it hardly bears mention. But just because it's obvious doesn't mean it's easy to explain. Think of another perfectly obvious, well-known phenomenon: the fact that metals turn red when you heat them enough. Why does this happen? It could be otherwise—

they might just as well turn green or not change color at all. It's a simple phenomenon, easily observable, but the explanation isn't simple at all. It turns out to involve at the very least the theories of electromagnetic radiation and quantum mechanics, two of the more amazing intellectual advances of the past century. So it is, I want to suggest, with the human ability to use language.

The basic parameters underlying a theory of language ability were first laid out in the late 1950s and early 1960s by Noam Chomsky, who can justifiably be called the creator of modern linguistic theory (and who is, at the time of this writing, still doing pathbreaking research). I am going to lay these parameters out in a form that I'll call the two Fundamental Arguments. Just to give you an idea of where we are going, let me state them in very abbreviated form:

The Argument for Mental Grammar:
The expressive variety of language use implies that a language user's brain contains a set of unconscious grammatical principles.

The Argument for Innate Knowledge:
The way children learn to talk implies that the human brain contains a genetically determined specialization for language.

These two arguments lead us to the conclusion that the ability to speak and understand a human language (say English) is a complex combination of nature and nurture. Moreover, the part coming from nature involves more than a big brain: it is a specific human adaptation for language learning and use. The next two chapters will work through the Fundamental Arguments; Parts II and III will be spent explaining, qualifying, and elaborating them.

Part IV places the Fundamental Arguments in a larger context. It asks: If the human brain contains unconscious grammatical principles and a genetically determined specialization for language, what are the implications for other aspects of human behavior and experience? We will see that language is a revealing microcosm of the mind as a whole—that similar characteristics emerge in activities as disparate as seeing, thinking, listening to music, and taking part in a social environment. Along the way, we will present a third Fundamental Argument, whose consequences are perhaps even more radical than those of the first two:

The Argument for the Construction of Experience:
Our experience of the world is actively constructed by the
unconscious principles that operate in the brain.

I am shaping this book around the Fundamental Arguments because, of all the starting points I know for investigating language, they motivate the deepest possible scientific inquiry. On one hand, as we will see, they force us to integrate all sorts of issues from the broadest range of sources. And on the other hand, they yield the greatest insight into human nature in general: they allow us to see language as part of an integrated whole.

2 The argument for mental grammar

The communicative situation

Let's start with a fairly crude picture of the communicative situation—what goes on when one person says something to another.

Figure 2.1 *The communicative situation: Harry tells Sam about a tree*

In this picture (Figure 2.1), a pattern of light reflected off of a tree strikes the eyes of the person on the left (let's call him Harry). As a result of activity in Harry's nervous system, he comes to see the tree out there in the world. This is indicated in the picture by a tree inside a little cloud in Harry's head. Of course we know there are no clouds or trees in people's heads, and eventually (Chapter 13) we'll ask what's really there, but let this stand for the moment.

Once Harry has perceived a tree, it may occur to him that the word "tree" describes what he has seen—that is, the word "tree" is evoked from his memory. (If Harry spoke French rather than English, of course, the word "arbre" would be evoked instead.) This is indicated in the picture by the word "tree" in another little cloud in Harry's head. Again, we know there are really no little clouds, but this will have to do for now (we'll come back to it in Chapter 4).

Perhaps Harry decides to say something about the tree to the person on the right (let's call him Sam). Then Harry's nervous system causes his lungs to expel air, his vocal cords to tighten, and his tongue and jaw and lips to go through some gyrations. As a result, he produces some sound waves which travel through the air, striking Sam's ears, Sam's eyes, the furniture, and everything else.

But unlike Sam's eyes and the furniture, Sam's ears react to these sound waves by activating Sam's nervous system, so that he comes to perceive Harry uttering the word "tree." Assuming Sam also speaks English, his nervous system very likely goes on to produce a visual image of a tree—Sam is able to imagine what Harry sees, though probably not in many of its particulars.

Even this little dissection of the obvious has revealed quite a lot of complexity. There are a lot of parts to this simple communicative act, and each one of them involves tough puzzles. (For example: What is really in Harry's and Sam's brains instead of the little clouds? Exactly what gyrations of Harry's tongue, jaw, and lips take place? What happens in Sam's ears?) But we still haven't seen the full difficulty of the problem.

Suppose Harry wants to say something a little more interesting about what he sees than the single word "tree." Here are some things he might say (I'll put numbers and letters in front of example sentences so we can refer back to them later):

(1) *a* There's a bird in the tree.
 b A bird was in the tree yesterday.
 c Are there any birds in that tree?
 d A bird might be in the tree.
 e Birds like that tree.
 f That tree looks like a bird.

This time it isn't so easy to draw pictures in little clouds that depict what Harry has in mind. What difference can we make in the pictures in order to distinguish sentences (1a), (1b), (1c), and (1d)? (If we start putting question marks and writing in a picture, that's cheating—it's not just a picture anymore!) For sentence (1e), how do we show that the birds *like* the tree rather than, say, merely swarm around it?

In all the cases so far, the picture at least has both a bird and a tree in it, whatever its other failings. But what about sentence (1f)? What seems to come to mind is something like a bird-shaped tree. But such a picture has only one object corresponding to both words—yet another complication.

These examples illustrate some of the *expressive variety* of language—the number of different things we can say by combining words in different ways. Moreover, this expressive variety in many respects can't be conveyed by pictures, whether on a piece of paper or in the head. That is, significant parts of the messages that language conveys are abstract, or nonsensory, in nature.

Here we see a significant difference between human language and any of the forms of animal communication. To be sure, many kinds of animals convey information to each other. But in none of the known systems—birds, bees, whales, nonhuman primates, or whatever—is there an inventory of elements like words that can be combined and recombined in limitless new ways to express new messages. There are no elements that indicate points in time ("yesterday"), a desire for information ("are there . . . "), or possibility ("might"). Animals may have a way to indicate their own desires or feelings, but they can't convey someone else's, as in "Birds like that tree." Nor can animal communication systems explicitly draw resemblances among different objects, as in "That tree looks like a bird."

So, although people often speak loosely of animal communication as a kind of language, in fact the way animals communicate is orders of magnitude different from the way humans do. To make this distinction clear, I will adopt the policy of using the word "language" to mean only "human language (Spanish, Chinese, Navajo, etc.)," and I will use the more general word "communication" for any means by which information is conveyed, including both language and animal systems. (I will mention some attempts to teach human languages to apes in Chapter 10.)

The argument for mental grammar: The expressive variety of language use implies that a language user's brain contains unconscious grammatical principles

The expressive variety of language is the springboard for the first of the Fundamental Arguments. Any normal human being can understand and create an indefinitely large number of sentences in his or her native language. Aside from stereotyped utterances like "Hi, how are you?" and "Please pass the salt," most of the sentences we speak in the course of a day are sentences we have never heard or spoken in their entirety before. The same is true of most of the sentences we hear. For example, I doubt that you have ever heard or spoken any of the sentences on this page before. Yet you have no difficulty understanding them.

Let's think about what must be going on in your head that makes this possible. In the previous section we assumed that Harry and Sam could simply pull the word "tree" out of their memories when needed. Could this be true of whole sentences as well?

No. The number of sentences we are capable of using is just too large to store them individually. Let me run up the number in some rather stupid ways, just as a sample. Consider this series of sentences, all of which are perfectly comprehensible.

(2) Amy ate two peanuts.
    Amy ate three peanuts.
    Amy ate four peanuts.
       . . .
    Amy ate forty-three million, five hundred nine peanuts.
       . . .
       . . .

There are as many sentences in this series as there are nameable integers. The biggest number name listed in my Webster's Collegiate is a vigintillion (10^{63} in US/French usage; 10^{120} in British/German usage). With all the numbers up to this at our disposal, we can create more sentences in this series than there are elementary particles in the universe.

Here's another way to make lots of sentences. There are at least some tens of thousands of nouns in English. Let's be conservative and say we know ten thousand (10^4). Now let's construct all the sentences we can by putting in different nouns for X and Y in "An X is not a Y." Here are some of them.

(3) A numeral is not a numbskull.
    A numeral is not a nun.
    A numeral is not a nunnery.
       . . .
    A numbskull is not a numeral.
    A numbskull is not a nun.
    A numbskull is not a nunnery.
       . . .

A nun is not a nursery.

. . .

An oboe is not an octopus.

. . .

These are all completely absurd, but they *are* sentences of English nevertheless. There will be something like $10^4 \times 10^4$ of them $= 10^8$. Now let's put pairs of these sentences together with "since," like this:

(4) Since a numeral is not a numbskull, a numbskull is not a nun.

Since a numeral is not a numbskull, a numbskull is not a nunnery.

Since a numeral is not a numbskull, a numbskull is not a nuptial.

. . .

Since a numeral is not a nursery, a numbskull is not a nun.

. . .

Since an oboe is not an octopus, a numeral is not a numbskull.

. . .

And so on it goes, giving us $10^8 \times 10^8 = 10^{16}$ absolutely ridiculous sentences. Given that there are on the order of ten billion (10^{10}) neurons in the entire human brain, this divides out to 10^6, or one million sentences per neuron. Thus it would be impossible for us to store them all in our brains, in the unlikely event that we should ever want to use or understand any of them. But still, you did just understand a sampling of them. And these lists are only a minute proportion of the sentences you can understand. What lists include the sentences of this paragraph, for instance?

In short, we can't possibly keep in memory all the sentences we are likely to encounter or want to use—not to mention all the unlikely ones such as the sentences in (2)–(4). On the other hand, we are apparently ready to encounter them—we seem to know what the possibilities are.

The way the brain seems to achieve expressive variety is to store not whole sentences, but rather words and their meanings, plus *patterns* into which words can be placed. For example, it is only by using patterns that we can reasonably store the sets of sentences of which (2), (3), and (4) form a tiny sample: the pattern for the sentences in (2) is "Amy ate N peanuts"; that for the sentences in (3) is "An X is not a Y"; and that for the sentences in (4) is "Since an X is not a Y, a Z is not a W." With such patterns, plus a list of words to insert into them, we can specify a large number of possibilities at minimal cost in storage. Moreover, such a system is prepared for *novelty*: it can recognize or create examples of the pattern on the spur of the moment, whether or not they have been encountered before.

But even using these kinds of fixed patterns isn't quite good enough. Consider the list of sentences in (5).

(5) *a* Bill thinks that Beth is a genius.
  b Sue suspects that Bill thinks that Beth is a genius.
  c Charlie said that Sue suspects that Bill thinks that Beth is a genius.
  d Jean knows that Charlie said that Sue suspects that Bill thinks that Beth is a genius.
      . . .

This sequence can be extended as long as we have the patience—that is, it is effectively infinite. (To be more precise, there is no longest sentence in this sequence, because we can always add one more.) As a result, we can't specify a single pattern for this list the way we could for the lists sampled in (2)–(4). Rather, each sentence has to come from a different pattern, and the patterns get longer and longer. (6) shows the first three of these patterns; the term "Verbs" stands for one of the words "thinks," "suspects," "knows," and so forth.

(6) X Verbs that Y is a Z.
  W Verbs that X Verbs that Y is a Z.
  T Verbs that W Verbs that X Verbs that Y is a Z.
      . . .

Can we store all these patterns in our heads? Again, no, because no matter how many we store, there is always a longer one. On the other hand, there is clearly a more basic pattern involved: given any declarative sentence, we can make another declarative sentence by placing "X Verbs that . . . " in front of it. For instance, we can apply this pattern to any of the sentences in (2)–(4) above to get whole new classes of sentences. Here are some of them (marking in italics the sentence we started with): "Bill knows that *Amy ate two peanuts*," "Wolfgang realizes that *an oboe is not an octopus*," "Ludwig suspects that *since a numbskull is not a nunnery, a nun is not a nuptial*," and so on. This pattern can be summarized as the formula given in (7).

(7) X Verbs that S. (where S is any declarative sentence)

Going back to the sequence of sentences in (5), we can apply formula (7) to the sentence "Beth is a genius" to get "Bill thinks that *Beth is a genius*," sentence (5a). And then comes the fun: we can use our new sentence as the sentence *S* in formula (7), giving us "Sue suspects that *Bill thinks that Beth is a genius*," sentence (5b); then we can use *this* sentence as *S* in (7), giving us "Charlie said that *Sue suspects that Bill thinks Beth is a genius*," and so on as long as we want. That is, we get longer and longer sentences by applying formula (7) over and over to its own output, or *recursively*. What makes (7) different from the earlier patterns is that it contains another pattern within it: instead of just putting words into the slots in the pattern, we insert another pattern—in this case a whole declarative sentence.

This is a typical case of what we find in the course of investigating the expressive variety of language. The sequences in (8) and (9) show two more patterns with patterns inside them; as in (5), we can go on applying them recursively till our patience runs out.

(8) *a* Ben's father is a linguist.
     b Ben's father's older brother is a linguist.
     c Ben's father's older brother's best friend is a linguist.
     d Ben's father's older brother's best friend's former lover is a linguist.
          . . .

(9) *a* This is the house that Jack built.
     b This is the refrigerator that sits in the house that Jack built.
     c This is the cheese that fell out of the refrigerator that sits in the house that Jack built.
     d This is the mold that grew on the cheese that fell out of the refrigerator that sits in the house that Jack built.
          . . .

In short, in order for us to be able to speak and understand novel sentences, we have to store in our heads not just the words of our language but also the patterns of sentences possible in our language. These patterns, in turn, describe not just patterns of *words* but also patterns of *patterns*. Linguists refer to these patterns as the *rules* of language stored in memory; they refer to the complete collection of rules as the *mental grammar* of the language, or *grammar* for short.

This demonstration of the expressive variety of English, complete with recursive patterns, can be reproduced in any of the human languages of the world. The particular patterns of mental grammar may not be the same from one language to the next, but patterns of comparable complexity can always be found. In this respect, there is no difference between the languages of contemporary Western societies, those of present-day "primitive" cultures, and those of the distant past that can be recovered from written records. (An important exception arises in "pidgin" languages, to be discussed in Chapter 10.)

Clarifying the notion of mental grammar

The notion of a mental grammar stored in the brain of a language user is *the* central theoretical construct of modern linguistics. So it's important to make it as clear as possible before going on. Let me engage in a dialogue with an imaginary skeptic who raises some of the most common questions and objections.

Why should I believe that I store a grammar in my head? I just understand sentences because they make sense.

In reply I ask you: Why do some combinations of words "make sense" and others not? For instance, if we interchange adjacent words in the sentences in (2)–(5), to form chains of words like (10), we find that the sentences don't "make sense" anymore.

(10) Amy two ate peanuts.
A is numeral not a numbskull.
Bill that thinks Beth is a genius.
etc.

Why don't they make sense?

Well, these are sentences I've never heard before.

But look: You never heard the sentences in (2)–(5) before either, and even so, they "make sense" (albeit of a stupid sort).

What's the difference?

The difference is that the sentences in (2)–(5) are examples of patterns of English that we know, and the strings of words in (10) are not. That is, "making sense" involves, among other things, conformity to known patterns. In other words, the mental grammar plays some sort of role after all.

This is not to say that conformity to the patterns of English is the only factor involved in "making sense." Lots of sentences conform to the grammatical patterns of English but still don't "make sense."

(11) Colorless green ideas sleep furiously.
Bill elapsed three times this month.

I'm memorizing the score of the sonata I hope to
compose someday.
The harvest was clever to agree with you.

These examples (drawn from early writings of Chomsky's) are
certainly nonsense. But they do conform to the grammatical patterns
of English, as we can see by substituting one or two more "sensible"
words in each one:

(12) Large green lizards sleep soundly.
Bill sneezed three times this month.
I'm memorizing the score of the sonata I hope to
perform someday.
The lawyer was clever to agree with you.

On the other hand, notice that if we exchange adjacent words in the
sentences in (11), so that they violate the grammatical patterns of
English, they sound far worse: "Colorless green sleep ideas furiously," "Bill three elapsed times this month," etc. In this case, it's not
that they have strange meanings; rather, it's hard to say what they
mean at all. So the mental grammar seems to be involved even in
sentences like (11) that don't make sense.

In fact, we can recognize patterns of English even if not all the
words are real English words. This is the basis of Lewis Carroll's
famous poem *Jabberwocky*:

'Twas brillig, and the slithy toves
Did gyre and gimble in the wabe . . .

These lines are clearly an example of the same pattern as the
following, which contains all real words:

'Twas evening, and the slimy toads
Did squirm and wiggle in the cage . . .

This shows that the patterns themselves have a degree of life
independent of the words that make them up. Indeed, if you start
exchanging words at random in *Jabberwocky*, again the patterns fall
apart altogether.

Why do you want to call it a **grammar** *that I store in my
head? Why couldn't I just have a bunch of* **habits** *that I
follow in speaking and understanding English?*

My return question is: What is a habit anyway? It's something
stored in memory that guides behavior on appropriate occasions. If

the "habitual" behavior varies from occasion to occasion, as it does in the case of language, what is stored in memory has got to be a pattern. Why? Because the brain can't store all the individual examples—and even if it could, there would be no reason to call this random collection of behaviors a unified "habit."

Once we realize that habits must themselves be stored patterns, we shouldn't have a problem acknowledging that the "habits" of speaking English involve storing the patterns of English. That is, claiming that our knowledge of English is a kind of habit doesn't eliminate the need for us to have grammars in our heads.

What about people who speak ungrammatically, who say things like "We ain't got no bananas"? They *don't have grammars in their heads.*

This question points up an important difference between the ordinary use of the term "grammar" and the linguists' theoretical construct "mental grammar." In ordinary usage, "grammar" refers to a set of rules taught in school that tell us how we should speak in order to conform to the norms of polite (roughly, educated middle-class) society. "Proper grammar" frowns on the use of "ain't," the use of "got" for "have," and the use of double negatives; the "proper" way to say this sentence is "We don't have any bananas" or "We have no bananas." In the sense of "school grammar," then, speaking ungrammatically is a violation of a social norm, sort of like spitting in public.

The concept of "mental grammar" provides a different perspective on this issue. The mental grammar in our heads is what enables us to put words together into sentences. So it has to specify not just which patterns are socially acceptable and which are not, but *all* the patterns of the language. This includes some patterns that are much more basic than they ever had to teach us in school, for instance that the subject precedes the verb in English, or that adjectives precede the nouns they apply to ("ripe banana," not "banana ripe"). But it also includes some patterns that are much more complex than those taught in school, as we will see in the next few chapters.

What about the people who don't speak "correct English"? A moment's reflection suggests that their speech does in fact fall into consistent patterns. Someone who says "We ain't got no bananas" still doesn't produce monstrosities like "ain't no we got bananas" or "no got ain't bananas we": the words come in a well-defined order. More subtly, such a speaker won't substitute the so-called correct term "have" for "got," saying "We ain't have no bananas." In other words, there are principles that govern the use of "incorrect" English too, even if it violates the canons of school grammar.

This means that such speakers don't *lack* a mental grammar; they just have a mental grammar that is slightly different from that of speakers of "correct" English. Setting aside the issue of social approbation, the situation is exactly parallel to the difference between "proper" British and American English. Speakers of these two dialects have slightly different mental grammars, so the patterns they produce don't match up exactly. Consequently, each sounds somewhat exotic (or sloppy) to the other.

In short, although my imaginary critic may wish to deplore certain people's language from the point of view of school grammar, it is hard to deny that they have a mental grammar in their heads that governs their patterns of speech.

When I talk, the talk just comes out—I'm not consulting any "grammar in my head." If I look into my mind, I may find some scraps of school grammar, but you're trying to tell me that's not what mental grammar is supposed to be. So what is it supposed to be?

The answer to this question is potentially the most troubling. Here's the situation. We have just seen that an explanation of language ability demands that the patterns of language be stored in our memory somehow. We're now faced with the apparently conflicting fact that our memory reveals no such patterns to us. So something has got to give.

Can we give up the idea of a mental grammar? No: I've tried to convince you that just about any other way of thinking about the expressive variety of language amounts to the same thing. So let's grasp the other horn of the dilemma, and explore the hypothesis that the rules of language are not conscious, and are not available to introspection.

What could such a hypothesis mean? In this post-Freudian age, we are certainly accustomed to speaking of unconsciously (or subconsciously) guided behavior: "Willy has low self-esteem because he unconsciously identifies with his father." The premise of Freudian analysis, as well as most subsequent forms of psychotherapy, is that unconscious beliefs of this sort can be made conscious through suitable therapeutic procedures, and that in becoming conscious they cease to exert the same pernicious influence on one's experience and behavior.

Freud's notion that parts of the mind are not accessible to consciousness challenges the standard Cartesian identification of the *mind* with *consciousness*: there is a lot more going on in our minds than we are ever aware of. This is upsetting not only because it goes against intuition ("I *know* what I think!") but also because it tells us we are not altogether in conscious control of our behavior. What's more, the Freudian unconscious is full of dark and uncomfortable motives. (Freud stressed the sexual underpinnings of those motives, perhaps because of his social milieu; modern psychodynamic theory recognizes many other themes as well.)

In a way, the unconsciousness of mental grammar is still more radical than Freud's notion of the unconscious: mental grammar isn't available to consciousness under *any* conditions, therapeutic or otherwise. On the other hand, an unconscious mental grammar that guides our behavior is a good deal less personally threatening than an Oedipus Complex or a Death Instinct. Unlike these Freudian constructs, mental grammar doesn't have pernicious effects. On the contrary, we couldn't speak without it, except in terms of stereotyped fixed expressions. It is mental grammar that makes possible the expressive variety of our language.

You're telling me that a mental grammar is present in my mind but that I'll never find it by looking there? Aren't you trying to pull a fast one?

Well, consider: there are lots of other things going on in our brains of which we aren't conscious either. Think about getting from an intention such as "I think I'll wiggle my fingers now" into commands to be sent to the muscles, so that our fingers wiggle. Just how do we do it? From the point of view of introspection, the experience is entirely immediate: we decide to wiggle the finger, and the finger wiggles, unless there is some obstruction or paralysis. How the mind actually accomplishes this is entirely opaque to awareness. In fact, without studying anatomy, we can't even tell which muscles we've activated. So it is, I want to suggest, with the use of mental grammar.

If mental grammar can't be studied by introspection, then we have to find some other, less direct way to study it. I will take up this problem in Part II, showing how the investigation of mental grammar is an experimental science, and describing some of the organization that has been revealed by linguistic research. For now, the point is that if at least some other processes in the mind are not open to consciousness, it shouldn't be too distasteful to say that parts of language ability are unconscious too.

This, then, is our first inference about human nature on the basis of the nature of language. In order to account for the human ability to speak and understand novel sentences, we must ascribe to the speaker's mind a mental grammar that specifies possible sentence patterns. But in order to account for the fact that we have no direct access to this mental grammar, we must admit the possibility that some essential and highly structured parts of our abilities are completely unconscious.

3 The argument for innate knowledge

The character of language acquisition

We now turn to the preliminaries to the second Fundamental Argument. Suppose, following the discussion of the previous chapter, that we have mental grammars in our heads. The next question is: How did they get there?

Observation: All normal human children end up being able to speak whatever language is spoken in the community where they grow up. (If more than one language is spoken regularly, they usually end up speaking them all—but let's stick to the monolingual case for now.) And the language they speak has nothing to do with where their parents came from: a child of American parents growing up in Israel as part of a Hebrew-speaking community will become a native speaker of Hebrew; a Vietnamese baby adopted in Holland will become a native speaker of Dutch. So it's pretty obvious that children learn their language from the other speakers around them.

How do children do it? Many people immediately assume that the parents taught it. To be sure, parents often engage in teaching *words* to their kids: "What's this, Amy? It's a *BIRDIE*! Say 'birdie,' Amy!" But language learning can't be entirely the result of teaching words. For one thing, there are lots of words that it is hard to imagine parents teaching, notably those one can't point to: "Say 'from,' Amy!" "This is *ANY*, Amy!"

Think also about children of immigrants, say the Americans who move to Israel. The adults often never feel comfortable with the language of the adopted country. They speak with an accent, they express themselves with hesitation, they admit to not quite following the news on television, and so forth. Yet their children become fully fluent native speakers of the new language. Evidently the children have learned something their parents don't know. So the parents couldn't have taught them. Nor is the children's knowledge necessarily a result of teaching in school—and of course in nonliterate

21

societies it *can't* be the result of teaching in school. More often, the children just "pick up" the language from being with other children. (This example also touches on another phenomenon, the fact that adults usually have much more difficulty learning a new language than children do. I'll return to this in Chapter 9.)

Although children often learn *words* as a result of parental instruction, it is less clear that they learn *grammatical patterns* this way. Anyone who has attempted to correct a two-year-old's grammar will know that it can't be done. The following dialogue, recorded by the linguist David McNeill, is a famous illustration.

CHILD: Nobody don't like me.
MOTHER: No, say "nobody like*s* me."
CHILD: Nobody don't like me.
. . .
(eight repetitions of this dialogue)
. . .
MOTHER: No, now listen carefully; say "*nobody likes me.*"
CHILD: Oh! Nobody don't like*s* me.

(Of course, we can be sure that this child eventually got it right. But it may well have been at a time when the mother wasn't even paying attention.)

It is true that certain grammatical patterns *are* taught as part of school grammar, for example the rule that a preposition is something you must never end a sentence with. However, English speakers violate this rule all the time, and have for hundreds of years. I just did, two sentences ago. The idea that a preposition shouldn't occur at the end of a sentence seems to have arisen during the eighteenth century, when for the first time "authorities on English usage" sought to determine the "correct" way to speak, on the basis of the models of the classical languages Latin and Greek.

Now Latin and Greek genuinely do not allow sentences that end with prepositions. Neither do most modern European languages (for instance French, Italian, Spanish, and, with some caveats, German; Swedish, however, is more like English). If we translate "Who did she arrive with?" word for word into those languages—say, "Qui est-elle arrivée avec?" in French—it sounds as barbarous as "Harry ate peanuts a hundred" does in English.

By analogy, the "authorities" ruled that prepositions shouldn't end sentences in English either. Since that time, generations of children have been drilled on this rule, with little effect except in their formal writing. And ending sentences with prepositions is still very much alive in English.

Such proscriptive teaching of grammar, which evidently doesn't work very well, contrasts strikingly with aspects of English sentence patterns that probably nobody has ever thought to teach. Here's an example. Look at the four sentences in (1).

(1) *a* Joan appeared to Moira to like herself.
    b Joan appeared to Moira to like her.
    c Joan appealed to Moira to like herself.
    d Joan appealed to Moira to like her.

Without thinking about it consciously, you have automatically inferred that each of these sentences has a different combination of who is to like whom. In (1a), Joan likes Joan; in (1b), Joan likes Moira or some unspecified third party; in (1c), Moira is to like Moira; in (1d), Moira is to like Joan or a third party.

How do we come to understand these sentences this way? It obviously depends somehow on the difference between ordinary pronouns such as "her" and reflexive pronouns such as "herself," and also on the difference between the verbs "appear" and "appeal." But how? Whatever reasons there may be, I'm sure no one is ever taught about contrasts like this by their parents or teachers or anyone else. Yet this aspect of English grammatical patterns is deeply ingrained, much more so than the taught prohibition against ending a sentence with a preposition.

I can't resist another example, because it's so striking. There is an alteration called "expletive infixation" that many speakers perform on words of English under conditions of extreme exasperation, as in (2).

(2) How many times do I have to tell you? I'm not talking about the *Allegheny* River! Can't you get it into your stupid head that I'm talking about the *Susque-goddam-hanna*?

Even if you're too refined ever to use an expression like this, I'm sure you recognize it. Now the interesting thing is that we have pretty clear intuitions about how to use this infix. It sounds natural in the examples in (3), but decidedly odd in those in (4).

(3) uni-goddam-versity
    manu-fuckin-facturer
(4) Jacken-bloody-doff
    ele-goddam-phant

In addition, for those words that allow us to use the infix, we are very particular about where it has to go. If we try moving the infix to different places in the words in (3) ("un-goddam-iversity," "manufac-fuckin-turer," etc.) we can see that only the versions given in (3) sound at all acceptable.

I'm fairly certain none of us was ever *taught* the principle (or pattern) that says where it is possible to insert an expletive infix into English words. Yet we readily use this principle to make intuitive judgments about new cases. At the same time, the principle is not so obvious to conscious introspection.

(In case you're wondering, the infix sounds right only when it immediately precedes the syllable of the word with main stress— "Susque*han*na," "uni*ver*sity," and "manu*fac*turer." Since "*Jack*en-doff" and "*el*ephant" have main stress on the first syllable, there is no place to put the infix. But this is only a first approximation; there are further complexities that we can't go into here.)

We see, then, that much that we know about the grammatical patterns of English has not been taught. But this leads to a further problem about how children acquire language. Chapter 2 showed not only that we have a mental grammar, but that most of it isn't available to conscious introspection. Since adults aren't consciously aware of the principles of mental grammar (and the examples just presented provide further illustration), they certainly can't explain these principles to children—if children could understand the explanations in any event!

In fact, the most an adult can do is supply the child with *examples* of the patterns, in the form of grammatical sentences, or corrections to the child's sentences. For instance, notice that in the dialogue I quoted above, the mother isn't saying " 'Nobody' and 'not' are both negative words, and you shouldn't use two negatives in a sentence." She is just supplying the child with a correct *form*. This means that the child has to *figure out* the patterns of the language— that is, <u>the child has to construct his or her own mental grammar</u>.
 How?

Children are probably no more conscious of the patterns than adults. For instance, it doesn't make much sense to think that a child would confront sentences like "Joan appeared to Moira to like herself" by thinking "Hmm. I wonder who 'herself' is supposed to be. Well, 'herself' is a reflexive pronoun, so that probably makes a difference . . ." To be sure, children eventually learn the words "noun" and "verb," and maybe even "reflexive pronoun," but usually not until the age of ten or so, long after gaining command of the grammatical distinctions these words refer to.

Even simpler phenomena show the disparity between children's command of language and their *conscious* command of it. For instance, by the age of three or four, children can be taught to count syllables in a word, but they are certainly making use of syllables long before that. Similarly, learning to read depends in part on being conscious of sequences of speech sounds, in order to sound out words. For many children, this is difficult at age six and even later; that's why *Sesame Street* spends so much time on it. But at the same time, children couldn't discriminate and understand thousands of words by this age—not to mention appreciate rhymes—if they didn't have a sensitive ability to discriminate and sequence speech sounds. (We will see in Chapter 5 how this ability is organized.) So we're evidently faced with the same problem for children as for adults: their learning is backed by unconscious principles that are unavailable for conscious introspection. And if anything, we're tempted to suspect that children's abilities at introspection are less well developed than adults'.

Where does that leave the learning of language? On the basis of what the child hears in the environment, and in the (near-) absence of teaching and of conscious awareness of what is being learned, the child manages to acquire a command of the grammatical patterns of the language—that is, manages to construct a mental grammar. This isn't the way we're accustomed to thinking of language learning. We usually think of it in terms of something like French class in school, a highly structured situation in which teacher and learner bring a lot of conscious attention to bear on rules and regulations. The child's learning of grammatical structure just doesn't seem to be like that. The child learns just by speaking and being spoken to.

As a result, we can draw another conclusion about human nature: *We can acquire unconscious patterns unconsciously, with little or no deliberate training.* Perhaps we shouldn't even call such a process "learning," but for lack of a better word, let's leave the terminology alone.

A suggestive parallel to the unconscious learning of language might be the process of learning to skip, which requires complicated patterns of muscle coordination. It's impossible to describe to a child how to do it; the best we can do is demonstrate. And when the child figures out how to skip, it will be impossible to get him or her to explain it. Rather, the process of constructing the patterns takes place outside of consciousness; the major part of the learning is experienced as "just intuitive."

The argument for innate knowledge: The way children learn to talk implies that the human brain contains a genetically determined specialization for language

Here is what makes the child's acquisition of language even more remarkable. Thousands of linguists throughout the world have been trying for decades to figure out the principles behind the grammatical patterns of various languages, the very same grammatical principles that children acquire unconsciously. But any linguist will tell you that we are nowhere near a complete account of the mental grammar for any language. In other words, an entire community of highly trained professionals, bringing to bear years of conscious attention and sharing of information, has been unable to duplicate the feat that every normal child accomplishes by the age of ten or so, unconsciously and unaided. This contrast is so striking and so fundamental that it deserves a name. I like to call it the Paradox of Language Acquisition.

! ! !

What are we to make of this? How could linguists apparently be so inept compared to children, including the children they once were? Unfortunately, one commonly held attitude is that in fact linguists are just misguided, and that the complications they are struggling with simply don't exist. "Language just has to be simple: even a child can do it."

But if language is so simple, why hasn't anybody else, maybe someone without linguists' methodological blinders, figured it out either? As a case in point, one of the early predictions of the computer revolution was that we would have computers that talked to us and understood us within five years or so, as soon as we could build a machine big and fast enough.* But at the time of writing, forty years later, state-of-the-art computer understanding of spoken

---

* In fact, Chomsky's first book, *Syntactic Structures*, which appeared in 1957, acknowledges support from the US armed forces, who were at that time funding research on computer analysis of language. Why were the armed forces interested? Among other things, a "voice-writer," a computer that could take dictation, would be pretty handy for tapping phones.

and written language is pretty rudimentary, and one still often hears the prediction that a full solution is only five years off! So the computer people are evidently no better than linguists at figuring out the organization of language—they are just more optimistic.

A more romantic approach to the Paradox might go something like this: "Children are just so wonderfully open and unselfconscious about the world around them! Look! They can pick up language without thinking about it, while we poor adults are hobbled by our self-conscious hangups." Now while there may be a grain of truth in this, it has to be an oversimplification. Why can we think more clearly than children about simple things like income taxes and going to the dentist, but not about the organization of language? Along with our "self-conscious hangups" does come some sophistication, after all. So the Paradox remains: there is something special about language learning that isn't available to adults, and it still remains to be explained what mechanisms permit children to pull off the feat. Saying that it's wonderful and unconscious doesn't *explain* it, it just restates the problem. We still want to know how it works.

There are three steps involved in escaping the Paradox. The first two have already been touched on. First, as shown in Chapter 2, what the child ends up with is a mental grammar that is completely inaccessible to consciousness. Hence adult linguists can't figure out the principles of mental grammar just by looking into their minds. Second, as shown in the last section, a substantial part of the language-learning process is also unconscious, so linguists can neither directly observe it nor ask children about it.

But to escape the Paradox, a third step is needed. Remember: children can't just "absorb" mental grammar from the surroundings. All they can hear in the surroundings are sentences; they must (unconsciously) discover for themselves the patterns that permit them both to understand these sentences and to construct new sentences for other people to respond to. Whether this process of discovery goes on unconsciously in the child or consciously in the linguist, the very same problems have to be solved. That is, doing it unconsciously still gives the child no advantage over the linguist.

About the only way anyone has devised to overcome this difficulty is to suppose that *children have a head start on linguists*: children's unconscious strategies for language learning include some substantial hints about how a mental grammar ought to be constructed. These hints make it relatively easy for them to figure out principles that fit the examples of language they are hearing around them. (Only *relatively* easy: it still takes them eight or ten years!) By contrast, though, linguists have no such hints at their conscious disposal, so the problem is much harder for them. To invoke a crude metaphor, linguists are in the position of searching for a needle in a haystack, but children have a powerful magnet that pulls the needle right out.

For a more biological analogy, perhaps language acquisition is something like reproduction. Just about everybody figures out how to reproduce—it seems pretty easy! But it has nevertheless taken centuries of research to understand the actual mechanisms of reproduction, and we don't have a complete account even yet. Does that mean that biologists are inept? Of course not. We don't expect them to have conscious access to the biological mechanisms of reproduction. Somehow, though, because language is in the *mind*, we are more prone to thinking we should be able to understand it readily. Again I want to stress that we have to give up this preconception. We must realize that some parts of our minds are as distant from awareness as our chromosomes are.

Somewhat more technically, the claim is that all of us as children come to the task of language learning equipped with a body of innate knowledge pertaining to language. Using this knowledge, children can find patterns in the stream of language being beamed at them from the environment, and can use these patterns as a mental grammar. Because this innate knowledge must be sufficient to construct a mental grammar for any of the languages of the world, linguists call it *Universal Grammar* or *UG*.

Well, fine, but how is that different from the "romantic" solution? The difference is that it doesn't just revel in the mystery of the child's ability. Rather, it leads to three important questions for research:

1. What do children know (unconsciously) about language in advance of language learning? That is, what is Universal Grammar?
2. How do they use Universal Grammar to construct a mental grammar?
3. How do they acquire Universal Grammar?

I'll set questions 1 and 2 aside until subsequent chapters, when we have a better idea of what a mental grammar is. At the moment I want to think about question 3, the issue of how there could be such a thing as "innate knowledge"—knowledge that is not learned.

First I have to deal with a couple of simple matters. For one thing, we have to keep remembering that Universal Grammar is every bit as unconscious and inaccessible to introspection as the final mental grammar the child achieves and we adults use. So we have to tolerate a certain degree of strangeness in the use of the term "knowledge."*

"Innate" is also used a little loosely, in that I am not necessarily committed to its presence immediately at birth. Like the teeth or body hair or walking, Universal Grammar could just as well develop at some considerable time after birth; what is important is that its development is conditioned by a biological timetable. In fact, children usually begin acquiring grammatical patterns sometime toward their second birthday (although, as will be mentioned in Chapter 8, there are earlier precursors).

However we describe it, though, the point is that Universal Grammar is not learned. Rather, it is the machinery that makes learning possible. So question 3 amounts to this: How can knowledge or cognitive organization be available to the child *before learning*?

Fortunately, the outlines of a mechanism behind innate knowledge are available. Two components are involved: the determination of brain structure by genetic information, and the determination of mental functioning by brain structure. Let me take these up briefly in turn.

First component: Until relatively recently, it was a major mystery how organisms reproduce their own kind—how it is that people give birth to little people and pigs to little pigs, but not the other way around. One of the major achievements of twentieth-century science is some understanding of the mechanisms that determine inheritance of the physical structure of organisms: genetic material, coded in the cells' DNA and passed on from generation to generation, determines the physical arrangement and functioning of the body. Although the precise steps by which the genetic material guides the development of the body are as yet mostly unknown, we have for the first time a way of describing the physical basis of reproduction, inherited characteristics, mutation, and evolution.

* The philosopher Gilbert Ryle has made a distinction between "knowing that" (for instance, knowing that Grant's wife is buried in Grant's Tomb) and "knowing how" (for instance, knowing how to swim). The latter might be called "operational knowledge" or "skill"—it is not necessarily verbalizable. And perhaps we can best think of the child's knowledge of *how* to learn language as like this. (There are some tricky caveats in this, though, because Ryle himself intended the term purely behaviorally: it's not clear he would have been willing to say that someone who has been paralyzed still "knows how to swim." I would.) In any event, for lack of a better term, I'll continue to use the term "knowledge," though it should be clear that I intend the term in the very special sense we have been working out here.

Among the parts of the body determined by the DNA is, of course, the brain. Its anatomical structure is highly complex—at least as complex as that of, say, the little finger. So, although there is some plasticity in the brain's physical organization, there is good reason to believe that substantial aspects of this organization are genetic. As Chomsky often puts it, we don't *learn* to have arms rather than wings. Why, then, should we suppose that our brains acquire their fundamental structure through learning rather than genetic inheritance?

Second component: The way we think is partly constrained by the way our brains are built. Hardly anyone disputes this: for instance, you are relying on this assumption when you claim that we are smarter than animals because we have bigger brains. Now the idea of innate knowledge of Universal Grammar can be rephrased, if you like, as saying that children have a certain "way of thinking" that enables them unconsciously to construct a mental grammar, given appropriate inputs in the surroundings. The hypothesis, then, is that this "way of thinking" is a consequence of the physical organization of some part of the brain—which is in turn determined by genetic structure. In short, *the mechanism for acquiring innate knowledge is genetic transmission, through the medium of brain structure.*

This hypothesis—let me call it the *Genetic Hypothesis*—leads us into a rich range of issues. For it says that the ability to learn language is rooted in our biology, a genetic characteristic of the human species, just like an opposable thumb and a pelvis adapted for upright stance. This means that we can draw freely on biological precedents in trying to explain language.

For example, think of all the surprising structural specializations in the organisms of the world—the elephant's trunk, the bat's sonar, or the little bones of our middle ear. Given such biological precedents, it hardly seems outlandish that there might be a structural specialization in the brain for language (and language learning).

Next consider the fact that the "innate knowledge of language" doesn't seem to be present at birth, but begins to manifest itself at around the age of two. According to the Genetic Hypothesis, this knowledge is determined by brain structure, so it is present only when the supporting brain structures are present. Now development of the physical structure of the body, including the neural structure of the brain, is by no means complete at birth. Among other things, in the newborn's brain the myelin sheaths that serve to electrically insulate the neurons from each other are not yet fully developed. Further, as suggested earlier, the physical growth of various parts of the body follows a fairly predictable timetable: think of the developmental sequence of baby teeth followed by adult teeth, or the body changes of puberty, not to mention more dramatic developments in other species such as tadpoles turning into frogs. There is no reason why the development of the particular brain structures that support innate knowledge about language couldn't be like that. In other words, gradual development of innate knowledge over several years of life is very much in line with other developmental phenomena.

This is not to say that we should go out and start looking for the "gene for language." The connections between DNA sequences in the chromosomes and the body's structure are exceedingly indirect. Biologists are just beginning to figure out how the genes guide the differentiation of the embryo into head, middle, and tail, about the crudest of all body structures. When it comes to the exquisite differentiation of the brain (or heart, or ear, or wrist), we are very much in the dark. In addition, we know almost nothing about how brain structure governs the nature of thought. So both components of the Genetic Hypothesis leave a lot of questions at the moment. Still, the Genetic Hypothesis seems to be a plausible way—and maybe the *only* plausible way—of providing the child with innate knowledge. It can hardly be said to be *proven*, but all the pieces of it look reasonable.

Let's try to put this all together, tracing our argument back to our initial questions. (1) We arrived at the Genetic Hypothesis as a potential answer to the question of how there could be such a thing as innate knowledge. (2) Why did we need innate knowledge? We needed it in order to solve the Paradox of Language Acquisition —how it is that all children can unconsciously "pick up" a mental grammar on their own, while linguists as a community can't figure out completely how the mental grammar works. That is, the Paradox shows how difficult the task is that children accomplish. Innate knowledge of some aspects of language would give children a head start on learning the language spoken in the environment.

(3) Why does the Paradox of Language Acquisition arise? Because, as we showed, children mostly don't learn language by being taught. Rather, they must be unconsciously figuring out a mental grammar that gives them the patterns for forming sentences. (4) How do we know that children must be figuring out an unconscious mental grammar? Because that's what they have to end up with as adults, in order to account for their ability to speak and understand an unlimited range of sentences they have never heard before.

Questions about innate knowledge

For some reason, the hypothesis of a genetically determined Universal Grammar has provoked various degrees of astonishment, disbelief and outrage since the time it was proposed by Chomsky. Let me try to defuse some of the more common reactions, once again through a conversation with my imaginary skeptic.

> *The child's acquisition of language clearly depends on exposure to language in the environment. So why should we believe that it is genetically determined?*

The answer is that one's language ability is a complex combination of nature and nurture. A biological comparison may be helpful here. Our bone structure is obviously genetically determined, but it can't develop properly without nourishment and exercise. In this case it's clear that environmental interaction complements genetic endowment: both are necessary. Why shouldn't the same be true of the brain structure that supports language, where "nourishment" includes a sufficient quantity and variety of incoming information, and "exercise" includes the opportunity to converse with people?

> *I don't mind the idea of a genetic component to learning, so long as none of it is specifically linguistic, that is, if it consists only of general-purpose learning strategies such as stimulus–response learning or principles of association or analogy. But why do you insist that there is a genetic component of learning that has to do specifically with language?*

The problem is that general-purpose learning strategies alone can't solve the Paradox of Language Acquisition. Adults, including adult linguists, have access to plenty of general purpose strategies, but they can't figure out the organization of mental grammar. We have to suppose that children know something more, something specifically about *language*. Still, this is not to say that language acquisition doesn't make use of more general learning strategies. It is just that this cannot be all there is.

> *But how could a brain structure for Universal Grammar have originally come to be coded into the genes?*

The only possible answer is evolution. Unfortunately, there isn't any record of the evolution of language: we can't dig up fossil vowels or verbs, and the earliest written documents already display the full expressive variety and grammatical complexity of modern languages. So the route by which language evolved is pretty mysterious. It is easy to see how having language would confer a selective advantage in the course of evolution, but presumably it didn't spring into existence full-blown. What are the steps on the way? There are not just one but many missing links.

On the other hand, evolution gives us an interesting angle on the Paradox of Language Acquisition. For it says that language acquisition doesn't just take ten years of the child's life. Those ten years are backed up by a couple of million years that evolution has spent developing in the brain the Universal Grammar that children start with—more time than linguists will ever have!

Isn't the Genetic Hypothesis just a "null hypothesis," a desperate move to explain away all this embarrassing complexity?

Remember: we're stuck between a rock and a hard place. On one hand, the expressive variety of language demands a complex mental grammar that linguists can't entirely figure out. But on the other hand, children manage to acquire this grammar. Thus, in a sense the Genetic Hypothesis *is* a move of desperation. As I said earlier, it's the only answer anybody has been able to think of; different schools of thought disagree mainly in exactly what and how much they think is innate.

Still, I don't think the Genetic Hypothesis is an attempt to explain the complexity *away*. One can imagine a similar criticism of the theory of gravitation: "The theory postulates an occult, invisible force; it just restates the facts of the interaction of physical bodies without explaining them." In fact, the Genetic Hypothesis plays much the same role in linguistics as the hypothesis of gravitation does in physics. It is a construct which, as we will see, serves to unify a large body of diverse facts from language structure, language universals, and language acquisition.

In turn, like the theory of gravitation, the Genetic Hypothesis calls for eventual deeper explanation. But remember, it is over three centuries since Newton postulated a gravitational force, and we don't yet have an entirely satisfactory theory of how gravity works. So I'm inclined to counsel patience.

Conclusions

Putting together all the considerations of the past sections, our proposed account of mental grammar takes the following overall form:

Mental Grammar = Innate Part (Universal Grammar)
               + Learned Part

In trying to understand the mental grammar of English (or Chinese, or whatever), linguists try always to find the simplest possible account, consistent with the complexity of the facts of the language. At the same time, rather than insisting that language is all learned (or all innate), we leave it as an empirical question to determine how the mental grammar is parceled out between innate and learned parts. Three basic criteria are involved.

1. If the language in question is different from other languages in some respect, the child must be able to acquire this difference, so it must fall into the learned part.
2. If certain aspects of all languages we have examined are alike, these aspects are *likely* to fall into the innate part. Of course, there is always the possibility that they are alike purely by accident. In practice, this can be checked out by examining more languages, preferably unrelated ones.
3. Suppose there is some aspect of language that children couldn't possibly figure out from the evidence in the speech they hear around them. Then this aspect can't be learned; it has to fall under the innate part of the language.

The last of these criteria has been called the "poverty of the stimulus" argument. Its use requires a certain amount of care, and in fact there is a running debate on what sorts of evidence children are capable of using. We have already encountered this debate in discussing the character of language learning; there is more to come in succeeding chapters.

We can go a step further and decompose the innate part of language like this:

Innate part of language = Part due to special purpose
                          endowment for language
                        + Part due to general properties of
                          the mind

Again, rather than insisting that language is based entirely on general-purpose principles, or entirely on principles peculiar to language, we leave it to be decided by research how the work is divided up.

I sympathize with those who are suspicious of a specific

language capacity: we *should* try to minimize the first factor. A special-purpose endowment for language, after all, demands an evolutionary jump during the time since we diverged from the apes, and we would like to think that the jump was not too extraordinary. But that doesn't mean we can eliminate it altogether: *something* has to account for the Paradox of Language Acquisition.

To close this chapter, let's recall our initial question: What does human nature have to be like in order for us to be able to use language? Two more answers, having to do with the nature of learning, have emerged from the Argument for Innate Knowledge.

First, the learning of language isn't just a passive "soaking up" of information from the environment. Rather, language learners actively construct unconscious principles that permit them to make sense of the information coming from the environment. These principles make it possible not just to reproduce the input parrotlike, but to use language in novel ways. What is learned comes as much from inside the learner as from the environment.

Second, we have spent considerable time chewing over the idea that certain aspects of our knowledge of language must be derived genetically, rather than through learning *per se*. We have concluded that the child's language ability comes from a combination of environmental influence, which is obvious, and heredity, which is far less so. The fact that language learning is supported by a genetic component is what makes the task possible for every normal child, despite the complexity of the resulting knowledge.

Is the learning of language just a curious exception in the story of human learning, or are other kinds of learning like this too? If they are, there are strong implications for one's approach to education: one should see the learner as an active agent of learning, not just a vessel to be filled with facts. Education should stress the learner's engagement and creativity, for ultimately the learner must construct the knowledge in his or her own mind.

Similarly, we can ask if other kinds of learning are, like language acquisition, supported by some sort of special-purpose innate endowment. If this is the way language is, what about all the other things we do? We will return to this question in Part IV, after working out our ideas about language itself more clearly. But in the meantime, it should remain lurking in the background, for this is ultimately the issue that makes the study of language absolutely crucial to understanding ourselves.

PART II
The organization of mental grammar

4 Overview

Language as a conversion between thought and sound

Let's return to the basic communicative act sketched in Chapter 2—
one person saying something to another. To begin with, I'll simplify it
even more.

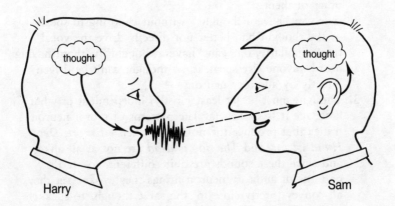

Figure 4.1 *A speech event*

Something in Harry's brain that we might as well call a "thought"
results in movements of his vocal tract (lungs, vocal cords, tongue,
jaw, and lips), which in turn create a sound wave that is transmitted
through the air. This sound wave, striking Sam's ear, results in Sam's
having the same "thought" (or a similar one) in his brain.

Of course the brain doesn't move the vocal tract by magic. It
employs its usual means of bringing about motor activity: neural
activation of the muscles. In other words, Harry's brain creates

patterns of neural firings that drive the muscles of his vocal tract. His vocal tract, by being so activated, creates and broadcasts the acoustic patterns that we hear as speech.

Noises going into Sam's ears don't create thoughts in his brain by magic either. Rather, the inner ear turns acoustic waveforms into patterns of neural firings that are transmitted to the brain.

Consider now the patterns of neural firings that activate the vocal tract, and those that reach the brain from the ears. Neither of these patterns can in itself be the thought transmitted by the speech event. In case this isn't ridiculously obvious, here are three reasons why.

1. The form of the thought must be neutral between spoken and heard language—we must be able both to speak the thought and to hear it—so it had better not be a pattern of neural firings that pertains specifically to one or the other of them.

2. One can "have a thought" without choosing to speak it, so the thought had better not directly drive the vocal tract. Similarly, one can "have a thought" without having heard anyone else speak it, so thought can't be driven directly by auditory neurons.

3. Thought must be (at least mostly) independent of what language it is spoken in. The patterns of motor neuron firings that produce the noises *Le chien est mort, Der Hund ist tot*, and *The dog is dead* are not at all alike; and since these sounds are quite different, so are the patterns of auditory neuron firings they evoke. Yet they all convey (pretty close to) the same thought to speakers of French, German, and English respectively. In order for us to be able to translate among languages, there must be a constancy in the thought being expressed that isn't present in the motor or auditory patterns. In short, we have to identify the thought with a pattern of neural firings that is distinct from both the motor and auditory patterns.

(By the way, what can it mean to say a thought is a pattern of neural firings? If you find this idea troublesome, please bear with me until Chapter 14, when we confront this issue a little more closely.)

This conclusion requires us to add a further piece to the picture: the brain has to have a way to convert the patterns of neural firings that constitute the thought into the patterns that drive the vocal tract, plus a way to convert the patterns of firings produced by the inner ear into those that constitute thought. Figure 4.2 sums up our analysis so far. (The heads in Figure 4.1 are cute but a nuisance to draw, so I'll schematize a little: the solid line indicates the boundary between the person's body and the outside world; the dotted line indicates the boundary between the brain and the rest of the body.)

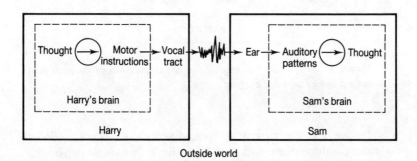

Figure 4.2 *Conversion of thought into sound waves and back again*

We now begin to home in on where language fits in: it is the brain's means of translating in a principled way between thoughts on one hand and auditory and motor patterns on the other. In other words, we can locate it within the circled arrows in Figure 4.2. (Of course, Figure 4.2 is incomplete, since each person has the capability of performing both translations. We'll fix that in a moment.) The process of going from thought to motor instructions is *speech production*; that from auditory patterns to thought is *speech perception*. We can think of different languages as different ways of converting thought into motor patterns and auditory patterns back into thought.

One of the basic insights of linguistic theory is that these translations or conversions are not carried out by the brain in one fell swoop. Rather, two major intermediate steps are involved in the conversion: *phonological structure* (or sound structure) and *syntactic structure* (or phrase structure). Zooming in more closely on Harry's and Sam's brains in Figure 4.2, the general configuration looks like Figure 4.3: the circled arrows of Figure 4.2 have been elaborated to include these intermediate steps of conversion.

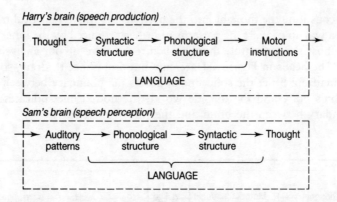

Figure 4.3 *The place of language in the conversion of thought into sound waves and back again*

Notice that most parts of these diagrams are shared. We can therefore combine them, and portray the brain of a single person who is able both to produce and to perceive language, simply by allowing some of the conversions to go in either direction, as in Figure 4.4.

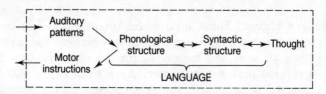

Figure 4.4 *Information flow in the brain of a combined speaker-hearer*

How are we to understand Figure 4.4? To help get a sense of it, think of what goes on when you play a videotape on your VCR. The videotape contains information stored as patterns of magnetization on the oxide of the tape; its organization is essentially linear and spatial. The VCR playing the tape translates this organization into a temporal pattern of electrical impulses that it feeds into the television set. In turn, the television set translates this pattern of impulses into a pattern of dots on the screen, arrayed in two dimensions in space plus one dimension in time.

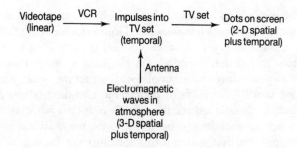

Figure 4.5 *Information flow in a VCR–antenna–TV configuration*

Each of the information formats—videotape, electrical impulses, and dots on the screen—has its own intrinsic organization; a specialized device is necessary to turn each of these types of information into one of the others.

Figure 4.5 shows another format of information relevant to this system. TV broadcasts involve a signal being transmitted in the form of an electromagnetic wave, which is three-dimensional and temporal in its organization. The antenna is a device that converts this signal into one of the formats already mentioned: the electrical impulses entering the TV set. Videodiscs are yet another format for information, requiring yet another specialized device to convert their patterns into inputs for the TV.

Finally, we should remember that there exist several different formats for videotape—VHS and Betamax, for example. Each of these needs a slightly different device to transform it into properly coded impulses for the television set. (One could think of these as different "languages" or "dialects" of videotape.) Similarly, the patterns of dots on the screen can be organized differently, depending on whether one is dealing with black-and-white or color television, or with ordinary versus high-resolution video.

Going back to Figure 4.4, a similar story emerges, except that each of the formats of information consists of patterns of neural firings. Again, each format has its own characteristics, and specialized devices—different parts of the brain this time—are required to convert the information from one format to the next. Again, each pairing of formats requires a different conversion device. For example, converting auditory patterns into phonological structure is quite a different process from converting phonological structure into motor patterns, even though the two processes share phonological structure as a common format of information. And different conversion procedures are needed if the phonological and syntactic structures are those of Vietnamese or Hopi instead of English.

We could add yet another component to Figure 4.4: the relationship to written language. Alphabetic written language is basically an encoding of phonological structure—one learns to "sound out words"—though of course the encoding is not perfect, and English spelling is especially notorious for its idiosyncrasy. In order for such an encoding to be useful to us, we must have another conversion process that gets information into the format of phonological structure, through the visual system rather than the auditory system—namely, reading. That is, reading can be seen as an additional branching in Figure 4.4, analogous to the antenna in Figure 4.5.*

It is worth pointing out an important psychological distinction between the reading/writing system and the speaking/hearing system. Acquiring the ability to read and write usually requires extensive instruction and practice, and not everyone achieves this ability; by contrast, every normal person learns to speak fluently. This helps to underline the important point in Chapter 3 that spoken language is not explicitly taught: compare the relatively laborious task of teaching reading with the effortless task of letting children learn to talk. The contrast highlights how special the learning of spoken language is.

The most prominent issues of modern linguistic theory concern the organization of phonological and syntactic structure, the mental codes that serve as way-stations between thought and the auditory and motor codes. Not surprisingly, these structures are far more complex than the ones employed in the VCR–TV system of Figure 4.5. The next two chapters will present a very sketchy idea of what these structures are like.

Functionalism

But before discussing phonological and syntactic structures, I had better say a word about how we manage to study them, even though we don't know very much about how they are physically encoded in the brain as patterns of neural firings. This general approach to studying mental capacities goes under the name of *functionalism*, and

---

* Nonalphabetic writing systems such as Chinese characters also require a conversion process whose input is the visual system, but the output of the process is possibly syntactic instead of phonological structure.

it is a leading strategy in much of cognitive psychology and artificial intelligence as well as linguistics.

To help us see what functionalism is about, let's think about the videotape again. In order to store TV pictures, a videotape must carry a code that expresses certain distinctions, and this code must be stored in terms of basically one-dimensional patterns of magnetization on a tape. So we can ask how the code could be organized so that the videotape can do its job. As a pattern, it doesn't matter too much whether we put the code on a magnetic tape or on something else comparably one-dimensional, say a punched paper tape or a bar-code that can be read by an optical scanner: it's the pattern that counts. Similarly, we can study the patterning of speech sounds—their order, the differences and similarities among them, and their contributions to understanding—to a certain degree independently of the neural medium in which they are physically encoded.

In a functionalist theory, what does it mean to say we have a certain principle in our mental grammars, as part of the equipment we bring to understanding and creating novel sentences of English? Let's take a very simple principle of English—for instance, that the subject of a sentence (normally) precedes the verb. If this principle is somehow in our heads, then the terms "sentence," "subject," and "verb" must be too. What does it mean to say we unconsciously know and use these terms?

Well, for one thing, it doesn't mean that we know them *in English*! It's in the nature of the communicative situation that we as theorists have to state the principles in English, or in Japanese, or, if we want to get fancy, in terms of some mathematical formalism. That's the only way we have of stating theories about anything. But if we're developing a theory of physics and we happen to use the symbol *e* for an electron, it's not as though we expect actually to find electrons with little *e*'s on them. Similarly, we don't expect to look in the brain and find the sentence "Amy loves Uncle Sparky" stored with a little sign on "loves" that says "verb." In fact, we don't even expect to look in the brain and recognize the word "loves."

Suppose we think of our stored knowledge as the contents of some curious sort of filing cabinet in the brain. The information in the filing cabinet isn't stored in a form readable by us outside observers. Why should it be? It's not there for the benefit of outside observers, it's there for the use of the rest of the brain.

So when we state a rule of mental grammar, we're doing something like this: We use a term like "verb" to distinguish some class of words from everything else. The claim is that, whatever way the brain uses to store words, it has a way of distinguishing these particular words from everything else. We use a term like "sentence" to distinguish a particular class of word *sequences* from everything else; the claim is that the brain makes the same distinction. We use terms like "subject" and "object" to pick out word sequences that are particular *parts* of sentences; the claim is that the brain can pick out the same parts. Finally, the whole condition, "the subject of a sentence precedes the verb," states a relation among various parts of the sentence; the claim is that the brain—however it identifies and stores these parts—imposes the same relation.

We can't find out if our claim is right by going in and looking at the brain, because we don't know how. However, if the claim is right, it also has certain consequences for how the brain is going to regard certain sequences of words—and we can test these consequences by doing experiments.

What is a linguistic experiment? As in other sciences, the strategy is to study unobservable phenomena by relating them to things that *are* observable. If we want to measure the mass of an electron or the sun, we can't just weigh them on a scale. We have to use some sort of indirect means to get at what we want to measure—we have to think of something else we *can* measure that is connected to what we really want to know, in what we think is a reliable way. The same is true with the mental principles behind language. The only difference is that linguistic experiments have to do with the inside of our heads instead of external objects.

It turns out that among the kinds of experiments that can be done on language, one kind is very simple, reliable, and cheap: simply present native speakers of a language with a sentence or phrase, and ask them to judge whether or not it is grammatical in their language, or whether it can have some particular meaning. In fact, we have already done a number of these experiments in the course of the previous chapters. I presented various strings of words such as "Harry thinks Beth is a genius" and "Amy nine ate peanuts," and I judged whether they were or were not possible sentences of English. If all went well, you had no trouble agreeing with my judgments. That's all there is to it. The idea is that although we can't observe the mental grammar of English itself, we *can* observe the judgments of grammaticality and meaning that are produced by using it.

This experiment is so simple that you may have hardly even noticed it as such. But it isn't so different from other experiments that study what's going on in the head—for instance, such well known visual phenomena as the Müller-Lyer illusion, the duck–rabbit, the

Necker cube, and various "impossible figures." In the Müller-Lyer illusion, shown in Figure 4.6, the horizontal line on the left looks shorter than the one on the right. But if we measure them with a ruler, they turn out to be the same length.

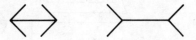

Figure 4.6 *The Müller-Lyer illusion: The two horizontal lines don't look the same length*

Figure 4.7 is the duck–rabbit, which can look alternately like a duck or a rabbit, and as you look at it, it can periodically switch back and forth.

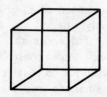

Figure 4.7 *The duck–rabbit ambiguity*

Figure 4.8 is the Necker cube, which looks alternately like a wire cube seen from the right and above or one seen from the left and below.

Figure 4.8 *A Necker cube*

Figure 4.9 presents three "impossible figures"—line drawings that can't be interpreted as drawings of actual objects.

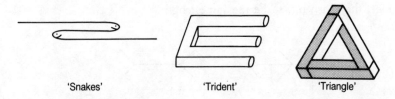

'Snakes'   'Trident'   'Triangle'

Figure 4.9 *Three impossible figures*

These experiments are so simple and reliable that all we have to do is present them to observers and ask them what they see. Moreover, it is clear that our judgments of these figures have nothing to do with what we were "taught about seeing"; that these judgments require no conscious thought; and that at the same time it's very hard to be explicit about why the figures look the way they do. That is, these visual judgments have all the same symptoms as judgments about sentences. I'm suggesting, then, that the two kinds of judgments have similar status as experimental evidence.

A linguistic example very much like Figures 4.7 and 4.8 is the ambiguous sentence (1a). On one interpretation, your relatives are visiting you, and the sentence means about the same as (1b). On the other, you are visiting your relatives, and the sentence means about the same as (1c).

(1) *a* Visiting relatives can be boring.
   b Relatives who are visiting you can be boring.
   c Going to visit relatives can be boring.

Parallel to the impossible visual examples in Figure 4.9 are all the ungrammatical sentences of the last chapter, such as "An oboe not is octopus an." We know immediately, intuitively, that there is something the matter with them. ("Intuitive" judgments are just judgments that follow from unconscious principles. We make the judgment but can't say exactly why.)

Ideally, we might want to check these experiments out by asking large numbers of people under controlled circumstances, and so forth. But in fact the method is so reliable that, for a very good first approximation, linguists tend to trust their own judgments and those of their colleagues. So in a couple of hours it is possible to dream up and perform dozens of these low-tech experiments.

On the other hand, there are cases where these experiments aren't so simple. The most obvious is when you are working on some language other than your own. You then have to find an informant, a native speaker of Turkish or Kwakiutl or whatever, and ask him or her for judgments. In this situation it's much harder to make up sentences to check, and harder to guess what to try next; the process is trickier, but it can be done. (It works both ways. I once spent an entire Kyoto-to-Tokyo train trip being asked by a Japanese linguist for judgments about hundreds of English sentences.)

Another problematic situation arises when the judgments of crucial sentences aren't so crystal-clear and reliable. For instance, a certain line of recent research on so-called "long-distance dependencies" (see Chapter 6) depends on judgments of sentences like those in (2).

(2) *a* What did he wonder whether to fix?
     b These are the only vegetables which I don't know
          where to find out how to plant.

Here I'm not so sure what your judgments are going to be like. To me, the sentences are pretty awkward. On the other hand, they sound better than the slightly different sentences in (3), which I find horrible.

(3) *a* What did he meet a man who can fix?
     b These are the only vegetables which I don't know
          anyone who planted last year.

In such cases the researcher tries to proceed with sensitivity, perhaps trying more possibilities and consulting more people before making a judgment on what the mental grammar is telling us about the sentences.

Of course, other kinds of experiments can be used to explore properties of the mental grammar, including computer simulations, various reaction-time procedures borrowed from experimental psychology, and even measurement of brain waves during language processing. (People who do these kinds of experiments are called *psycholinguists*.) Often these other procedures provide crucial evidence. Their disadvantage is their relative inefficiency: it takes a great deal of time and energy to set up the experiment. By contrast, when the experiment consists of making judgments of grammaticality, there is nothing simpler than devising and judging some more sentences. (Unless, of course, you're working on Inuit and have to go back up to Hudson Bay to see your informant.) So grammaticality judgments remain the most widely used experimental technique in contemporary linguistics.

You have to bear in mind, of course, that it is possible to make up and judge sentences from now until doomsday without getting any closer to understanding mental grammar. But the same is true in any experimental science: experiments are worthwhile only if they help us to figure out what's going on.

Drawing this all together: the functionalist approach to mental grammar is to make experimentally testable hypotheses about the organization of information and knowledge in the brain, without too much concern for the moment about how the brain physically encodes this information.

Some researchers have gone even further and suggested that functionalist research should divorce itself from *any* consideration of how the brain actually functions: we should be interested in intelligence in the abstract, in organizations of information that could be equally well embodied in computers or in Martians. From this point of view, it is essentially beside the point how the human brain in particular encodes language.

I would rather not buy into such an extreme version of functionalism. I am interested in how *we* work. If someday someone shows that the neural circuitry of the brain is capable of encoding certain kinds of patterns and not others, I will be damned sure that this constrains my hypotheses about the principles of language. The problem is hard; I need all the help I can get. Conversely, I would hope that an understanding of the functional organization of language would inform research into how the brain encodes information: however the brain works, it must be able to encode information with *these* sorts of patterns.

The Modularity Hypothesis

The organization of language sketched in Figure 4.4 already illustrates an important hypothesis of modern cognitive science and neuroscience: the differentiation of the brain. Think again of the VCR–TV system. Each translation from one format into another requires a specialized device. We need a VCR to translate from videotape into electrical impulses; we can't use the circuitry of a TV set or a computer printer. And it can't be just any old VCR, it has to be one that can read the kind of videotape we happen to have. Likewise, if the production and perception of language require several complex specialized codes, the brain must include complex specialized devices to deal with each of them, and with the translations among them.

This hypothesis has been called the *Modularity Hypothesis*: the idea that the brain is divided into many separate units or *modules*, each with the capacity to deal with a specialized kind of information. It is not just the way the modules are connected up with each other that makes the brain function as it does. The nature of the circuitry inside each module is absolutely crucial, for it is the particular circuitry that makes a module act as a phonology processor or a visual shape identifier or a finger wiggler or whatever.

Notice how the Modularity Hypothesis connects up with the Genetic Hypothesis of Chapter 3—the idea that a great deal of the structure of language is transmitted genetically, through the inheritance of brain structure. The more the brain consists of specialized parts, the less likely it is that these parts are acquired through learning, especially learning of a simple stimulus–response nature. The brain thus comes to look a lot like the rest of the body, with exquisitely specialized complex physical structure.

To repeat Chomsky's point from Chapter 3: we aren't tempted to think that, by trying hard enough to fly, we can learn to have wings rather than arms. We can strengthen our arms and learn to use them in complex tasks such as doing gymnastics or playing the cello, but we're not going to be able to alter their basic organization. Likewise, under the Modularity Hypothesis, we shouldn't believe that our brains can develop entirely new specialized parts in response to new and unusual tasks. We can strengthen and refine the use of the parts that are there—say, by learning mathematics or chess or real estate law—but the basic functional organization can't change. (It *can* change, of course, through evolution. Just as birds evolved a structural specialization of the forelimbs for flying, humans evolved a structural specialization of the brain for learning language.)

This way of looking at learning is even more radical than the view developed in Chapter 3. Language perception and production require specialized devices for processing information in different formats and for translating information from one format to another. We're now saying that in learning language, children don't build these specialized devices from scratch. Rather, they just "tune up" or strengthen or adjust devices that are already present by virtue of biological structure. (And a speaker of two languages may be thought of as having the ability to "change channels" within the same specialized device.) Under this view, our solution to the Paradox of

Language Acquisition is perfectly natural. Compare the problem of adjusting your TV to the problem of inventing it (or figuring out how it works). The former is more like the child's task; the latter more like the linguist's. No wonder there's a disparity.

In Part IV we will come back to the Modularity Hypothesis in the context of abilities other than language. Right now, our task is to get a sense of (1) the complexity and specialization of the codes employed in speech production and perception and (2) the relative contribution made to these codes by Universal Grammar (or prebuilt structure) and by learning (or tuning). This will give us an overall idea of the degree to which the brain is specialized for language, and it will set a standard by which we can judge the plausibility of the Modularity Hypothesis for other domains of human nature.

5 Phonological structure

We now delve into some of the actual content of the organization of language. This chapter deals with phonological structure, one of the two intermediate steps of conversion between thought and sound. The next chapter deals with the other, syntactic structure. The structure of thought (or meaning) is more controversial, and I have put it off until Chapter 14.

Phonological structure is neither an auditory nor a motor pattern

One of the primary intuitions we have about language is that it comes divided into words, and that the words can be neatly divided into syllables and individual speech sounds. The phonological structure of language is an encoding of this sequence of sounds. It turns out that this sequence is a considerable abstraction of what physically takes place in speech. The acoustic stream we hear as speech shows no such neat divisions. To understand why, it's useful to see how speech is produced.

For a convenient analogy, think about how a trumpet works. The player presses his or her lips together and forces a stream of air through them, producing a sort of buzzing sound. When the trumpet is placed against the vibrating lips, the air column in the trumpet is forced into vibration as well. The way the air column vibrates is a function of the vibration of the lips interacting with the resonant frequencies of the tube; the tone quality we hear has to do with which natural harmonics of the tube are produced in what proportions. If we change the tightness of the lips, the pitch of the whole system changes; if we place a mute in the trumpet's bell, we change the mix of resonant frequencies of the tube, and so the tone quality changes.

Now let's imagine a trumpet whose tube is made out of rubber instead of brass, so it can be stretched and pinched in various ways.

Let's also imagine that a second tube branches off somewhere in the middle, and that air can be directed out of either tube or both. Such a horn probably won't have the clear resonances of a regular trumpet, but it will be able to produce a much greater variety of tone colors, because its resonant frequencies can be altered so much.

Next let's shove this trumpet down the player's throat. Instead of the lips, the vocal cords down in the larynx set the tube into vibration. The tube consists of the throat and its branches into the oral and nasal cavities. The nasal cavity can be disconnected by raising the velum (or soft palate), which functions as a valve. The oral cavity can be constricted or closed off by closing the lips or by raising different parts of the tongue. The sound produced is a function of the vibration of the vocal cords coupled with the very complicated resonances of this tube. As the muscles of the vocal tract change the shape of the tube, the resonances change correspondingly, and these differences are perceived as different speech sounds.

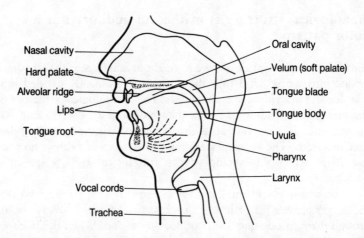

Figure 5.1 *The vocal tract*

During speech, the movements of the vocal tract are smooth and continuous. For instance, try saying the word *wow*, and pay attention to what your mouth is doing. You don't hold a *w* (or *oo*) sound, with pursed lips, then suddenly switch to an *ah* sound, with mouth and lips open, then instantaneously switch back to the *w*. Trying say it that way: *oo-ah-oo*, with sharp transitions between the sounds. You can hear how unnatural it is. In the normal pronunciation of the word, your lips and mouth open smoothly and then close smoothly, with virtually no holding of either the closed *w* or the open *ah* sound.

As a result of the smooth transition between positions of the vocal tract, the acoustic signal produced by the vocal tract also shows a smooth transition from one sound to the next, without any abrupt boundaries. Consequently, the signal that the hearer *perceives* as neatly divided speech sounds is actually far from it. The waveform undergoes continuous change as a result of continuous change in the shape of the vocal tract.

But then what *do* the separate speech sounds correspond to? As it turns out, they correspond rather closely to beginning and end configurations of vocal tract movements—for instance, in the word *wow*, the sequence lip-pursing followed by open mouth followed by lip-pursing. This sequence is obviously different from the auditory information. But it is also different from the motor instructions driving the vocal tract: ultimately, the vocal tract must be told not what sequence of positions to attain, but what muscles to tense and relax in order to obtain that sequence.

Nevertheless, in order to structure speech, it is necessary for the brain to code the sequence of speech sounds and their combinations into words and sentences. This code of speech sounds is referred to as *phonological structure*. In this section we have seen that phonological structure is a distinct kind of mental organization from either vocal tract instructions or auditory patterns (see Figure 5.2).

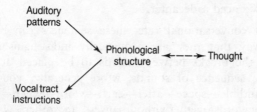

Figure 5.2 *The place of phonological structure in the information flow of language*

When speaking, then, one has a phonological structure (as well as a thought) in mind. The phonological structure specifies a sequence of vocal tract configurations, and the brain must convert this sequence into instructions that tell the muscles of the vocal tract how to move. When *hearing* speech, the brain must convert the continuous, smeary information coming from the auditory nerve into such a sequence of vocal tract positions—in effect reconstructing configurations of the speaker's vocal tract, that is, perceiving the phonological structure that the speaker has in mind.

Psychological reality vs. physical reality of phonological structure

Alert readers may be getting slightly uneasy at this point. At the outset of this chapter I observed that we intuitively sense utterances as divided into words, and words as divided into syllables and individual speech sounds. Yet we've spent the last few pages showing that the acoustic signal out in the world shows no such neat divisions—that the actual sounds of speech undergo continuous change, so that each one smears into the next.

To make this more vivid, think about the divisions between words. In writing, of course, we leave spaces between words, and this mirrors perception: we (almost) never have trouble hearing where one word ends and the next begins. But listen to yourself say the following pairs of sentences:

(1) *a* I don't really think it's a parent.
    b I don't really think it's apparent.
(2) *a* Have you looked at this guy yet?
    b Have you looked at the sky yet?
(3) *a* We needed a cantor.
    b We need a decanter.*

At a normal conversational rate, these sentences can be spoken in such a way that they are acoustically indistinguishable. Yet they require the breaks between words to be placed at different points in the sequence of sounds. More generally, you—don't—leave—an—audible—space—after—each—word—when—speaking. Youjustjamthewordstogetherwithoutpauses. In other words, the boundaries between words, though undeniably part of phonological structure, are not present in either the motor instructions or the auditory information.

In case these examples from English don't convince you, think about the last time you heard people speaking a language you didn't know. Could you tell where one word ended and the next began?

---

* This is a real-life example. During my friend Michael Bennett's wedding ceremony, the rabbi was having trouble pouring the wine, and Michael quipped, "We have a rabbi, but we ..."

There were pauses here and there, but for the most part it probably sounded like just a great rush. This shows that you have to know the language in order to be able to perceive the word boundaries.

A profound point is lurking here. We have discovered that the words we consciously hear and pronounce are not in any physical sense "out in the world." We can't find them through physical measurement of acoustic waveforms. Rather, the way we experience the stream of language seems to have more to do with the patterns of phonological structure in our heads, in which the speech sounds and words are clearly demarcated.

I won't stress this observation too much for now. But we will come back to it in Chapter 12, where we will ask: Are there more general implications about the relation between the physical world and what we perceive? This question will serve as the starting point for the third Fundamental Argument, the Argument for the Construction of Experience.

The internal structure of speech sounds

We now go back to speech sounds themselves. Recall that phonological structure encodes speech sounds as a sequence of vocal tract configurations—successive positions of the larynx, jaw, lips, tongue, and velum. How does the brain specify these configurations, and how are they stored in memory?

Yet again we have to break with intuition. Intuitively, speech sounds are unitary: the sound *z* is just that, a single sound. However, one of the major discoveries of phonological theory, originally developed by Nicholas Trubetzkoy and Roman Jakobson in the 1920s and 1930s, is that speech sounds are encoded in the brain in terms of more primitive specifications called the *distinctive features* of speech sounds. Some of these features are listed in (4). If you pay very careful attention to what is going on in your mouth and throat as you make different sounds, you can verify the features for yourself.

(4) *a* Significant constriction of the vocal tract (consonants)
        vs.
        Vocal tract unconstricted (vowels)
    b Vocal cords tensed and therefore in vibration (sounds such as *b*, *g*, *d*, *z*, *n*, *th* as in "there," all vowels)
        vs.
        Vocal cords relaxed and therefore not vibrating (*p*, *t*, *k*, *ch*, *f*, *sh*, *th* as in "thin")

  c Velum lowered so air passes through nose (*m, n, ng* as
     in "sing," vowels in French "on" and "fin")
     vs.
     Velum raised so air passes only through mouth (all
     other sounds)
  d Air flow through mouth completely blocked (*p, b, m,
     t, d, n, k, g, ng, ch, j*)
     vs.
     Air flow through mouth not completely blocked (all
     other sounds)
  e Most constricted part of mouth at lips (*p, b, m, f, v,
     w, u*)
     vs. at tip of tongue (*t, d, n, s, z, l, th*)
     vs. at body of tongue (*ch, sh, j*)
     vs. at back of tongue (*k, g, ng*, German *ch* as in
     "Bach")

Each speech sound can be described in terms of a combination of the
distinctive features. The sound *d*, for instance, codes a configuration
in which the vocal tract is significantly constricted, the vocal cords
are tensed, the velum is raised, air flow through the mouth is blocked,
and the main constriction is at the tip of the tongue. The sound *t*
differs minimally from *d* in that the vocal cords are relaxed; *n* differs
minimally from *d* in that the velum is lowered so air passes through
the nose. The sound *z* differs minimally from *d* in that the mouth is
not completely blocked, so air continues to pass through; *b* differs
minimally from *d* in that the constriction is at the lips. Thus the
similarities and differences among speech sounds can be specified in
terms of distinctive-feature analysis.

    The relations among sounds provided by distinctive features
enable us to explain many curious aspects of pronunciation. For a
simple example, the plural suffix for English nouns is pronounced
three different ways: as a *z* sound in words like "dogs," as an *s* sound
in words like "cats," and as an *uhz* sound in words like "horses." (It
is always *spelled* "s" or "es"; but I want to pay attention to how it is
actually *pronounced*. For simplicity, I am disregarding irregular
plurals like "oxen," "mice," and "sheep.") What decides among
these three choices in any given word?

    It turns out to depend on the final sound of the noun to which
the plural is attached.

(5) *a* If the noun ends with one of the sounds *s, z, sh, ch, j,* the plural is pronounced *uhz*.

  b If the noun ends with one of the sounds *p, t, k, f,* or *th* as in "death," the plural is pronounced *s*.

  c If the noun ends with anything else, the plural is pronounced *z*.

These classes of sounds may look arbitrary, but in fact distinctive-feature analysis shows us the method behind the madness. The class in (5b) consists of sounds that are "unvoiced"—that is, in which the vocal cords are not vibrating. The class in (5c) consists entirely of sounds that are "voiced"—in which the vocal cords vibrate. Two of the pronunciations of the plural, *s* and *z*, are articulated identically except for this feature of voicing; we can see the pronunciation of the plural as "agreeing" in voicing with the end of the word it is attached to.

What about the class in (5a), which includes both voiced sounds (*z* and *j*) and unvoiced ones (*s, sh,* and *ch*)? This class includes sounds whose articulation is very close to that of the plural ending: *s* and *z* themselves plus the sounds articulated with the body of the tongue. Here a vowel sound is inserted before the plural ending to prevent interference between the two consonants—and the plural itself is pronounced *z* to agree with the voicing of this vowel.

There is a small class of words ending in *f*, such as "wolf" and "half," in whose plurals the final consonant changes to *v*: "wolves" and "halves." What has happened here? Notice that the sound *v* is articulated exactly like *f*, except that it has vocal cord vibration. So in these words, exceptionally, the last consonant of the word changes its sound slightly in the plural, becoming voiced. The plural ending is then pronounced *z* to agree with it.

Not only can the choice among the three pronunciations of the plural be predicted from the features of the final sound of the word, but the choice is *productive*—that is, we can produce plurals for new nouns on the spot. We don't just memorize the plural ending for every noun we know (though we probably *do* memorize the irregular cases). To see this, suppose I introduce new words to you and ask you what their plurals are. If you had to learn the plural form by memorization, you couldn't carry out this task. Here are some words (they happen to be borrowed from Yiddish).

(6) *a* kvetch
  b dybbuk
  c shmeggeggie

Whatever "kvetch" might mean, you know its plural is "kvetches," with the plural pronounced *uhz*. This follows from the fact that the last sound of the word falls into group (5a). Similarly, the plural of "dybbuk" is "dybbuks," with the plural pronounced *s*, because the word ends in an unvoiced sound; that of "shmeggeggie" is "shmeggeggies," with the plural pronounced *z*, because the word ends in a voiced sound.

Even more striking is what happens when a new word ends with a sound not present in English. "What a big family of composers! There was Johann Sebastian Bach, and Carl Philip Emmanuel Bach, and Wilhelm Friedemann Bach, and even P.D.Q. Bach. There sure were a lot of __!" Fill in the blank. The word is "Bachs," with the plural pronounced *s*. Why? Because even though the *ch* sound is not a sound of English, English speakers can tell (unconsciously or intuitively) that it is unvoiced, and that it is not made with the body of the tongue. It therefore falls in with the sounds in group (5b), whose plural is pronounced *s*. In other words, we don't even memorize the plural rule in terms of the list of sounds—we use the distinctive-feature analysis, which can extend to sounds not even present in our own language.

These observations deal with only a tiny aspect of the sound pattern of English. But they are a microcosm of the larger picture: using distinctive-feature analysis, we have been able to describe the pronunciation of the plural fairly simply, rather than as a complex list of special cases. This kind of result is replicated in case after case in many different languages, suggesting that this is indeed the way the brain encodes speech sounds.

You probably had no conscious awareness of distinctive features before I pointed them out a moment ago. The conscious awareness of the sound pattern of language extends as far down as individual speech sounds (and perhaps not that far in nonliterate societies), but it does not include the further analysis of the speech sounds themselves. Nor do we have any conscious awareness of principles such as the one governing the pronunciation of the plural; yet everyone adheres to them. Thus the features and the way they are put to use in language had to be discovered by experiment. In fact, in our discussion above, we have replicated some of the simpler experiments in this domain. More generally, I would consider the discovery of distinctive features, and the continual refinement of their formulation over some decades, to be a scientific achievement on the order of the discovery and verification of the periodic table in chemistry.

There is a great deal more to phonological structure than just distinctive features. In addition to a sequence of speech sounds, words and phrases carry stress, or relative emphasis among their syllables. In many languages (such as Chinese, Vietnamese, and many West African languages), words carry with them an inherent melody (or sequence of tones) that is as much a part of the word as its speech sounds. Words and phrases also have an inherent rhythm that determines their temporal flow. For each of these aspects of the sound structure of language there is a growing literature of analysis and theory, with much lively dispute. I have tried to illustrate here only the basic spirit of the analysis.

The Paradox again

If the system of distinctive features is such a great scientific discovery, what does this say about the child's learning of language? How did we as children learn the principles of the English plural, including its application to "shmeggeggie" and "Bach"? We had to figure out at least three things.

1. We had to notice that describing a multiplicity of objects is correlated with changes in the way the names of the objects are pronounced. What in the world do three cats, five apples, and fourteen clouds have in common? Not much other than multiplicity (or plurality). Yet this really very abstract notion is correlated with the use of some special noise tacked onto the names for the animal, the fruit, and the meteorological phenomenon respectively. This has to do with meaning, so it's not, strictly speaking, within the ambit of this chapter. But it *is* part of the learning process.

2. We had to guess that there is some relation among the noises tacked onto the different names for objects—that is, that there is a standard way to form plurals and not just a million different ways. (Why couldn't the plural of "cat" be "cattis," the plural of "apple" be "akkle," and the plural of "cloud" be "cleez"? That *could* be memorized, though it would be a pain.) Guessing that there is a regularity is probably not specific to language, though—children try to find regularities in everything.

3. We had to figure out that the regularity in use of the sounds z, s, and *uhz* to denote multiplicity has to do with

the last sound of the words they are attached to, and in particular to the distinctive features of those sounds. And here it is necessary to invoke Universal Grammar. For in order to figure out that the pronunciation is dependent on distinctive features, the child must either figure out the distinctive features or else know them in advance. Given that linguists just figured them out sixty years ago, but children have been learning the English plural rule for hundreds of years, we have to suppose that children have access to distinctive-feature analysis of sounds in order to be able to learn to speak.

Naturally, since the child doesn't know in advance which of the languages of the world he or she is going to be learning, the system of distinctive-feature analysis had better be able to accommodate all the speech sounds of all languages, including the German *ch* sound, the French nasal vowels in "fin" and "on," and even the click sounds of the South African languages Xhosa and Zulu. Any single language chooses only a subset of these possibilities. That is, we can think of distinctive features as a part of Universal Grammar that provides a "menu" of speech sounds, plus the relationships among these sounds that come from shared features.

In learning a language, then, the child selects certain speech sounds from this menu to match those in the environment. Having selected these sounds, the child already "instinctively" or "intuitively" (i.e. unconsciously) knows how to sort them out—for example, which ones are voiced and which unvoiced, which are made with the tip of the tongue and which with the back, and so forth. It is this classification that makes it possible to figure out the principles that govern regularities of pronunciation like the English plural.

I've dwelt on the plural not because it's such a big deal in and of itself. It is one of the simpler cases of hundreds (maybe thousands) of phonological regularities that have been studied in the languages of the world, each of which presents similar problems to the child. And, as it happens, the English plural rule has played an interesting role in studies of language acquisition, which we will come back to in Part III. So it's worth concentrating on it a little bit here.

What else besides speech is in the auditory signal?

I've tried to show so far that speech is encoded in the brain as a sequence of distinctive-feature configurations. Recalling our functionalist orientation from Chapter 4, we won't worry too much how the brain neurologically accomplishes this encoding. But it is worth remembering that contemporary neuroscience is silent on this problem. We know that speech is encoded in some particular *part* of the brain, but we have no idea of how the neurons in this part of the brain encode distinctive features and all the principles that depend on them. We'll return to this issue in Chapter 11.

Meanwhile, on to further complications. Let's return to speech perception—how the brain gets from the activation of auditory neurons to a perception of discrete speech sounds. We've already noted how smeared the auditory input is, and how this presents a severe problem for perception, which has to locate the boundaries between speech sounds and even between words. But that isn't the only problem that speech perception faces.

For one thing, everyone's voice is different. Because of differences in the size of the vocal cords and the anatomy of the vocal tract, there is considerable variation from person to person in the resonant frequencies that are crucial for defining vowel sounds. This means that speech perception can't just define a vowel in terms of some fixed set of frequencies. Rather, the frequencies have to be quickly adjusted to the overall range of frequencies we hear coming from the speaker. We obviously do this without thought.

In addition, the acoustic signal presented by someone speaking in a slow, sweet voice is quite different from that of the same person saying the same thing in a rapid angry voice or a measured ironic voice or a casual bantering voice. The possible variations are immense, and somehow the process of speech perception can ignore all that and pick out the speech sounds. Again, much more easily done than explained.

On the other hand, the brain doesn't simply regard these variations as noise that gets in the way of perceiving what the person is saying. Rather, the process of auditory perception analyzes the acoustic signal into three separate but simultaneous factors: *who* is speaking (voice recognition), *what* the speaker is saying (language perception), and *how* it is being said (the speaker's tone of voice or emotional affect). Each of these factors appears to be picked out by a separate module of the brain. For instance, we can recognize voices and tones of voice in a foreign film whose language we don't understand. We even "instinctively" (i.e. without conscious effort or intent) attribute emotional tone to acoustic events like a rumble of thunder or bird song, which in and of themselves are not meant to convey emotional tone. Moreover, each of these factors can be disrupted by brain damage, leaving the other two intact: there are stroke victims who cannot understand language anymore but do respond to tone of voice, while others cannot recognize voices anymore but do understand what people are saying.

These extra factors in auditory perception can be added to our earlier diagram of the flow of information in language, as shown in Figure 5.3.

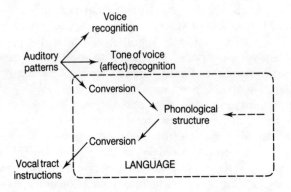

Figure 5.3 *The auditory signal feeds language and two other specialized processors*

The idea is that there are three different specialized processors awaiting the auditory signal. Each one is eager to find what it is prepared to find: the linguistic processor finds speech segments, voice recognition finds the overall mix of frequencies that identifies a speaker's voice, and affect recognition finds the variation in frequencies that characterizes tone of voice.

To help us see what this process is like, let's return to our VCR–TV assembly (Figure 4.5, p. 43), in which I ignored an important complication. The VCR feeds a unified train of electrical impulses into the TV set. But the TV set, in fact, has to sort this train into two independent factors, the picture and the sound, each of which requires its own specialized processor to convert the appropriate part of the electrical impulses into the appropriate kind of output. So it is with the auditory system, but instead of pictures and sound we get three different aspects of the same sound.

It is often said that the brain filters incoming information, attending to only a small part of what impinges on the sense organs.

This is taken to be an impressive feat. What we have found here is somewhat different: out of a unified, smeary acoustic signal, the brain derives three distinct kinds of information, at least one of which, speech, is discrete and highly complex.* Nothing goes to waste! Personally, I find this feat a great deal more impressive.

---

* The other two types of information may turn out to be equally complex, but so far hardly anything is known about them.

6 Syntactic structure

Syntactic structure is distinct from phonological structure

Phonological structure allows us to build up speech sounds into words and string them together. But it doesn't help us to describe the kinds of patterns we discussed in Chapter 2, shown again in (1).

(1) *a* An X is not a Y.
b Since an X is not a Y, a Z is not a W.
c X Verbs that S.

What fits into the slots marked "X," "Y," "Verb," and "S" in these patterns? We can't describe these just in terms of their sound. Rather, we need the notion, familiar from traditional grammar, of "parts of speech" such as noun, verb, adjective, and preposition—plus ways of combining them. X, Y, Z, and W in patterns (1a) and (1b) have to be filled by nouns such as "nunnery," "banana," "oboe," and so forth; *Verb* in pattern (1c) has to be filled by a verb such as "thinks," "believes," "expects," and so forth.

There is a further complication in pattern (1c). As we saw in Chapter 2, *S* has to be filled with another pattern, a sentence that can stand on its own. In the examples in Chapter 2, *X* was filled by a name (or proper noun) such as "Larry," "Moe," or "Curly." But it can also be filled by a larger pattern of words consisting of a common noun and a collection of modifiers—a so-called *noun phrase*. In the sentences in (2), I've underlined the noun phrase that takes the place of X in pattern (1c), and I've marked in bold the *head noun*, the noun that everything else modifies.

(2) *a* <u>The big black **bear**</u> thinks that you won't shoot him.
b <u>A **woman** in the lobby with a book under her arm</u> believes that an oboe is not an octopus.
c <u>The tall **boy** who Bill met yesterday</u> expects that the world economy will disintegrate within a year.

So, in order to describe X in (1c), we need a pattern made of further patterns, just as we do for S.

It should be fairly obvious that these syntactic categories and patterns—noun, verb, noun phrase, and so forth—can't be characterized in terms of phonological structure. For one thing, the very same sequence of sounds can serve as different parts of speech, as seen in the sentences in (3); you can doubtless multiply examples *ad libitum*.

(3) *a* We're going to **rock** around the clock. (rock = verb)
    b We put some **rock** around the clock. (rock = noun)
    c Beth **threw** the ball. (threw = verb)
    d It went **through** the window. (through = preposition)

Consequently, if we (and our brains) are to be able to characterize the patterns of phrases and sentences, we need an additional layer of structure beyond that provided by phonological structure, a layer in which the basic units of analysis are parts of speech, and in which they are combined into phrases and sentences. Just as the auditory signal is factored into voice recognition, affect recognition, and speech perception, the speech analysis is factored into phonological structure and this further analysis, which we'll call *syntactic structure*.

On the other hand, syntactic structure can't be related as directly to the auditory signal as phonological structure is. In order to determine the part of speech of a word, first the word has to be identified. What word is being spoken obviously doesn't depend on who is saying it or their tone of voice—that all has to be filtered out already. But this is exactly what phonological structure does. That is, identifying the word depends not on its auditory characteristics but, rather, on its *phonological* characteristics. So our functional diagram of information flow in language is elaborated to Figure 6.1.

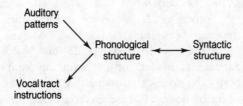

Figure 6.1 *The place of syntactic structure in the information flow of language*

Syntactic structure is distinct from meaning

School grammar defines a noun as "the name of a person, place, or thing" and a verb as "an action or state of being." According to these definitions, the units of syntactic structure are actually elements of meaning (or thought). And many people (some eminent psychologists and computer scientists included) think that syntactic analysis is nothing but a stripped-down description of meaning: if we characterize the meaning properly, there is nothing left to be said about syntactic structure.

It would indeed be nice if we didn't have to posit a level of syntactic analysis in between phonological structure and meaning—if the brain's analysis were maximally simple. But the facts of language don't let us off the hook so easily. Syntactic structure is closer to meaning than sound is—it's the last way-station enroute from sound to meaning—so it strongly reflects certain aspects of meaning. But, as I want to show, there are other properties of syntactic structure that don't have much to do with meaning. Rather, they have to do with organizing the elements of meaning into linear order so that they can be pronounced, and at the same time marking the relations among these elements so that they can be re-identified by the hearer.

To start with, let's ask whether each part of speech really denotes a consistent kind of meaning. Some of the most common matchings of entities of meaning with parts of speech are shown in (4).

(4) Object = Noun (*dog, skyscraper, ocean, molecule*)
Action = Verb (*breathe, enter, provide, interpret*)
Property = Adjective (*hot, jealous, quiet, insubstantial*)
Location = Preposition (or prepositional phrase) (**in the house, on the ceiling, between** NY **and** LA)

Now it is true that any word that names an object will be a noun. But on the other hand, not every noun names an object. "Earthquake" names, if anything, an action, as does "concert"; "redness" and "size" name properties; "place" and "location" pretty obviously name locations. In fact, for just about any kind of entity we can think of, there exist nouns that name that kind of entity. So the grammatical notion of noun can't be given a definition in terms of what kind of entity it names.

Similarly, prepositions can be used to name not only locations but also times ("**after** lunch," "**through** the night") and properties ("**out of** luck," "**in** a good mood"). So prepositions don't correspond to any fixed sort of entity either.

These examples also show that a particular kind of entity need not correspond to a single part of speech either. Actions can be named by either verbs or nouns; properties can be named by adjectives, nouns, or prepositions. In fact, the very same property can be expressed by an adjective or an adverb, depending whether it modifies a noun or a verb:

> (5) *a* a **violent** earthquake, a **beautiful** concert
> *b* The earth shook **violently**; The orchestra played **beautifully**

We conclude that parts of speech, the basic units of syntactic structure, are not definable in terms of meaning.

Here's another reason why syntactic structure isn't predictable from meaning. In Chapter 4 we noticed that meaning or thought is independent of the language that is being spoken. Otherwise it makes no sense to speak of translating from one language to another, conveying the same meaning.* It follows, then, that any difference between the original and the translation isn't part of the meaning they share.

Of course, languages don't share the *phonology* that goes with the same thought. That's why we have to study vocabulary like crazy when we're learning foreign languages: what noise means the same thing in Portuguese that "umbrella" means in English? But in addition to learning phonology, we have to learn what order to put the words in, and that's a *syntactic* property of the languages in question.

For example, English adjectives normally precede the nouns they modify, but French adjectives (with some exceptions) normally follow the nouns they modify.

> (6) le chat noir = the cat black ("the black cat")

English verbs normally follow the subject and precede the object, but Japanese verbs always follow both subject and object.

> (7) Bill-ga hon-o utta = Bill book sold ("Bill sold the book")

In English, one can form a question by placing an "auxiliary verb"

---

* *Almost* the same meaning, at any rate. In Chapter 14 I'll mention some circumstances where completely accurate translation is not possible.

("do," "will," "be," etc.) in front of the subject, but in German questions, the main verb can be placed before the subject.

   (8) Liebt Wozzeck Marie? = loves Wozzeck Marie?
       ("Does Wozzeck love Marie?")

These patterns of word order depend on knowing the parts of speech of the words, so they have to do with syntactic structure. On the other hand, since they differ from language to language, they can't depend on the meaning. So again we see that syntactic structure has properties that are independent of meaning.

Some syntactic patterns

If parts of speech don't have to do with meaning, what *do* they have to do with? It should be evident by now that the classification of words into parts of speech determines their roles in patterns.

Let's briefly explore some syntactic patterns in English. As we go through them, it is important to bear in mind that these patterns are part of mental grammar—that we somehow have these patterns stored in our brains, and that we had to learn them.

As we saw in Chapter 5, a noun can appear with a plural ending: "dogs," "bananas," "earthquakes." A verb, on the other hand, can appear with a past tense ending: "helped," "believed," "procrastinated." Notice that our ability to use these endings is *syntactic* knowledge, and doesn't follow from the meanings of the words. In terms of meaning, it would make sense if nouns that name actions could appear with a past tense. But there are no words "earthquaked" or "concerted" which name an earthquake or a concert that occurred in the past. Likewise, in terms of meaning, it would make sense to be able to put a plural ending on a verb to mean that the action was performed more than once. But we can't say "Bill will dances" to mean he will dance several times. (The "-s" ending in "Bill dances", of course, indicates not plural, but that there is a third-person-singular subject.) In other words, the availability of past tense and plural endings correlates with the syntactic distinction between verbs and nouns, not with the distinction in meaning between objects and actions.

Another case: in English, a verb is preceded by its subject and followed by its object, if there is one. Both the subject and object are noun phrases. As we saw a minute ago, the verb can also be modified by an adverb. So we find sentences like (9).

(9) The enemy   rapidly   destroyed   the city.

  subject noun phrase   adverb   verb   object noun phrase

Now it so happens that there is a noun, "destruction," which describes the same action as the verb "destroy." But if we want to express something similar to (9) using this noun, the phrase comes out somewhat differently: not "the enemy rapidly destruction the city," which is gibberish, but (10).

(10) the enemy 's   rapid   destruction of   the city

   "subject" possessive   noun   "object"
   noun phrase   adjective   preposition noun phrase

These differences can't have anything to do with meaning, since the meanings of (9) and (10) are parallel. Rather, they have to do with the syntactic patterns that go with verbs and nouns.

Let's look next at how subpatterns are put together into larger patterns. It is customary to notate the way a sentence or phrase is composed of patterns and subpatterns by drawing a "tree," like this:

(11)

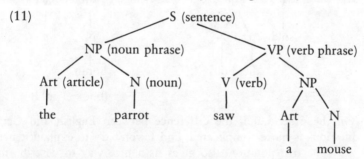

This notation is similar to old-fashioned sentence diagrams in the way it breaks the sentence into parts. It is different in that it labels each part as belonging to a particular syntactic type such as N, VP, or Art. (11) says that the sentence "the parrot saw a mouse" is composed of two main parts, a noun phrase (the subject) and a verb phrase (the predicate). The noun phrase consists of two parts, the article "the" and the noun "parrot." The verb phrase also consists of two parts, the verb "saw" and the noun phrase "a mouse," which itself breaks into two parts, the article "a" and the noun "mouse."

Many variations in word order among the languages of the world become transparent when they are viewed in terms of tree structures. For example, the relative order of French adjectives and nouns differs from English in that the A under NP is swung around to the other side of the N.

(12)　　　English　　　　　　　　　　　　French

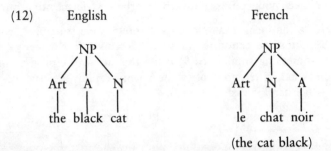

(the cat black)

The relative order of the Japanese verb and direct object results from reversing the V and NP that hang from VP.

(13)　　　English　　　　　　　　　　　Japanese

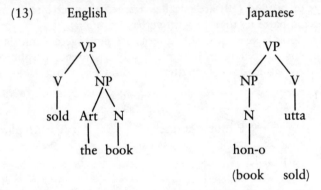

(book　sold)

(On the other hand, the difference between English and German questions is more complicated, and I won't try to explain it here.)

The tree notation also gives us a nice way to describe many cases of ambiguity. A typical case is shown in (14).

(14) the old man in the chair with a broken leg

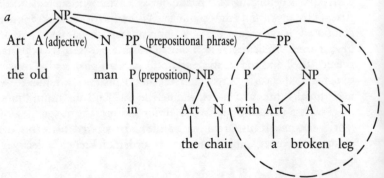

The phrase in (14) is ambiguous: Does the old man have a broken leg, or does the chair? These two possibilities show up as the two trees in (14). The crucial difference is where the circled prepositional phrase "with a broken leg" is attached to the phrase. If it is attached to the upper noun phrase, it modifies "man"; if it is attached to the lower, it modifies "chair." The phrase is ambiguous because both structures result in the same string of words. In other words, the difference in meaning shows in the syntactic structure, but not in the phonological structure.

It is a continuing issue in linguistic theory to determine exactly which ambiguities in language are to be explained this way. For instance, the sentence in (15a) can be interpreted as (15b) or (15c).

(15) *a* Many people here have read two books.
    b There are two particular books (say, *Gone with the Wind* and *Fear of Flying*) that many people here have read.
    c Many people here have read two books, but not necessarily the same two.

The question is whether sentence (15a), like the phrase in (14), has different syntactic structures for these different interpretations, or whether it has just a single syntactic structure that can be interpreted either way. I can't begin to go into the complexities of this case here; suffice it to say that the jury is out after nearly thirty years of investigation. This research has revealed a great deal about what the correct solution has to be able to account for, and about what possible solutions *won't* work, but there is still substantial disagreement among theorists on what the proper solution *is*. (A notable case of the Paradox of Language Acquisition: children trying to learn language probably don't have to make up their minds about this, even unconsciously!)

Recursion and syntactic movement

Let me continue a little more with tree structures.

When we first discussed syntactic patterns in Chapter 2, we talked about the property of *recursion*, the ability of sentences to occur inside of other sentences *ad infinitum*, as in "Harry said that Amy thinks that Sam predicted that Mildred would believe that Beth is a genius." Tree structures give us a nice way to account for this pattern. Notice, for instance, that the trees in (14) have an NP inside another NP, and in fact (14b) continues the pattern to a second step. This pattern, too, can go on indefinitely, forming unwieldy but comprehensible phrases like "the cover of a book about the mother of the man in the chair with a broken leg." Here's a tree for part of this phrase.

(16)

In similar fashion, our pattern "X Verbs that S" enters into tree structures like this:

(17)

We see, then, more explicitly than in Chapter 2, that long and complex sentences can be built up from a collection of relatively simple patterns. In fact, to a great extent, the basic syntactic patterns of the language can be thought of as subtrees only one layer deep, like these:

(18) *a*   S   *b*   VP   *c*   NP
   NP VP   V NP   Art A N PP

 d PP   *e* VP   *f* SC
   P NP   V SC   that S

By putting these together like Lego pieces, trees of great complexity can be constructed. In addition, we can characterize the patterns of different languages by supplying them with a different stock of basic subtrees—as shown, for example, in (12) and (13).

This approach also enables us to show why not every combination is possible in every language. For instance, in English there is no subtree like (19a). As a result, a noun cannot occur with a "direct object" as in the ungrammatical (19b). Rather, the closest parallel to the verb phrase "destroy the city" is to use a prepositional phrase, as in (19c).

(19) *a* Not in English:

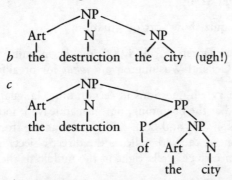

 b the destruction the city (ugh!)

 c

As usual, this organization of mental grammar is verified by extensive experimentation with speakers' intuitions about sentences, of the sort discussed in Chapter 4. In addition, this way of describing the patterns is claimed to be parallel to the way the brain organizes them, even if we are ignorant of how the neurons accomplish such organization.

Experiment also reveals that there are cases where subtrees like (18) are not enough to characterize our syntactic knowledge. The

examples in (20) are so-called *wh-questions*, which begin with one of
the *wh-words* "who," "what," "where," "when," and "which."

> (20) *a* What did Beth eat for breakfast?
>   *b* Whom did Harry think that Nancy met at the store?
>   *c* Which book does your mother say that the teachers
>   think that the children will read over the summer?

In (20a), "what" is understood as the direct object of the verb "eat,"
even though it is at the beginning of the sentence instead of after the
verb. We can see this because an appropriate answer is something like
"Beth ate octopus for breakfast," in which the noun phrase that
answers "what?" is in the usual position after the verb.

In order to account for the "understood" relation of "what" to
the verb, linguists have proposed that in mental grammar there is a
stage of analysis in which "what" really *is* the direct object of the
verb—"Beth did eat what for breakfast." Then "what" in some sense
"moves" to the front of the sentence. To help make sense of this idea,
notice that there are two kinds of situations in which the wh-word
actually is used as direct object instead of at the front. One is in a
situation of incredulity (so-called "echo-questions"):

> (21) Holy cow! Beth ate WHAT for breakfast?!
>   OCTOPUS??!!

The other is in a quiz-show sort of situation:

> (22) Mr. Van Doren, for $64,000: on the morning of July 4,
>   1776, General Washington ate *what* for breakfast?

In addition, ordinary wh-questions in certain other languages do not
place the wh-word at the beginning, but instead leave it in place, just
like the wh-words in (21) and (22). (23) is an example from Korean,
where, as in Japanese, the verb follows the direct object; notice that
the phrase "which college" falls right in the middle of the sentence.

> (23) Ne-nun Chelsoo-ka enu tayhak-ey kat-ta ko
>   sayngkakha-ni?
>   You Chelsoo which college went that think*
>   'Which college do you think that Chelsoo went to?'

---

* I am grateful to Soowon Kim for this example. For clarity, I have omitted the suffixes
from the translation. For completeness: "-nun" is a topic marker; "-ka" marks
nominative case; "-ey" marks dative case; "-ta" marks indicative; "-ni" marks the
sentence as a question.

The idea, then, is that echo-questions, quiz-show questions, and Korean questions show us the basic or "underlying" position of wh-words, from which they move to the front in ordinary English questions. This is one of the foundational ideas behind Chomsky's theory of *transformational grammar*: a sentence in the mind has an "underlying structure" or "deep structure" that is different from its surface form, and various principles of mental grammar can transform the sentence by moving certain parts such as wh-words around. This innovation, more than any other, is what permitted Chomsky's approach to syntactic structure to describe a wide range of linguistic phenomena that had remained relatively opaque to previous theories.*

According to current theory, when wh-words move, they leave behind a "trace," a sort of unpronounced pronoun, in the place where they came from. The idea of an "unpronounced pronoun" may seem rather mystical. But in fact, various techniques involving measuring reaction times and detecting brain waves have shown that people listening to sentences like (20) actually detect these traces of moved wh-words (unconsciously, of course). The trace is detected just at the point during the sentence where linguistic theory postulates it, and it has an interpretation appropriate to the wh-word that has been moved.

Constraints on long-distance dependencies

It turns out that wh-words can "move" to the beginning of the sentence from many different places. In "Whom did Harry think Nancy met at the store," "whom" is understood as the direct object of the subordinate clause "Nancy met ∧ at the store" (where the trace left by the moved wh-word is indicated by ∧). In the even longer sentence (20c), "which book" moves out of the doubly subordinate clause "the children will read ∧ over the summer." In fact, we can construct sentences in which a wh-word is understood as belonging

---

* Deep structure (now often termed "D-structure") has always been understood simply as an aspect of syntactic structure that expresses certain structural regularities. These regularities, since they include word order, have to be syntactic (i.e. distinct from meaning) and have to express variation among languages (i.e. they are not universal). However, because of the way deep structure was characterized at a certain stage of development of the theory during the mid and late 1960s, many commentators erroneously identified it with either meaning or Universal Grammar or both. However, this was never the intent of the term, except in certain circles for a certain brief time.

to a clause as deeply embedded as we want. (24) is very awkward, but nevertheless understandable.

(24) Whom did Sam say Harold thought the teacher had
   told us that Fred would get Susie to kiss ∧ last Tuesday?

Because it can involve many embeddings, the relation between a wh-word and its "original" or "understood" position cannot be expressed in terms of one-layer subtrees like those in (18). For this reason, the relation is called a *long-distance dependency*.

Oddly enough, though, a wh-word can't be moved from just anywhere in a sentence to form a question. Mental grammar is very particular on this point. To see what I mean, notice that the quiz-show questions in (25) are perfectly understandable.

(25) *a* For $64,000, Mr. Shmoo: General Washington ate
      kippers and *what* for breakfast?
   b For a chance to go on to the bonus round, Ms.
      Glurk: The Empire State Building was completed in
      the year that *what actress* married a future Prime
      Minister?

But if I try to make the very same inquiries using garden-variety wh-questions, I am completely incomprehensible.

(26) *a* What did General Washington eat kippers and ∧ for
      breakfast? (ugh!)
   b What actress was the Empire State Building
      completed in the year that ∧ married a future Prime
      Minister? (triple ugh!)

It's not that these are too long or complex to understand—they're shorter than the reasonably comprehensible sentence in (24). More-over, their difficulty appears to lie in their syntactic structure, not their meaning. We know what the questions in (26) *ought* to mean—the same as those in (25)—it's just that we can't ask them this way. That is, these examples seem to reveal "imperfections" in mental grammar, situations where it doesn't allow us to express our thoughts as freely as a completely general system might.

The problem is not limited to wh-questions. (27) illustrates two other kinds of long-distance dependency in English.

(27) *a* Topicalization:
      That kind of movie, I would never be caught dead
      sending my kids to ∧!

b Adjective + "though" construction:
Sophisticated though Susan thinks Bill is ∧, she'll still marry Clyde.

In example (27a), the topic of the sentence, "that kind of movie," appears at the beginning instead of in its normal position as the object of "to." (This construction may not be "proper" English, but we all say things like this in casual conversation.) In the more learned construction shown in (27b), "sophisticated" appears before "though" instead of in its normal position after "is." Like wh-questions, these constructions are thought of as involving a "movement" from the position indicated by ∧ to the front of the sentence.

However, the configurations from which movement can take place (indicated by ∧) are limited in the same way as in wh-questions. (28) provides examples analogous to to the unacceptable wh-questions in (26).

(28) *a* Topicalization:
That kind of cracker, I would never make my kids eat cheese and ∧ for breakfast! (ugh!)
b Adjective + "though" construction:
Sophisticated though Susan is aware of the fact that Bill is ∧, she'll still marry Clyde. (gack!)

Notice that we can see what these are supposed to mean: "I would never make my kids eat cheese and THAT KIND OF CRACKER for breakfast"; "Though Susan is aware of the fact that Bill is (very) sophisticated, . . ." It's just that we can't express these meanings using the long-distance-dependency constructions.

These sorts of situations were first pointed out (by Chomsky and, in much greater elaboration, by John Robert Ross) in the mid 1960s. It has turned out that, with minor variations, similar restrictions appear on *all* long-distance dependencies in *all* languages examined so far. Why should this be?

My imaginary skeptic breaks in:
Well, it's just that as children we never heard sentences like (26) and (28). If we had, we would have learned to make sense of them.

But look: we probably never heard sentences like (24) either, yet we can interpret (24) without too much trouble. The problem posed by sentences like (26) and (28) is: Exactly what patterns are in our mental grammars that make all these examples comprehensible *except* for those in (26) and (28)? Pushing it one step further, how did we acquire patterns for such a great variety of cases without happening to include patterns for (26) and (28) among them? Furthermore, why do the restrictions on these patterns appear universally, as far as we can tell?

These questions should be reminiscent of our discussion in Chapters 2 and 3: we are back in the world of the Fundamental Arguments. Unfortunately, even to begin to answer them would take us far beyond the scope of this book. Suffice it to say that they have been a central preoccupation of syntactic research for three decades, so they constitute a prime instance of the Paradox of Language Acquisition.

Universal Grammar in syntactic structure

I've presented only the barest minimum of syntactic phenomena of English and the thousands of other languages of the world. But already the description has become fairly complex; perhaps it's even a little tough to follow. If so, that too is evidence for the Paradox of Language Acquisition—remember that you have unconscious command of all these patterns that I have had such trouble describing to you.

Again, if it is so complex, we are driven to invoke the Argument for Innate Knowledge and ask: With what aspects of these patterns is the child endowed in advance? That is, what is the Universal Grammar for syntactic structure?

Throughout this chapter, I have been at pains to show that syntactic structure is to a degree independent of both sound and meaning. The syntactic structures of sentences that we speak and hear are in no sense present in the physical reality of speech sounds or in the world of objects and events of which we speak. They are just part of the mind's internal accounting system, a step in the calculations that relate sound to meaning.

Let's think about how hard this situation is for the language learner. Prelinguistic children can observe objects and events in the world, they can hear speech sounds in the world, and presumably they can even form associations between speech sounds and objects ("CAR, Beth! See the CAR?"). But they can't observe *nouns* and *verbs* in the world—these are only internal classifications that correlate with syntactic patterns, which themselves depend on other internal classifications. So how is the child to figure out the system, if it can't be observed?

Current theorizing suggests, at the very least, that children don't have to figure out that there are such things as nouns and verbs that fit into hierarchical tree patterns. Universal Grammar provides the child with a substantial skeleton of syntactic structure that gets the acquisition process off the ground. Like the Universal Grammar for phonological structure, it is useful to think of this as a collection of universal stipulations of the possible units and relations available to all human languages, plus a kind of menu (like a computer software menu) that helps to guide the learner through the possibilities.

Here, stated very informally, are some aspects of UG that pertain to phenomena we have looked at in this chapter.

1. UG lets the child know that the expressive variety of language is made possible by combining local subtrees into larger assemblies. The child does not have to figure out that words are not just strung together one after another.

2. UG stipulates that a language contains a class of *nouns*, that the names of physical objects (among other things) are found in this class, and that a noun plus its modifiers constitute a syntactic unit *noun phrase*. It leaves open, though, where the modifiers are placed: is a modifying adjective before the noun, as in English, or after, as in French? The child has to figure this part out, but it's a lot less than inventing the whole idea of a noun phrase from scratch.

3. UG stipulates that there is a class of *verbs*, and that a verb can combine with a noun phrase to form a *verb phrase* (or predicate). It leaves open whether the verb precedes the noun phrase (English) or follows it (Japanese).

4. UG stipulates that there is a set of wh-words used to ask questions. It leaves open whether they can be left in place (Korean and special constructions in English), moved to the front (ordinary English questions), or moved directly before the verb (Hungarian).

5. UG stipulates that the patterns of a language may contain long-distance dependencies of various sorts, subject to a number of innate restrictions.

More generally, the linguist's strategy in forming hypotheses about Universal Grammar is to try to reduce the things the child must figure out to those that can be observed in the physical and linguistic environment. Given a knowledge of words, a child can determine word order. But tree structures, and the categories present in them (NP, VP, etc.), can't be observed. They have to come from inside the mind, as it were "instinctively" or "intuitively." Universal Grammar is, if you like, the organization of that instinct.

7 American Sign Language

Basic facts about American Sign Language

I am concluding this part of the book with a brief discussion of American Sign Language (ASL), the language of the Deaf community in the United States and most of Canada. I have chosen to do so in part because of the intrinsic interest of signed languages, but more specifically because of the light they shed on language in general. In addition, research on ASL plays a prominent role in our discussion of the biological basis of language in Part III, so it makes sense for me to acquaint you first with some facts about the language.

The most important thing I want to stress is that *ASL is a language*. Of course, it seems completely different from familiar languages such as English, Russian, and Japanese. Its means of transmission is not through the speaker's vocal tract creating acoustic signals that are detected by the addressee's ears. Rather, the speaker's gestures create signals detected by the addressee's visual system.

Some people have found such communication altogether alien and magical. I'll try to show, though, that the differences are rather superficial. It is sort of like switching a VCR–TV system from videotape to videodisc—the peripheral system is different, but the inner workings are exactly the same.

Not exactly the same as *English*, though. ASL is emphatically not just a coding of English into manual signs. Such codings do exist, but they can be clearly distinguished from ASL. One is *fingerspelling*, in which each letter of the alphabet has a hand sign, so that English words can be spelled out letter by letter on the hand. This is used to sign names and technical terms of English for which there is no conventional ASL translation—much as words like "glasnost" and "perestroika" were borrowed whole into English some years back.

The other coding of English into signs is called *Manual English* (or, in one variant, Signing Exact English). It renders literally into signs the word order of English, even adding to its words suffixed signs for the English plural and past tense endings. Manual English was devised by educators as an aid in teaching English to deaf children. It is sometimes used in simultaneous translation of English into sign. However, as we will see, a word-for-word translation of English, complete with prefixes and suffixes, is quite different from ASL, which has its own grammatical organization. Native ASL speakers find Manual English awkward and unnatural, and its use is disfavored by the Deaf community.*

ASL itself exhibits the full expressive variety of spoken languages. It is not just pantomime, of the sort that speakers of, say, English and Mohawk might make up on the spot in order to communicate with each other. It has a standardized vocabulary and as fully complex a grammar (i.e. mental grammar) as spoken languages. It is a suitable vehicle for jokes, arguments, poetry, drama, and science (including linguistics).

Like vocal-auditory languages, there are many different sign languages spoken throughout the world. Japanese Sign Language and British Sign Language, for instance, are independent languages that cannot be understood by an ASL speaker. (When an ASL speaker and a Japanese or British Sign Language speaker want to communicate, then *they* have to resort to pantomime too!)

Interestingly, a sign language different from ASL was spoken on the island of Martha's Vineyard, off the coast of Massachusetts, for at least two centuries. Here there was a high incidence of inbred genetic deafness, which persisted into the early twentieth century owing to the island's isolation. But in Martha's Vineyard, unlike most of the rest of the world, the deaf were not at all socially stigmatized. Rather, it was taken for granted that the hearing were fluent in sign as well. With none of the usual linguistic barriers, the deaf were fully functioning and fully integrated members of the community.

Returning to ASL, its pedigree goes back at least to the mid eighteenth century in France. Charles Michel, the Abbé de l'Epée, undertook to educate the deaf, and discovered that the deaf of Paris

* To get a sense of what Manual English might feel like to an ASL speaker, imagine "Spoken Exact German," in which English words are used in German order and with German inflections for gender and case. In this language, "The man didn't give the book to the woman" would be rendered as something like "The-masculine-nominative man has the-feminine-dative woman the-neuter-accusative book not given," in parallel to the German "Der Mann hat der Frau das Buch nicht gegeben." It's uncomfortable indeed.

had an indigenous sign language that they used to communicate with each other. Using this as a basis of instruction, he developed methods for teaching the deaf to read and write French. His pupils astonished and excited the European intellectual community: l'Epée had shown that the deaf were neither mentally retarded nor incapable of reason, as had been widely assumed. L'Epée's school, founded in 1755, trained teachers who spread his methods of teaching—as well as the use of French Sign Language—to schools for the deaf throughout much of Europe.

In 1817 the first American school for the deaf was opened in Hartford, Connecticut. Its language of instruction was French Sign Language, introduced by Laurent Clerc, a deaf graduate of L'Epée's school. This school was quickly followed by other residential schools throughout the country, and 1864 saw the founding of the National Deaf Mute College, now Gallaudet University. In these schools, students speaking a variety of sign languages (including Martha's Vineyard Sign) were brought together, and elements of their languages blended with French Sign Language to form ASL. (Such blending doesn't take place by design; it is a natural outcome of intimate contact between languages. The English of Chaucer formed from a similar blending of Old English with Norman French in the centuries after the Norman Conquest.)

The status of sign—and of the Deaf community—was dealt a severe and long-lasting blow in 1880, when the International Congress on the Education of the Deaf voted overwhelmingly against the use of sign and in favor of oral instruction (after first denying the deaf among them the right to vote!). The philosophy behind the resolution was that only with the use of speech could the deaf be integrated into society. The actual outcome was the degradation of deaf education. (Imagine trying to learn anything from a television set with the sound turned off. Remember: lip-reading gives access only to what the lips and perhaps the tip of the tongue are doing, not to features of voicing, nasality, or movement of the body of the tongue. Consequently, the sounds *p*, *b*, and *m* look identical, as do *t*, *d*, and *n*, for instance. Not so easy, even to a fluent user of a spoken language.)

Despite the official suppression of ASL in schools for the deaf, the language was used in the dormitories and passed on to new generations of speakers. The schools in fact have played a focal role in the use of ASL: most deaf students come from families with hearing parents, so that their first exposure to the Deaf community and to sign (and thus to any comprehensible language at all) occurs when they go to school.*

The current rebirth of respect for ASL is generally acknowledged to have begun in 1960, with the publication of William Stokoe's *Sign Language Structure: An Outline of the Visual Communication System of the American Deaf.* Stokoe showed that ASL gestures have systematic organization that strongly parallels the phonological structure of spoken languages. By the 1970s his work had been taken up by a substantial number of linguists, both deaf and hearing, and there is now a vibrant community of researchers examining ASL and other sign languages.

Among other things, this research has served as public legitimation of ASL as a real language. It has helped to empower the Deaf community to take pride in their language and culture, and to demand the respect and political rights accorded other minorities. Yet, despite progress, there is much still to be done to improve the general perception of the Deaf and their language. Oral teaching is still the method of choice in most schools for the deaf. And awareness on the part of the general public leaves much to be desired. Not too many years ago, a colleague of mine, an otherwise well-informed and politically enlightened man, wondered whether my deaf graduate student was really answering the questions addressed to him in a colloquium—whether his interpreter might not actually be doing the thinking. Upsetting, to say the least.

Elements of ASL grammatical organization

Stokoe's discovery, which inaugurated the modern study of ASL linguistics, was that signs can be factored into a combination of parts: handshape, hand orientation, location of the hands in space, and movement of the hands. Like the distinctive features of phonological structure, these factors are themselves meaningless.

---

* This has recently come to serve as an argument against "mainstreaming" deaf children in public schools in the USA. The reasoning is that the residential schools provide a linguistic and cultural community with which deaf children can identify, and in which they can interact freely with their peers. In an ordinary public school classroom, with at best the part-time help of an interpreter, linguistic support and social interaction for the deaf child are meager. Not only does this produce a sense of isolation and severely hinder the educational process, it destroys one of the main mechanisms for transmission of Deaf culture.

To give an idea of how they work, here are some samples of signs that differ in only one of the factors. Figure 7.1 shows the signs for "candy," "apple," and "jealous." They have identical location, movement, and orientation, differing only in handshape.

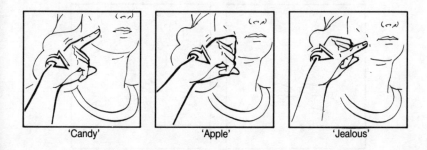

Figure 7.1 *Signs that differ only in handshape (Illustration, copyright © Ursula Bellugi, The Salk Institute for Biological Studies, La Jolla, CA 92037, USA)*

Figure 7.2 shows the signs for "Chinese" and "onion," which have handshapes and twisting motion identical to "candy" and "apple" respectively, but in a different location.

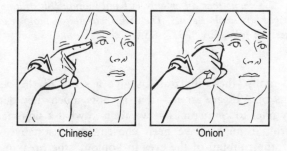

Figure 7.2 *Signs that differ only in location from those in Figure 7.1 (Illustration, copyright © Ursula Bellugi, The Salk Institute for Biological Studies, La Jolla, CA 92037, USA)*

Figure 7.3 shows the signs for "name," "short," and "egg." They are all made with the same handshape, location, and orientation. The first two are made with different motions of the right hand; the last is made with motion of both hands.

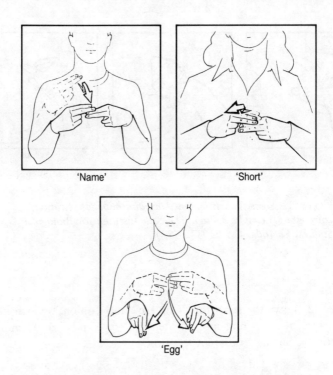

'Name'   'Short'

'Egg'

Figure 7.3 *Signs that differ only in hand motion (Illustration, copyright © Ursula Bellugi, The Salk Institute for Biological Studies, La Jolla, CA 92037, USA)*

Incidentally, these illustrations give a sense of the degree to which signs of ASL are *iconic*—that is, how much they depict the things they refer to. Sometimes, if we are told what a sign means, we can see why it might have been chosen: the distinctive eyes in "Chinese," the rubbing of the eyes in "onion," the breaking of the egg. But it would probably be difficult to *guess* what the signs mean if we didn't know. Furthermore, why those twists of the hand in "Chinese" and "onion"? And do the signs for "name" and "short" make any sense at all?

These examples show that although *sometimes* signs *partly* depict what they refer to, hardly ever are the forms of signs completely determined by what they mean. So ASL vocabulary has to be learned just like that of a spoken language—though it sometimes has a little more mnemonic power than the arbitrary sounds of spoken language.

Stokoe's analysis of signs shows that there are distinctive features of manual articulation analogous to the distinctive features of vocal articulation. More recent research has found a rhythmic structure in sign similar to that in spoken language. The basic rhythmic unit of spoken language is the syllable—roughly, a vowel plus whatever consonants (if any) surround it. The corresponding rhythmic unit in sign is a motion plus whatever held positions (if any) precede and follow it. Just as speakers of spoken languages tend to slow down at the end of a sentence, so do speakers of sign. Just as speakers of spoken languages tend to pronounce an emphasized word more loudly, speakers of sign tend to make an emphasized sign larger. We see, then, that ASL preserves significant aspects of phonological structure, while adapting the parts having to do with motor articulation so as to make use of the rather different possibilities inherent in the manual-to-visual channel of communication.

Turning to syntactic structure, ASL, like spoken languages, classifies signs into parts of speech, and it strings parts of speech together with modifiers to form larger constituents and clauses. It also displays long-distance dependencies such as wh-questions. As it happens, though, ASL forms wh-questions by putting the wh-word at the end of the sentence instead of the beginning—for instance, "Bill buy yesterday what?" instead of "What did Bill buy yesterday?"

I'd like to run through a few examples of phenomena in ASL syntax that look very different from English. I'll try to show that in almost all respects they have analogues in other spoken languages, and are therefore recognizable as variants available in the menu of Universal Grammar.

The signs for "I" and "you" are pointing gestures directed at the speaker and addressee respectively. So far, apparently iconic. But further probing reveals more structure in the pronouns. First, changing the handshape from a pointing index finger to a flat palm makes the pronouns into the possessives "my" and "your," and making the movement arc-like makes the pronouns into the plurals "we" and "you-all." So the apparently iconic gestures actually form part of a grammatical system. (English, of course, doesn't have separate forms for singular and plural "you"; but many languages of the world do, for instance Hebrew.)

Now let's look at the third-person pronouns. A grammatical strategy found in ASL is to sign the name or description of each character at a different location in the "signing space" in front of the speaker. Then, when the speaker wishes to refer back to a character previously named (the function of a third-person pronoun like "he" or "she"), it is necessary only to point at that character's designated location in signing space. Like the first- and second-person pronouns, this reference can be made possessive or plural by changing the handshape or motion respectively. The effect is that there are as many different third-person pronouns available as there are discernible locations in signing space.

This is actually a grammatical device not found in spoken languages. In "John told Bill that Susan likes him," who does Susan allegedly like? We can't tell. But in ASL, the pointing gesture corresponding to "him" would pick out the answer unambiguously.

One of the most intensively studied phenomena in ASL has been the forms of the verb. English verbs have only a few different forms: infinitive ("write" or "to write"), present and past tenses ("writes" and "wrote"), present and past participles ("writing" and "written"). ASL verbs, in contrast, can have a vast number of different forms, which incorporate information that would be expressed in English by separate words or phrases. For instance:

1. The direction of motion in the verb's sign can be altered, so that it begins at the location in signing space for the subject and ends at that for the object. If the subject and object are pronouns, they can be omitted altogether as separate signs. Figure 7.4 shows the signs for "ask," "I ask you," "I ask him," and "you ask me."

2. The motion of the verb can be inflected to show whether the action takes place at a point in time, over a long period of time, incessantly, repeatedly, or habitually. Figure 7.5 illustrates some of these variants ("stacked" arrows indicate repeated motion).

3. The motion of the verb can express how the action is distributed among a group of individuals over time. Figure 7.6 shows a few possibilities.

(text continues on p. 94)

Figure 7.4 *Modification of a verb's motion to incorporate subject and object pronouns (Illustration, copyright © Ursula Bellugi, The Salk Institute for Biological Studies, La Jolla, CA 92037, USA)*

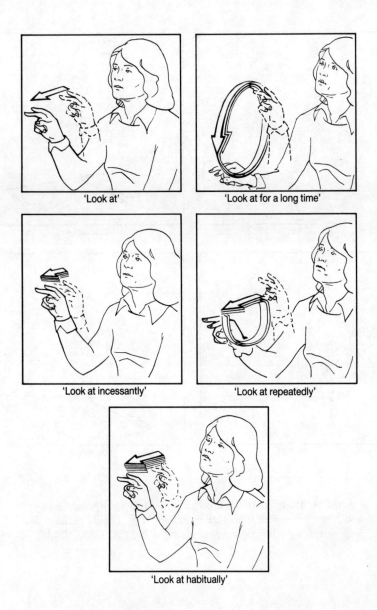

Figure 7.5 *Modification of a verb's motion to express duration and repetition of action (Illustration, copyright © Ursula Bellugi, The Salk Institute for Biological Studies, La Jolla, CA 92037, USA)*

'Preach to each of them'

'Preach to selected ones at different times'

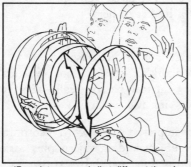

'Preach to any and all at different times'

Figure 7.6 *Modification of a verb's motion to express distribution of action among a group of individuals over time (Illustration, copyright © Ursula Bellugi, The Salk Institute for Biological Studies, La Jolla, CA 92037, USA)*

This strategy of incorporating all sorts of modifying information into the verb looks altogether exotic from the point of view of English and most other European languages. But it is by all means an option in the menu of Universal Grammar: there are many so-called *agglutinative* languages with similar possibilities. Here are some examples from such languages, with analyses and translations.*

> *Hungarian*:
> beadogattathattuk
> be-ad - o -   gat - tat - hat- t - uk
> in -give-them-distributive-cause-can- past-we
> "we could make someone hand them in piece by piece"

> *Onandaga*:
> tashako?ahsv:?
>   t - a - shako - ?ahs - v: - ?
> cause-past-he to her-basket-give-past
> "he handed a basket to her"

> *K^{w}ak$^{w'}$ala:*
> ai k'əlxlk' axsu?əm̱xat' ida q'isina
>   a   -i k'əlxlik'ax - su? - əm - x̱at-ida q'isina
> auxiliary-they eat raw-passive-really-also-the currant
> "raw currants are also eaten"

In each of these examples, a single word incorporates the verb of the sentence plus the subject and/or object, plus various other markers that would be expressed in English by extra verbs, auxiliary verbs, or adverbs. Such combinations are comparable to those of ASL in both complexity and content.

In these languages, all the extra information appears as prefixes and suffixes on the verb. In ASL, though, it is *inside* the verb, changing the motion of the hands. But in fact there are spoken languages that use a parallel to this strategy too. The most notable examples are Semitic languages such as Arabic and Hebrew, in which different forms of the verb preserve the order of the consonants but change the vowels and the length of the consonants. Here is a small

---

* The Hungarian example is courtesy of Piroska Csuri. The example from Onandaga, a language spoken in the vicinity of the Great Lakes, appears in Mark Baker, *Incorporation*, University of Chicago Press, 1988, p. 76, citing H. Woodbury, *Noun Incorporation in Onandaga*, a Yale Ph.D. dissertation of 1975. The example from K^{w}ak$^{w'}$ala, a language of British Columbia, is cited in Stephen Anderson, *A-Morphous Morphology*, Cambridge University Press, 1992, p. 92.

sample of the vast number of forms for the Arabic verb "to write," whose basic consonants are *k-t-b*.

(1) *a* kataba "he wrote"
     b kaataba "he corresponded"
     c kutib "was written"
     d kattaba "he caused to write"

So even the way verbal modification is accomplished in ASL parallels a possibility in the phonology of spoken languages.

The last wrinkle in ASL which I want to mention is that it is not all done with the hands. Facial expression also plays a crucial role in syntactic structure. For instance, the following three sentences of English are translated into ASL with the very same sequence of hand signs:

(2) *a* The woman left her book.
     b Did the woman leave her book?
     c The woman didn't leave her book.

The difference is signaled by the face. The simple statement (2a) is accompanied by a neutral expression. The question (2b) is signaled by a brow raise, widened eyes, and frequently a tilting forward of the head or whole body. The negative sentence (2c) is signaled by a side-to-side headshake and frequently by drawing the brows together. These gestures make different use of the facial muscles from ordinary facial expressions, which is why ASL speakers may seem to be grimacing as they speak.

Like the features of the pronoun system, ASL facial gestures function combinatorially. For instance, to ask a negative question ("Didn't the woman leave her book?"), a speaker uses both gestures at once: drawing the brows together and raising them, widening the eyes, and tilting the head forward while shaking it from side to side.

Lest it should seem strange that questions and negations can be formed without changing word order, let me remind you that English can signal questions by intonation alone: "The woman left her book?" Here, just as in ASL, the questioning is carried on a separate channel from the words, conveyed simultaneously. Simple negation can't be expressed in English by intonation, but sarcastic disbelief can: "Oh, yeah, sure—you really won the lottery (. . . and I'm the Queen of England)." So even these devices of ASL have spoken analogues (though probably without the rich combinatorial possibilities).

The Fundamental Arguments again

Even with this tiny amount of information about the language, it's not hard to restate the Fundamental Arguments in terms of ASL. The Argument for Mental Grammar: What do ASL speakers know that enables them to speak and understand an indefinitely large number of sentences? They can't just be memorizing signs, since even a single verb can occur in an unbelievable number of variants (of which we have seen only a few here). Rather, speakers must have in their heads a mental grammar—a basic vocabulary of signs, plus a set of patterns for combining signs sequentially and simultaneously. The difference in modality serves to make the complexity of the patterns all the more vivid: once we see that ASL goes beyond pantomime, the skill displayed by its speakers is harder to take for granted than mastery of a spoken language, if only because the complexity can literally be seen.

The Argument for Innate Knowledge: How, then, do ASL speakers acquire these patterns? The facts of ASL learning militate against its being taught. Recall (1) that most ASL speakers have hearing parents who, prior to their child's education, were not even aware of the existence of the language; (2) that ASL has been primarily spread through the residential schools for the deaf; and (3) that until very recently the use of ASL in these schools has been officially discouraged and even punished. Consequently, people have had to learn the language not by instruction, but by "picking it up" from fellow students. This is essentially parallel to the situation of immigrant children, except it involves learning a *first* rather than a second language: typically, there is no language a deaf child can use with hearing parents.*

Yet, as with spoken language, linguists are working overtime to discover the organization of ASL patterns, to find the units out of which ASL is built. The fact that it took until 1960 to begin to see these units is in itself striking. (Of course, for a long period, analysis was hampered by the prevailing ideology that ASL *had* no patterns. But the fact that such an ideology was believable also helps make my point.) So we are faced with the Paradox of Language Acquisition

---

* There is undoubtedly *communication* between deaf children and their parents through pantomime, body language, and the like. But, as stressed in Chapter 2, such communication does not constitute a *language*, in that it lacks the expressive variety and grammatical structure of spoken languages—and of ASL. See Chapter 10 for a discussion of how elaborate such communication can be.

again: children acquire an unconscious mental grammar of ASL, but linguists can't yet figure it out.

We conclude, as before, that children come equipped with unconscious hypotheses about what the mental grammar should be like. These hypotheses can't be specific to ASL, for deaf children learn whatever sign language they happen to come in contact with. So there has to be some sort of Universal Grammar for sign languages, just as for spoken languages.

But wait: remember that Universal Grammar itself isn't learned—it has to be transmitted genetically, and the genetic information has to be a product of evolution. It would seem bizarre for evolution to have provided us with a Universal Grammar for sign languages, to be drawn on just in case we happen to be deaf! Fortunately, as we have seen, there is a better answer: in almost all respects, the UG for sign languages is exactly the same as UG for spoken languages. Deaf children exposed to ASL don't have to draw on an entirely different body of innate knowledge. They expect the same organization in sign that they would have expected in spoken language, could they hear it. The very same special-purpose machinery kicks in. Children come prepared to learn *language*, in whatever modality.

The main adaptation of sign languages is replacing the distinctive features of vocal articulation by distinctive features of manual and facial articulation. An interesting by-product of this adaptation is a much greater use of simultaneity rather than sequencing, as we saw in the grammatical phenomena discussed in the previous section. Yet our comparison with spoken languages shows that ASL only takes the possibilities for simultaneity in the UG of spoken languages and extends them to a greater degree. This exploitation of simultaneity is possible because the hands and face have more independent degrees of freedom than the vocal tract—they can do more different things at once. But the abstract principles that organize these degrees of freedom are drawn from the same menu.

Returning to the main theme of this book: What does ASL tell us about language and about human nature? In previous chapters, we came to think of language as a complex relation between thought and speech, with two codings enroute, phonological and syntactic structure. We now have to generalize that characterization to include sensorimotor modalities other than speech. Figure 7.7 (next page) incorporates this revision into our earlier diagram of the overall organization of language.

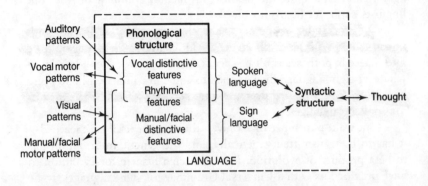

Figure 7.7 *Information flow in spoken and signed language*

Thus ASL serves to emphasize the *abstractness* of linguistic organization—its independence from sensorimotor modality. In using language, we're doing a lot more than simply associating sounds (or signs) with meanings. Most of the richness of language comes from *inside* the mind, from the way our mental grammars unconsciously create structure that gives meaning to sensory patterns. Moreover, much of the structure is now seen to be indifferent as to the modality of the sensory patterns. And it is learned on the basis of innate organization of the brain, built to tune itself to language-like patterns in the environment, whether auditory or visual.

As for human nature, we should continue to keep in mind the question: If the organization of language and language learning is this complex, rich, abstract, flexible, and unconscious, what about everything else we do? Stay tuned for Part IV. But first, we have some further business regarding language.

Evidence for the biological basis of language

8 How children learn language

Introduction to Part III

Part II primarily addressed the Argument for Mental Grammar, looking at the principles for language use that mature speakers carry around in their heads. However, we constantly kept in mind the Argument for Innate Knowledge, and we therefore made an effort to separate the aspects of mental grammar that have to be learned from those that are given to the language learner in advance.

The evidence we drew on in Part II came from the structure of mental grammar itself, in two ways. First, from the range of possibilities for grammatical features across the languages of the world, we get an idea of the menu presented by Universal Grammar. Second, the fact that grammatical structure is so abstract with respect to speech (and sign) shows us that language acquisition has to go far beyond just memorizing and reshuffling inputs one has heard. Much of the organization has to come from inside the brain.

We will now go into more direct evidence for the Argument for Innate Knowledge, looking at the process of language learning in normal children (this chapter) and in a wide variety of more unusual cases (Chapters 9 and 10). We will also look at different kinds of language loss due to brain damage (Chapter 11). The goals throughout will be (1) to figure out which aspects of language are learned and which innate; and (2) to factor language ability into the parts specific to language and the parts which can be accounted for by more general intelligence.

In turn, the point of all this is to establish a baseline in terms of which to think of human nature. If language consists of this complex mix of learned and innate, special-purpose and general-purpose, and if in language learning the effects of nurture are strongly guided by nature, then there is reason to look for similar organization in other abilities as well.

101

Basic stages of language acquisition

Let's start looking at language learning in terms of the simplest observable phenomena—what babies and young children say. Of course, the earliest vocalization is crying, which, as any parent will tell you, comes in many varieties. Though it obviously communicates, it isn't language by any means. The kind of information it conveys is more akin to tone of voice: essentially, emotional state.

Sometime in the first couple of months, babies develop a kind of vocalization usually called "cooing": "goo" or "gmp" sorts of sounds, or quiet whooping. This gradually gives way at about six months to a stage called "babbling," in which the baby makes a large range of meaningless sounds, often forming strings of syllables. Frequently, babbling children even make sounds that aren't present in the language of the environment.

The consensus on babbling is that it is basically a stage in which the baby is playing with its vocal tract, with no particular linguistic intention. Even deaf babies are observed to babble; on the other hand, not all babies do it (my older daughter didn't, to my deep disappointment). Still, there are hints of proto-linguistic behavior. Babies often babble in response to being spoken to, suggesting that they are catching on to the idea of taking turns speaking in conversation. And a couple of months into babbling, the strings of sounds begin to be uttered with intonation patterns characteristic of speaking, so that the baby almost seems to be talking.

As this period progresses, the baby's phonetic output gradually comes to be "tuned" to the language of the environment—and deaf children tend to fall silent. Ruth Weir and Jean Aitchison have reported research that demonstrates this tuning. Recorded babbling of an American, a Russian, and an Arab baby was played to mothers. The American mothers could often identify the American baby, the Russian mothers the Russian baby, and the Arab mothers the Arab baby. But none of them could distinguish between the remaining two babies. So the babies, even though they weren't saying anything meaningful, were evidently making noises that sounded like the language they had been hearing around them.

(Incidentally, deaf children exposed to sign start "babbling" with their hands, in a way very much parallel to spoken babbling, experimenting with handshape and movement.)

Sometime between ten and twenty months (with girls tending to be on the earlier side, boys later), babies really start to talk, albeit in single-word utterances. The words in their vocabulary include names like "Mommy" and "Cindy," object words like "spoon" and "car," pointing words like "that," action words like "eat" and "push," properties like "hot," directions such as "up" and "down," greetings like "bye-bye," and, of course, "no." There are no function words like "a," "is," or "to"; there are no inflections like plural and past tense. The child's vocabulary may grow to fifty or seventy-five or a hundred words over a period of six months or so. You can list the words your child knows, and each new word is a milestone: "Hey, Beth said 'turtle' today!" Despite the limitations of this one-word stage, a surprising amount gets communicated this way.

After a few months of this kind of talk, perhaps at two years of age or a little before, children start to put together two-word utterances, things like "Mommy sock," "drink soup," "no eat." Even though there is nothing like an adult grammar yet, we see fairly consistent use of word order, in a sort of stripped-down version of adult order. For instance, a child at this stage won't say "Mommy throw ball," because it's too long. But we may well hear the more reduced versions "Mommy throw" and "throw ball"; while the opposite orders, "throw Mommy" and "ball throw," are unlikely.

Around the same time, all of a sudden the child's vocabulary takes off. The parents can't keep track anymore of the words their child knows. The standard estimate is that a five-year-old knows on the order of 10,000 words. This means that between the ages of two and five (three years, about a thousand days), the child has averaged ten new words a day, or close to one every waking hour! Since a word may take a period of time to master, this also means the child is probably working on dozens of words at a time.

After maybe another few months of two-word utterances, we begin to see a steady growth of grammatical complexity along with vocabulary growth. The child starts constructing gradually longer and more complex sentences, and function words and inflections begin appearing. By age five the child is speaking with a very good approximation to adult grammar, though there are numerous wrinkles to be ironed out and complexities to be added by age ten or so. (And vocabulary learning continues throughout life, though at a less frenetic pace.)

I should add that this is the standard story, and there is a fair amount of variation, including anecdotes of children who don't speak at all till they are three or four, then start talking in whole sentences. (On the other hand, if *my* child didn't talk by the age of three, I would start getting worried.)

It is also worth mentioning that children who are exposed to a second language—say because they have moved to a new country—don't take as long to learn the new language. They tend to become relatively fluent within a year or so. This suggests that some of the protracted stages of language learning from ages one to four or so should be attributed to maturation of the brain—growth in the ability to learn language—rather than to the inherent difficulties of the language being learned.

In Chapter 3, we pointed out how little of this gradual growth of language ability can be attributed to teaching. To be sure, adults and even older children will teach individual words. (But one an hour? I doubt it.) In addition, adults tend to speak to children more clearly and in simpler sentences than they use with other adults. So to some extent, children don't have to deal with the full daunting complexity of the language all at once.

We also noted, though, that children get very little grammatical correction, and are liable to ignore or resist correction when it does take place. Here's another famous example, cited by Martin Braine.

> CHILD: Want other one spoon, Daddy.
> FATHER: You mean, you want the other spoon.
> CHILD: Yes, I want other one spoon, please Daddy.
> FATHER: Can you say "the other spoon"?
> CHILD: Other . . . one . . . spoon.
> FATHER: Say "other."
> CHILD: Other.
> FATHER: "Spoon."
> CHILD: Spoon.
> FATHER: "Other spoon."
> CHILD: Other . . . spoon. Now give me other one spoon?

This shows that the child is not just imitating—the imitation is, as it were, filtered through the child's own (unconscious) version of the language. In other words, we are seeing evidence of a mental grammar—maybe not the same as an adult's, but a mental grammar nonetheless—which governs the child's use of patterns.

So the real problem of language acquisition is not just to describe the child's behavior, but to induce from this behavior the nature of the unconscious grammar that guides it, and to discover how this grammar changes as the child matures. In the rest of the chapter, I'll describe some of the things we can find out about the development of the grammar. As usual, I'll only be able to skim over a few representative phenomena, in the hope of giving the flavor of the results of a flourishing body of research.

Children know more than they say

Impressionistically, one-and-a-half-year-old children understand an amazing amount of what you say to them—even if their speech consists only of one-word utterances and their spoken vocabulary contains only fifty words. That is, their comprehension is way ahead of their production. Some rather simple experiments show this in striking fashion.

First, consider their phonology. Where I have written whole words in transcribing babies' utterances above, I was not showing you any of the simplification that they wreak on the pronunciation. Typically clusters of consonants may be simplified ("spoon" is pronounced "puon") and final consonants may be omitted ("bus" is pronounced "buh"). The articulation of consonants may be altered to make them more like other consonants in the same word: "truck" may become "guck," where "g" and "k" are articulated in the same place in the mouth.* Some of the simplification is undoubtedly due to lack of adequate motor control of the vocal tract, since the child can be shown to perceive the adult sounds. For example, a child who says "guck" for both "truck" and "duck" won't have any problem distinguishing trucks from ducks on demand.

There are other cases that are even more intriguing. The linguist Neil Smith writes that his son consistently substituted "f" for "th," so that "thick" came out "fick." But it wasn't that he couldn't pronounce "th," since at the same time he used "th" instead of "s," so that "sick" came out "thick"! So there is evidently some system in place that goes beyond motor control alone.

A final complication is that children often don't hear what they're doing. If you deliberately pronounce a word the way your child does, he or she will get mad at you and tell you to say it right. If you tell your child to say "duck", not "guck," most of the time you'll get "guck" and a blank stare. Perhaps it's like not being able to hear your own accent. The point is, even at beginning stages, the child seems to grasp much of the sound system of the adult language, but maps it into motor control in an eccentric or degraded fashion.

---

* This is the standard account of why "truck" may be pronounced "guck." Recent research by Clara Levelt, examining a large number of such mispronunciations by children learning Dutch, suggests that it is actually the vowel that affects how the consonants are pronounced. On Levelt's account, vowels made in the back of the mouth, such as the "uh" in "truck," tend to pull adjacent consonants back to "g" and "k"; vowels made with lip-rounding, such as "oo," tend to change adjacent consonants to "b" and "p," which are also made with the lips.

Such phonological facts are easily observable. Testing syntactic understanding takes more sophisticated tests. It can be shown, though, that children as young as the one-word stage (seventeen months, say) appreciate some of the subtleties of syntactic structure.

Here's one kind of experiment, developed by Kathy Hirsh-Pasek and Roberta Golinkoff. Let's sit a very young child down in front of two side-by-side TV screens. The left-hand screen shows, say, Big Bird tickling Cookie Monster; the right-hand screen shows Cookie Monster tickling Big Bird. And out of a loudspeaker between the two screens, a voice says, "Look! Big Bird is tickling Cookie Monster!" (We have already made sure the child can identify Big Bird and Cookie Monster.) What happens? It turns out that the child will look much longer at the left-hand screen, which correctly depicts what the sentence describes. That is, the child appreciates the fact that in English the actor reliably precedes the verb and the patient follows it. Remember, not all languages have this order, so the child has to have learned something about *English*. And this effect can be observed as young as seventeen months—in many children barely the onset of the production of one-word utterances.

Experiments designed to elicit children's syntactic knowledge often involve using some nonsense word in a sentence. The child doesn't get upset about this—people are *always* using unfamiliar words. But because *we* know the child has never heard this word before, we can tell that the child's response is due to knowledge of the syntactic pattern in which the word is used.

An experiment of this genre, devised by Nancy Katz, Erica Baker, and John Macnamara, has to do with the distinction between names and common nouns. Suppose I hand you a doll and say one of the sentences in (1). (I'll use all capitals so as not to bias your interpretation.)

(1) *a* This is DAX.
    b This is a DAX.

In the first case you will probably take "DAX" to be the name of the doll; in the second, because of the indefinite article "a," you will probably take "DAX" to be a word for doll or for some special kind of doll.

Children in the one-word stage—again as early as seventeen months—can be shown to know this too. How? We take the doll back and put it with a bunch of other things—blocks, toy cars, and, crucially, another doll. Then we say:

(2) *a* Could you give me DAX?

or
   b Could you give me a DAX?
      (depending on whether we first said (1a) or (1b))

In the a. case they will tend to hand you the same doll you gave them in the first place—that is, the doll named DAX. But in the b. case they are as likely to give you one doll as the other: you are asking them for any old DAX. So they evidently know that an indefinite article signals a common noun, and its absence signals a name—more than a year before they will be using indefinite articles themselves.

There is a second part to this experiment. Suppose that instead of doing it with dolls we do it with, say, packages wrapped with a ribbon. This time, we don't find any difference between "DAX" and "a DAX." In both cases the children are likely to give you back either package. Did something go wrong? No: actually they are pretty clever. They apparently know that *packages don't have names*—only people (and people-like things such as pets and dolls) do. As a consequence, they interpret "DAX" as a common noun in both the a. and b. cases. So, not only do they know how to tell names and common nouns apart and how to respond differently to them, they know which sorts of things ought to have names and which shouldn't.

Experiments like these show that children have some grasp of the grammatical patterns of the language quite a while before they can use them in their own speech. They also show that children use this grasp to help them figure out what we're trying to tell them, even when they don't know all the words we've uttered. This is an important key to how they can learn all those words without being taught: using a combination of their understanding of the context in which a sentence is uttered plus the syntactic pattern of the sentence, they can often formulate fairly precise guesses about the meanings of unknown words.

Evidence for rules in sentence production

How can we tell whether children are using a rule of mental grammar in *producing* speech—how do we know they're not just imitating what they've heard? One way is by observing them saying things they've never heard.

There are at least two methods for doing this. One is analogous to the experiment we just discussed, using nonsense words.

Remember when we formed plurals of unfamiliar words like "shmeggeggie" in Chapter 4? Our ability to do this, immediately and reliably, showed that we don't just memorize all the plural nouns: we have a principle in mental grammar that permits us to form plurals productively. Jean Berko asked children to do the same thing, with a protocol like this:

EXPERIMENTER: This is a wug. [Pointing to a cartoon of a cute little bird-like object.] Now there is another one. There are two of them. There are two . . .
CHILD: Wug.

This child obviously doesn't know the pattern for forming plurals yet. Very roughly, about three-quarters of the four- and five-year-olds tested gave the correct answer "wugs" (with the ending pronounced *z*), while nearly all the six- and seven-year-olds got it right. Since they couldn't ever have heard the words "wug" and "wugs" before, they had to use a principle of mental grammar to construct the latter from the former. And we see that this rule is not reliably available for speech production till the age of six or so.

Now recall a complication in the plural rule: when the noun ends in "s," "z," "ch," or "j," the ending is pronounced *uhz*, as in "glasses," "churches," and so forth. It turns out that children are much slower to learn this part of the rule. Only about a quarter of the four- and five-year-olds thought the plural of "tass" was "tasses," or the plural of "gutch" was "gutches." (The most frequent incorrect answer was to leave the word unchanged.) And just over a third of the six- and seven-year-olds got it right. So this extra complication in the plural rule takes a good deal longer to be acquired than the simple part.

Interestingly, at the same time that the children couldn't produce a plural for the novel word "gutch," they could fairly reliably produce the plural "glasses" for "glass." That is, this was a word whose plural they *had* heard, so they could retrieve it from memory. What they couldn't do was produce a plural on the spot using the rule. So we can clearly see the difference between learning words by memorization and constructing words by using rules of mental grammar.

Another way to discover a child's mental grammar is to observe *systematic mistakes*: things the child says that show a consistent pattern different from adult speech. For instance, in learning to form wh-questions, children often go through a number of different stages. Here are some samples, reported by Edward Klima and Ursula Bellugi.

Stage 1 (around two and a half years):
  What book name?
  Why you smiling?
  What soldier marching?
Stage 2 (around three and a half years):
  What he can ride in?
  Which way they should go?
  Why kitty can't stand up?
Stage 3 (around five):
  Where will you go?
  Why can't kitty see?
  Why don't you know?

Stage 1 looks like a simplification of adult English, in which the auxiliary verb before the subject ("What *is* the book's name?") is simply omitted. Yet when auxiliary verbs appear in Stage 2, we see that the child doesn't know where to put them: they are put directly *after* the subject, as in a normal declarative sentence. Finally, in Stage 3, the adult order is achieved.

The crucial point is Stage 2. Here all the necessary verbs are present in the sentence, but in the order they would appear in the corresponding declarative sentence ("He *can* ride in something"; "They *should* go a different way"; "Kitty *can't* stand up because . . ."). From this we surmise that the child has a mental grammar—the utterances are grammatically systematic—but hasn't figured out the adult mental grammar yet. Again, this stage can't possibly be learned by imitation, because there are no sentences like this in the environment to imitate.

Parallel stages are found in the acquisition of negative sentences. Here are some of the patterns, again from Klima and Bellugi's work.

Stage 1
  No the sun shining.
  No a boy bed.
  No sit there.
Stage 2
  He no bite you.
  I no want envelope.
  I no taste them.
Stage 3
  I didn't did it.
  You didn't caught me.

These are progressively closer approximations to the adult pattern: each reveals a different mental grammar for dealing with negative sentences. In Stage 1, the principle is just to stick "no" in front of the sentence; in Stage 2, "no" goes where "not" appears in adult grammar, but without any auxiliary verb like "did." In Stage 3 the auxiliary is there all right, but the verb still appears in the past tense instead of the untensed forms "do" and "catch." These are all possible grammatical principles for languages of the world—but they aren't English. So the child at any of these stages must have constructed a mental grammar, since the systematicity of the utterances can't be a consequence of imitation.

A last classic case involves the acquisition of the English past tense. Most English verbs form the past tense by adding a regular ending spelled "-ed" and pronounced *d*, *t*, or *uhd*, depending on the final sound of the verb (more or less parallel to the pronunciation of the plural). But there are about 180 verbs that have an irregular past tense—remaining unchanged ("put," "fit"), changing the vowel ("held," "rang," "wrote"), or worse ("caught," "brought," "went"). Initially, children often learn some of the irregular past tense verbs correctly. But then suddenly they seem to regress, saying things like "comed" and "holded." Then sometimes there appear some real monstrosities like "helded" and "wented" before gradually the incorrect forms are replaced by correct ones again.

Stage 1   walked, played, came, went
Stage 2   walked, played, comed, goed, holded
Stage 3   walked, played, camed, wented
Stage 4   walked, played, came, went, held

What seems to be going on is this: At Stage 1, children are learning past tense verbs as separate words. They haven't yet figured out that there is a relation between the words "walk" and "walked"—they're as different as "Sue" and "suit." So they just copy the adult pronunciation.

But then they (unconsciously) realize that "walked" can be analyzed as "walk + past tense"—that is, it isn't a separate word at all but, rather, a complex pattern. They then apply this pattern to everything in sight: to form past tense, add "-ed" to any old verb. So the child can now forget about all those previously memorized forms and make them up from scratch. *Voilà*: Stage 2. This child is using a rule of English correctly, but hasn't yet realized that there are exceptions.

In Stage 3 we see an unsuccessful attempt to deal with the

exceptions: the child knows you have to do *something* different with the irregular verbs, but doesn't yet know what. Relics of this stage can persist late into childhood. We're familiar with correcting eight-year-olds who still say "brang" or "catched" or "rung." But finally most people get the irregularities figured out.

Again the interesting stage is Stage 2, for here we see a rule of mental grammar—a correct one this time—which is creating things the child has never heard. And children say these in preference to the correct forms that they *do* hear.

Conclusions

There are four general points I want to take from this discussion:

1. Children understand a great deal more than they can imitate, showing that they have constructed grammatical patterns.
2. Children *don't* just imitate what they've heard. They are always coming up with novel utterances, which are patterned—implying that they have a mental grammar.
3. The patterns of their utterances are to some extent stripped down from the adult patterns, in particular leaving out function words and inflections, and shortening utterances to within narrow limits of a few words.
4. BUT—Their patterns have their own life, a life that cannot be induced from the input.

So where are the patterns coming from? From the menu of Universal Grammar.

And—in line with our larger theme—if we look hard enough, how much other learning is like this?

9 Language acquisition in unusual circumstances I

Introduction

Chapter 3 developed the Genetic Hypothesis, the idea that some aspects of language are built into brain structure and transmitted genetically. This knowledge gives children a head start on constructing a mental grammar for the language(s) they hear in their environment. Now, some people (my imaginary critic among them) are skeptical about the idea of innate knowledge that is devoted specifically to learning language—but they don't mind positing innate knowledge as long as it is basically general-purpose. Back in Chapter 3, my main reply was the Paradox of Language Acquisition: adults are better than children at solving problems in general, but they can't figure out the principles of mental grammar consciously anywhere near as well as children do unconsciously. This seems to point to some specialization for language learning that falls outside of our abilities at solving general problems.

I think it's misguided to get into an argument about whether the innate knowledge that makes language acquisition possible is *all* specialized for language or *all* general-purpose. Rather, the issue ought to be how the two factors balance each other, as summarized in the equation I gave in chapter 3:

Innate part of language =
 Part due to special-purpose endowment for language
 + Part due to general properties of the mind

The all-or-nothing cases are when one part or the other is zero. But there are many possibilities in between.

Having looked at how normal language acquisition takes place, we are in a position to look further into the balance between special-purpose and general-purpose factors. Our evidence will be drawn from a variety of cases in which language acquisition does not proceed in normal fashion. In each case, we'll be able to see that the difficulties fall under the special-purpose part of the language faculty. As a result, we can show more vividly that general-purpose intelligence is not enough to accomplish the acquisition of mental grammar.

A genetic impairment of language acquisition

Some children who appear to be normal in every other respect are late in developing language. These children, when they do begin to speak, don't follow the normal course of acquisition we discussed in the last chapter. Such children are said to be "specific language impaired" (SLI) or "developmentally dysphasic." This diagnosis undoubtedly masks a wide range of disorders that could be distinguished with more sensitive techniques of testing; it is to be hoped that advances in linguistic theory can be used to help develop more detailed diagnostic and remedial tools for speech and language therapy.

A particular set of cases of specific language impairment has been examined in depth by the linguist Myrna Gopnik and her associates. This is a family of 30 members, extending over three generations, of whom 16 have been diagnosed as dysphasic. It is worth reproducing the genealogy of the family for what it shows about the distribution of the impairment. Figure 9.1 shows the impaired family members in bold face, and ages in 1992 in parentheses.

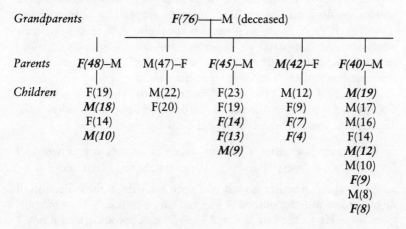

Figure 9.1

This is a classic instance of the inheritance of a dominant gene: those who have the gene are language impaired and have a 50 percent chance of passing it on to their descendants. The grandmother has passed it on to 4 of her 5 children. The one child who is not impaired has no impaired children. The 4 impaired children have passed it on to 11 of the 24 grandchildren, 5 of whom are male and 6 of whom are female.

Suppose instead we tried to explain this pattern on the basis of the environment in which the children grew up. "The grandmother talked strangely, so some of her children, imitating her, spoke strangely too; and some of their children, imitating them, did likewise." But consider: why did some of the children pay attention to the strange way one of their parents talked, and others didn't? In particular, the eight-year-old grandchildren in the lower right corner of Figure 9.1 are fraternal twins, exposed to the very same environmental inputs. Why did one come out language-impaired and the other not?

Remember also that children growing up in bilingual environments typically learn *both* languages they are exposed to. If the impairment were just a result of imitating an impaired parent, we might therefore guess that children in these families actually would be able to talk like *either* parent—that is, either normally or strangely. That isn't how it works at all. In short, a strictly environmental explanation seems impossible.

Although the degree of language impairment varied from one individual in the family to the next, the overall pattern of impairment was remarkably uniform. All of the impaired individuals had a noticeably slow rate of speech, and they stopped to correct themselves much more often than normal speakers (in 5 percent of their utterances, as compared to 1 percent for normal speakers). More remarkably, about half of their "corrections" actually made the sentence *less* rather than more grammatical!

To get a more precise understanding of what was going on, Gopnik ran a number of tests on the language-impaired individuals. There were some where everyone did all right:

1. When asked whether a certain string of sounds was a word of English ("wolf": yes; "barsen": no), everyone did satisfactorily.

2. When asked whether a verb was used with the right collection of direct and/or indirect objects ("The girl eats a cookie," "The nice girl gives a cookie to the boy": yes; "The girl eats a cookie to the boy," "The nice girl gives": no), everyone did satisfactorily.

So some basic aspects of language were not affected by the impairment. The main area where Gopnik found difficulty was in the use of inflections such as plural and tense.

3. The following sentences are missing inflections:

The boy eat three cookie.
Yesterday the girl pet a dog.

Asked whether these sentences are acceptable English, normal speakers (including those in the family) have no trouble detecting the problem. But the language-impaired members missed many of these, and even "corrected" acceptable sentences:

Example: Roses grow in the garden.
Response: "Wrong: The roses grow in the garden."

And even when their responses were correct, they often acted unsure of themselves, in a way that a normal speaker never would.

4. Recall the "wug" test in Chapter 8, in which children were asked to supply the plural for a nonsense word. Children perform essentially like adults by age eight or so. But the language-impaired family members, even the adults, had trouble with this test. For example, one adult subject pluralized "wug" as "wugs," pronouncing the ending as *s* instead of the correct *z*. She pluralized "sass" as "sasss," simply prolonging the final *s*. Another adult pluralized "wug" as "wugness," "zat" as "zackle," "zoop" as "zoopes," "tob" as "tobyes," and "zash" as "zatches." (Incidentally, this was not a problem of hearing, for which they all tested normal.)

5. The language-impaired members often used an untensed form of a verb where a past tense was called for.

Example: Every day he walks 8 miles. Yesterday he . . ."
Response: "Walk."

Tense was frequently absent in their spontaneous narratives as well—more frequently with regular verbs like "walk–walked" than with irregulars like "hold–held." By contrast, normal children, once they have learned the rule for past tense (see Chapter 8), *never* omit the past tense on regular verbs.

Obviously something strange is going on here. The language-impaired individuals persist in such errors and omissions, despite the fact that (with the exception of the grandmother) they have all undergone intensive language therapy in school, with constant correction of these very problems.

Gopnik's analysis of the situation is that *the language-impaired individuals basically have not caught onto the idea that there are rules of inflection*—they do not see that there is a standard way to alter a noun when it refers to a multiplicity and a standard way to alter a verb when it refers to past time. Rather, they are much like children in Stage 1 of learning the past tense (see Chapter 8). Either they treat the plural and past tense suffixes as uninterpreted noise, or else they treat the plural noun and past tense verb as entirely different words from the singular noun and present tense verb respectively.

This may or may not be precisely the right way to characterize the impairment: Gopnik's analysis is controversial, and at the time of this writing she has not yet systematically tested the individuals' abilities in dealing with larger syntactic constructions. But the fact remains that (1) the pattern of impairment is uniform across affected family members, (2) it is randomly distributed among children of affected family members, (3) it results in striking problems in the inflectional system, (4) it is impervious to teaching and correction, and (5) it persists through life. These results strongly suggest that the impairment is genetic, and that it specifically affects the ability to construct a mental grammar, leaving other cognitive abilities intact. In order for this to be possible, there must be at least one gene that is responsible for a special-purpose mental endowment for language acquisition. The part of Universal Grammar having to do with acquiring inflectional endings must not be a general-purpose learning strategy.

It is interesting to contrast these cases to others with opposite symptoms—where there is mental retardation but language ability is intact. One of these is *Turner's Syndrome*, in which one X chromosome of a female is damaged or absent. Turner's Syndrome individuals display distinctive physical characteristics such as short stature, infantile sexual development, heart defects, and drooping eyelids. Their cognitive development is often characterized as "uneven," usually involving impaired visuo–spatial abilities such as visual memory and drawing, but also sometimes including difficulty with number concepts and auditory memory. However, typically their language development appears normal for their age.

A similar situation appears in individuals with *Williams Syndrome*, who have a distinctive "elf-like" facial appearance, a particular heart defect, and, commonly, abnormalities of many other organ systems. Williams Syndrome individuals almost invariably show mild to moderate mental retardation; they uniformly require special educational placements as children, and for the most part acquire only rudimentary skills in reading, writing, and arithmetic. Particularly severe deficits show up in tests of spatial understanding such as copying patterns of blocks. Their language, though, is if anything more fluent and advanced than that of their age-mates; in fact, they tend to be so talkative and expressive that to the unwary observer they may not appear retarded at all (at least at first).

These syndromes give us further evidence for a difference between general intelligence and the ability to learn language. In Gopnik's cases of Specific Language Impairment, a genetic pattern produces deficits in language learning without affecting intelligence; while, by contrast, Turner's and Williams Syndromes produce the reverse. The combination of these two sorts of cases provides striking confirmation of the Genetic Hypothesis, the idea that part of our ability to learn and use language comes from specific genetic factors, not just from intelligence in general. That is, language is not a consequence merely of the size of our brains, but rather of the way particular parts of our brains work.

The critical period hypothesis

I've mentioned a number of times the fact that the children of immigrants usually manage to acquire the language of their new country faultlessly, even though the input from their parents is often far from perfect. Let's look at another aspect of this situation: the parents. Even if they are literate, well educated, attend language classes, and so forth, they still end up speaking with an accent and generally distorting the new language to some degree or another. Why do the children do better than the parents at learning the new language?

Looking at the situation more generally, we notice that the ability to learn a language the way a child does seems to tail off in the early teen years. The kind of conscious teaching that goes on in school French class is rarely effective—and (in the US at least) it comes too late in life for anyone to achieve genuine fluency. Many people undoubtedly learn to speak another language well enough to get by, and maybe even well enough to give lectures and write books, but it's rarely the same as their command of their first language. (One occasionally encounters people who go on being able to learn many languages fluently as an adult. I am not aware of any research on such prodigies, but my impression from the anecdotes is that they are mostly people who grew up constantly using three or four languages in their day-to-day life.)

In the late 1960s, the neurolinguist Eric Lenneberg proposed that there is a *critical period* for language acquisition, a time of life when our brains are prepared to construct mental grammars. He proposed that this period extends from about two-years-old, the onset of the two-word stage, to about twelve, the point when people stop being able to learn languages without effort.

In addition to the sort of evidence we have just cited, Lenneberg drew on cases of language recovery after brain damage. Children may suffer damage to the language areas of the brain under a variety of circumstances, including injury, tumors, and removal of brain tissue to halt epileptic seizures. Under these conditions, the children become *aphasic*: there is loss of language function—often complete loss. However, Lenneberg observed that the younger a child is, the more likely it is that the child will recover full use of language. Very young children tend to recover almost completely, teenagers much less so. This parallels the received wisdom about the learning of foreign languages, suggesting that the unconscious ability to construct a mental grammar degrades severely after puberty.

The critical period hypothesis is often taken to mean that language learning ability is switched on before age twelve and then switches off. What Lenneberg actually proposed—and what subsequent evidence also suggests—is that there is a steady decline in language learning ability, starting very early in life, so that by the teenage years it has become comparatively feeble (and subject to much more variation among individuals).

Why should there be a critical period? We don't know. But if there is one, it provides strong support for a specialized capacity for learning language, separate from the general-purpose learning capabilities that remain active throughout the lifespan. Consequently, the critical period hypothesis has become a focus for arguments about the special-purpose nature of the language capacity.

Still, the idea of a mental capacity gradually shutting down over the course of one's childhood seems rather outrageous. How could it possibly be true? Fortunately, nature has come to the rescue here, providing us with numerous cases of animal learning that behave like this. So the existence of a critical period for language turns out to be completely plausible on biological grounds, bizarre though it may sound at first.

Let me briefly mention three of the best-known examples of critical periods in animals.

1. If one eye of a kitten is covered up until the age of three months, the kitten never learns to see properly with that eye, and comes to view the world monocularly. In this case the mechanism is known: the neurons of the visual system are growing their connections to each other and to the rest of the brain before this age, and stop growing afterward. Since visual input helps to guide the growth and organization of the connections, they do not get fully established in its absence. (It is worth mentioning that something similar happens to a human child's eye affected by strabismus or cross-eye: if it is not corrected early enough, the brain areas driven by the eye do not develop properly and vision cannot be restored, even if the eye itself is fine.)

2. One of the most famous experiments of the ethologist Konrad Lorenz was on the "imprinting" of goslings—their acquisition of the ability to follow their mother around. Lorenz discovered that, early in goslings' lives, anything that makes an approximately goose-like noise and moves in an approximately goose-like fashion is sufficient to imprint them. He showed this by making noises and waddling around himself, and he ended up with a troop of goslings following him all over the place. Imprinting seems to be tuned to occur only during a particular period shortly after hatching.

3. Bird species differ radically in how they learn their songs. In some species, such as the cuckoo, the song is entirely innate. (It had better be: cuckoos lay their eggs in other birds' nests, so baby cuckoos do not grow up hearing parental cuckoo songs.) In other species, such as the bullfinch, the song appears to be entirely learned: a young bullfinch raised in a cage with a canary will end up singing the canary's song.

   More interesting are the species where there is an interplay of innate and learned characteristics. Chaffinches reared in isolation from birth sing only a rudimentary song. It is necessary for these birds to hear other chaffinches sing in order to acquire the full detail of the song. Acquisition goes on over a period of about ten months. If a chaffinch is isolated somewhere along the way until after it is ten months old, its song remains in its intermediate state, and no amount of exposure after the age of ten months helps the bird learn more. So here we have a critical period quite analogous to that posited for language learning, with an interaction between nature and nurture.

The crucial test for the critical period hypothesis for language would be to treat a person the way the chaffinches were treated: raise them without language until the age of twelve. The critical period hypothesis suggests that they could not learn language. Of course, such experiments are unethical; but unfortunately society has performed the experiments for us.

Genie and others

The literature contains quite a few cases of "wild children," children discovered after apparently having been reared by wolves or bears. One of the most famous is Victor, the "Wild Boy of Aveyron," discovered in 1799 at an age estimated to be eleven or twelve. He was taken under the care of Jean-Marc-Gaspard Itard—who, incidentally, served as physician at the school for the deaf mentioned in Chapter 7, and who shared that institution's belief in the educability of the disadvantaged. Itard's intensive training did succeed in bringing out many cognitive and social skills. However, Victor never developed language beyond a few isolated words. This outcome is typical of these sorts of cases.

More promising have been the children raised by humans but subjected to a brutally deprived environment. One case in the 1940s was a girl, called "Isabelle" in the literature, who had been hidden away from early infancy, was given minimal attention, and in particular was never spoken to. Discovered at the age of six, she had no language, and her cognitive skills measured below those of a two-year-old. Within a year, though, she had learned to speak and was able to function as a normal child in school. In other words, she managed to learn her first language about as fast as an immigrant child of comparable age learns a second language.

Isabelle was discovered within her critical period. A better-known case is that of "Genie," who was discovered in 1970 at the age of thirteen—well toward the end of the critical period. Unlike previous reported cases of children raised in isolation, Genie's language development was intensively studied for ten years by linguists, primarily Susan Curtiss and Victoria Fromkin.

Genie had been isolated in a small curtained room since the age of twenty months, tied into a potty chair by day and kept in a covered infant crib by night. She was minimally fed and never spoken to, and she was physically punished if she made any sounds. I'm not going to talk about the psychotic behavior of the family that led to such treatment; the curious reader is referred to more detailed sources. Here I will confine myself to the issues relevant to the critical period hypothesis.

At the time of her discovery, Genie was described as apathetic and socially unresponsive. Measures of cognitive development placed her at the fifteen-month level. Within a month, she had become alert, curious, and emotionally engaged, and she spoke a few words. Over the next year and a half, her cognitive abilities improved markedly, reaching a six- to eight-year-old level.

Genie's language ability initially went through analogues of the early stages of normal language acquisition. She spoke in one-word utterances almost immediately, and began producing two-word utterances within about seven months, with a vocabulary of about 200 words. In fact, her vocabulary was fairly sophisticated compared to her grammatical ability, including numbers, color terms, and questions with "how," "what," or "why"; these are all words that enter the normal child's vocabulary considerably later than the two-word stage. By a little more than a year after her discovery, Genie could produce larger sentences, including negation, some prepositions, and some plurals and possessives. So her "early" language development was quite rapid, and she did achieve the ability to produce an indefinite variety of new utterances by combining her vocabulary into patterns.

On the other hand, her progress more or less stopped there. For instance, she continued to form negative sentences by putting "no" at the beginning of the sentence, parallel to Stage 1 in the development of children's use of negation (Chapter 8). Her use of definite and indefinite articles remained minimal ("bathroom have big mirror"). Although she generally constructed sentences in the order subject-verb-object, her comprehension of the significance of this word order was erratic. In general, after many years of training, her language performance remained at about the level of a two-and-a-half-year old—despite general cognitive performance at a much higher level.

A number of questions remain in this case, having to do with Genie's severe social and sensory deprivation. In particular, it is certainly not true that Genie became cognitively and socially normal in all respects other than language. So although her linguistic achievements point to the effects of the critical period, there is still some room to argue about more general-purpose cognitive impairments being partially responsible for her problems in language learning.

In the past decade a somewhat less equivocal (and much less publicized) case has emerged. A woman, called "Chelsea" in the literature, was born profoundly hearing-impaired to hearing parents. She was misdiagnosed as retarded, but was brought up in an otherwise normal family with normal social interaction; her hearing loss was finally diagnosed and she was fitted with hearing aids at the age of thirty-one. After nine years with hearing aids and training, she was reported to have a vocabulary of about 2000 words, could read at a grade 2 or 3 level, and could speak clearly enough to shop, order in restaurants, and hold a part-time job as a veterinarian's assistant. Yet after twelve years, her production of syntactic structure was still at roughly the two-and-a-half-year-old level: she tended to leave out subjects of sentences, saying things like "hit ball" and "cupboard put food." The function words and inflections were largely absent, and her word order was extremely variable. In short, she did not acquire English syntax after many years of exposure and intensive training.

Whatever questions may arise in this case or Genie's, the important thing to notice is the robust similarity of the results. Vocabulary was acquired, communication came to take place, but mental grammar, in particular the fine details of word order and inflection, did not develop. To my mind, the two cases together constitute substantial evidence for the critical period hypothesis.

Many more cases of late exposure to language

Once ASL came to be recognized as a language, it became possible to study its acquisition by children in just the same way as the acquisition of spoken language. It has been found that deaf children in families that speak ASL go through essentially the same stages of language learning as children acquiring spoken languages. In addition, hearing children of deaf parents are very much like immigrant children: they grow up bilingual, acquiring sign from their parents and spoken language from others in the environment.

However, as mentioned in Chapter 7, something like 90 percent of deaf children are born to hearing parents, into homes where sign language is not spoken. Increasingly, hearing parents of deaf children are encouraged to learn ASL and speak it with their children. But there is still an attitude in many quarters that deaf babies are "not ready to learn to speak." In the majority of cases, a deaf child's first exposure to sign—and therefore to any language at all—is upon entering a residential school for the deaf, in many of which the language is spoken only surreptitiously. Many children are sent to these schools at the age of four to six, but many not until later.

These practices have provided us with valuable evidence regarding the critical period hypothesis, in that there are now large numbers of people who were deprived of language (but not of social interaction) until the point in their lives when they went to school. Elissa Newport and Ted Supalla investigated how the learning of ASL might be affected by the age at which deaf speakers began to learn it.

Newport and Supalla had the clever idea of testing adult speakers of ASL who had only limited skills in English—people who had been using ASL daily for thirty years or more, so they had had plenty of experience with it. These people differed in just one significant variable: the age at which they first came into contact with the language. Newport and Supalla classified them into three groups according to this variable. The "native" learners were children of deaf signing parents, so they were exposed to ASL from birth. The "early" learners were exposed to ASL first at ages four to six, upon arriving at a residential school. The "late" learners' first exposure was not until after age twelve, because they first attended strict oral schools before encountering ASL.

The subjects were tested for production and comprehension of a wide variety of grammatical constructions in ASL. These included basic and varied word order, as well as many forms of verbal inflection of the sort we discussed in Chapter 7—for instance, alteration of the motion of the verb to mark the spatial position of the subject and object, and alteration to mark repeated, drawn-out, incessant, or habitual motion.

Guess what happened. On tests of basic word order, everyone did well. But on tests of verbal inflection, the native speakers did somewhat better than the early learners, who in turn did considerably better than the late learners. In particular, late learners were inconsistent in their use of ASL inflections, sometimes using an inflection and sometimes not in contexts where it should always have appeared. Newport writes: "These results provide strong evidence for an effect of age of acquisition on control over a primary language: The later the language is learned, the less its use is native (with crisp and grammatically consistent forms) in character."

This pattern strongly resembles the patterns found with Genie and with the genetically impaired population. It shows that no matter how much experience people have with a language, they can get only so far learning it if that experience doesn't begin early enough—and the earlier the better. Even the people who began at age four were at a disadvantage relative to those born into ASL-speaking homes.

As a further angle on these results, Newport, in collaboration with Jacqueline Johnson, went back to the initial insight that motivated the critical period hypothesis: the difficulty that adults have learning a *second* language. They looked at speakers of Korean and Chinese who had come to the United States and learned English. All the people they looked at had been in the USA for over ten years, immersed in an English-speaking world. Again, the crucial difference among the subjects was the age at which they had come to the USA.

Newport and Johnson tested these subjects on their judgments of grammaticality ("Is the following sentence acceptable English: The boy eat the hot dog"). The tests involved issues like verb tense, noun plurals, basic word order, use of the articles "a" and "the," and permutations of word order for wh-questions.

The results paralleled those for ASL speakers. Just about everyone got basic word order correct. But on tests that involved grammar any more complex than that, the people who arrived in the USA by the age of seven or so did uniformly better than everyone else. There was a steady decline over the ages of seven to fifteen, and the subjects who arrived after the age of seventeen were scattered randomly, well below the early learners. In addition, Newport and Johnson were able to show that these results could not be attributed to formal instruction in English, length of experience with English, motivation to learn English, or identification with American culture. The only significant variable was age of arrival in the USA.

Now it is true that people learning a second language late in life often get a lot better than Genie or Chelsea. It may well be that learning a first language early helps one to learn a second language later on, though not as much as starting the second language earlier. But qualitatively, the results have a strongly similar flavor. Basic word order and the acquisition of vocabulary seem to be largely independent of the critical period effect. But you have to be the right age to acquire complete command of finely tuned phonology (i.e. accent-free speech), the systems of inflection, and non-basic syntax such as negation and wh-questions.

Now I want to trace our argument backward, to remind you of why we're going through all this. We've established that there are critical period effects in the acquisition of the more complex aspects of mental grammar. These effects appear in a variety of circumstances when language is acquired past puberty, and the various cases differ in degree, but not in their essential character.

Why were we interested in the existence of a critical period for language? Because we wanted to show that there are aspects of language learning that are not correlated with other kinds of learning. If parts of language learning stop being available after a certain age, while other kinds of learning continue, there must be something special about language learning—not all of it can be due to one's general-purpose ability to learn. So the critical period, like the Paradox of Language Acquisition, points to children having a specialized piece of their brains that is devoted to constructing a mental grammar. This piece is not only genetically programmed, but even genetically programmed to *turn off*. The picture is further confirmed by the genetically impaired language learners, who fail in some of the same ways as the late language learners. Evidently the same specialized parts of the brain are affected.

On the other hand, the jury is still out on the parts of language that *can* be learned by late learners and genetically impaired speakers. Are vocabulary and basic word order acquired by general-purpose learning? Or are they acquired by means of a different part of the specialized language capacity, a part that is not affected either by the critical period or by this particular genetic defect?

However the answers to these questions come out, we see that the ability to learn language is not monolithic. There is some sort of division between, on one hand, vocabulary and basic word order, and on the other, the more complex aspects of language such as inflection and altered word orders. The latter in some sense piggybacks on the former: inflection and altered word order depend on there being words and basic word order to start with.

I'm not done with this topic yet. The next chapter discusses some further cases of unusual language acquisition which are even more radical than the ones we have looked at so far.

10 Language acquisition in unusual circumstances II

Creation of language: Home Sign

In Chapter 8, we saw that children acquiring language produce utterances that are different from those they hear in the environment. They can create plurals for nouns they have never heard before ("wugs"), regular past tenses for irregular past tense verbs ("holded"), and nonstandard constructions for negative sentences ("Daddy not come home"). Such errors are important because they show that the child isn't just imitating the input, but is rather constructing *rules* of mental grammar. These particular rules don't happen to be exactly the ones employed by the adults in the environment—they can be regarded as a good first or second guess, to be revised in the light of further experience. They help us to see how much the learning of language is an act of construction for the child, not just a passive "soaking up" of data from the environment.

This section and the next deal with cases in which children construct rules in response to environmental input, *despite the fact that the environmental input is not systematically rule-governed.* The children actually end up *creating* a new grammar where there wasn't one (or much of one) in the adult models. These cases demonstrate dramatically that children are relentless grammar-constructors. They can't help but interpret language-like input as though it is a language, structured according to the dictates of Universal Grammar.

For the first case, let's return once again to deaf children. Remember that most deaf children are born to hearing parents, who may not even know there is such a thing as sign language. Sometimes the parents may begin to learn a little Manual English to use with their child. As we saw in Chapter 7, Manual English just follows English word order, complete with prefixes and suffixes. But it turns out that young children exposed only to Manual English often spontaneously improvise some of the distinctive grammatical characteristics of ASL and other sign languages. For instance, they may

126

modify the motion of a verb to indicate manner or speed of motion (which seems fairly natural), and they may even use spatial location in signing space to pick out different characters (which seems a bit more surprising). In a sense, the children instinctively reject the organization of Manual English as an appropriate grammar for a signed language, substituting something more in line with the natural proclivities of the signed modality.

Even more interesting are ten children who were studied intensively over several years of their development by Susan Goldin-Meadow and associates. These children, profoundly deaf at birth, were born to hearing parents and exposed to no sign language at all. Nevertheless, each of them invented a substantial system of signs with which to communicate with the parents. These "home sign" systems reveal some interesting aspects of the language acquisition process.

How could Goldin-Meadow tell that these children were using a *language* of sorts and not just random gestures? After all, each one invented something different. But there were characteristics in common. First of all, there was clearly an attempt at communication. The children didn't just stand around gesturing: they made a point of establishing eye contact with an addressee before performing the signs. Second, their gestures weren't performed on objects. For instance, the gesture signifying the opening of a jar would be made in the air, not on the jar. Third, the gestures came in strings separated by relaxation of the hand, just like sentences of sign language. Fourth, it was possible to read a meaning into the gestures—to guess consistently what the child had in mind.

Goldin-Meadow was able to separate the children's gestures into a number of types, of which I want to mention two. The children used *pointing* gestures predominantly to pick out objects, people, and places in the environment. They also used stylized pantomimes of actions, to characterize either an action itself or an object that characteristically performs that action (such as a bird, denoted by two hands flapping). Goldin-Meadow called such gestures *characterizing* gestures.

Interestingly, the children sometimes used pointing gestures to "point" to things not present in the environment. For instance, one child pointed to an empty jar, then gave the gesture for "blow," in order to request that an absent jar full of bubble liquid be produced. Another child used a "round" gesture to signify a Christmas tree ball, then pointed to a place on the imaginary object to refer to the little hook on top of the ornament. These examples, which are typical of what was found in "home sign," go beyond the usual here-and-now function of pointing. In one case studied in detail, the child started using pointing gestures to indicate absent objects shortly after age three, and started pointing at features of imaginary objects shortly before age five. Guess what: children exposed to ASL start using pointing gestures in these ways at just about the same ages. This hardly seems like a coincidence.

What made the children's behavior especially language-like is that they strung gestures together into longer utterances. And here again their development parallels normal language acquisition. Goldin-Meadow happened to start observing two of the children at a stage when they produced only one sign at a time. They began producing two-gesture strings at ages one and a half and two and a half, both well within the range for the onset of the two-word stage in normal language acquisition. Similarly, during the study, four children progressed from a two-gesture stage to production of more complex utterances. Three of them were between two and two and a half; the third was about three and a half. Again these fall in the normal range for progression from the two-word stage to more complex language.

Let's see what kind of language the children eventually arrived at. In fact none of them went much further than the two-gesture stage. Like the two-word stage of normal acquisition, their utterances left a lot out. For instance, the act of X giving Y to Z might be signed by "X – Z," "Y – give," "give – Z," or "Y – Z," that is, just about any combination of two of the relevant four signs. However, as in the two-word stage of spoken language, the signs appeared in fairly consistent order. For instance, the sign for "give" tended to appear after the thing given but before the person doing the receiving: "Y – give" and "give – Z", but not the other way around.

When the children did create more complex sentences, they tended to express multiple actions as in (1a), multiple actors as in (1b), and multiple events without shared characters, as in (1c).

(1) *a* climb - sleep - point [to horse]
   "The horse climbed and then slept."
   b point [to pear] - point [to banana] - no - roll
   "The pear but not the banana should roll forward."
   c sip - point [to toy cowboy] - point [to toy soldier] - beat
   "The cowboy sips a straw and the soldier beats a drum."

In the case of one child who was studied especially carefully, it actually proved possible to classify his signs as nouns, verbs, and adjectives, where each part of speech had its own particular grammatical properties. For instance, his verbs developed an analytic treatment in terms of handshape and location, paralleling the grammatical structure of the ASL verb. Like deaf children exposed to Manual English, he invented a spatial inflection of action signs, displacing them toward the position in signing space occupied by the object in motion. This systematicity began to appear between three and three and a half, comparable to the age at which children learning English start using plural and past tense systematically. (By the way, it is not as though the other children didn't have such structure too; it is just that discovering it is extremely labor-intensive, given that each child is different and there is no translator to help out.)

On the other hand, even by the age of nearly six, none of the children developed recursive structures parallel to "Bill said that Harry thought Sue was a genius." Nor did they develop abstract connectives like "if," "before," or "because"; and generally their utterances never got longer than four or five gestures. This contrasts with children learning language in normal circumstances, who by the age of five are chattering away in complex sentences full of recursion and abstraction.

Still, the fact that the children got this far is fairly amazing if we look at the sort of input they got. To be sure, their mothers gestured, using both pointing and characterizing (pantomimic) gestures. But the mothers had far smaller vocabularies of characterizing gestures, overlapping no more than 33 percent with the vocabularies of their children. Yes, the mothers did produce strings of gestures—but far less frequently than their children. The children were fairly reliable in the order of their gestures, but the mothers were not. And when children began producing complex utterances like those cited above, it was not as a result of modeling their mothers: the mothers started doing it *later* than their children. As for the child whose signs were shown to have internal structure, his mother's signs were found to have a far less systematic analysis. In short, *the children had a much more elaborate and consistent mental grammar than their mothers.*

These children illustrate all the more vividly a point I was making in Chapter 3. Children can't get rules of mental grammar from the environment—the most they can get is *examples* of utterances, from which they construct their own mental grammar. In these cases, the parents provide lots of gestures, but the structuring of these gestures in rule-governed fashion can't come from anywhere but the children themselves.

In order to explain the invention of these systems of home sign, we have to suppose that children are looking for something—*anything*—in the environment that looks remotely like language, something out of which their Universal Grammar can construct a mental grammar. If the auditory–vocal channel doesn't provide any useful material (because the child is deaf), Universal Grammar seizes on the manual–visual channel as the only kind of input with enough richness in it. As a result, the mother's relatively unstructured gestures become the raw material out of which the child's Universal Grammar constructs a language—a rudimentary one, to be sure, but at least paralleling the normal linguistic achievements of a child up to the age of three or so.

One final angle. Not only do the mothers not teach the grammar to their children, they don't learn it from their children either. The disparities between the children's systematic use of gesture and the mothers' unsystematic use persist over two years and more of the study. The mothers just don't get any better. Why?

Goldin-Meadow observes that the mothers always use their gestures as accompaniment to speech. She suggests that gesture tied to speech does not itself have language-like properties. For instance, in the course of normal speech we tend to use only one characterizing (pantomimic) gesture per sentence. So perhaps the fact that they're speaking prevents the mothers from using (or from developing) use of sign as rich as their children's.

Another possibility is that the mothers are victims of the critical period. Although their children can't help interpreting gestures in the environment as a language, this interpretation is not open to the mothers: they're too old to acquire a second language. (I should stress, though, that both these explanations are just guesses at the moment. Maybe we'll know better in ten years.)

Creation of language: Creole

A very complicated and curious linguistic situation has occurred a number of times over the past three centuries. Hawaii provides a typical example. In the 1870s, a tremendous expansion of the sugar plantations brought an influx of laborers from China, Japan, Korea, the Philippines, Portugal, Puerto Rico, and elsewhere; by 1900 these laborers outnumbered other groups in Hawaii by a ratio of two to one. At home, everyone spoke their own native language; but out in the community, it was necessary to communicate with speakers of all the languages present. The result was the development of a so-called *pidgin* language, a makeshift that served as the means of communication in multilingual situations.

By 1900 the pidgin in use in Hawaii was based mostly on English vocabulary—I'll give some examples in a moment. Elsewhere in the world, pidgins developed based on other languages, usually that of the predominant colonial power in the region. For instance, in certain areas of the Caribbean, the pidgin that developed was based on English; in other areas, on French; in yet others, on Spanish.

Hawaiian pidgin was in widespread use in the early 1900s, so in the early 1970s, the linguist Derek Bickerton (on whose work this section is based) was still able to interview and record surviving speakers of the language. Two features of pidgin are significant for our present purposes. First, pidgin is syntactically impoverished. It lacks functional vocabulary: there is no systematic use of articles, auxiliary verbs, or inflections. There are no subordinate clauses, and the verb is frequently omitted.

Second, the basic word order is extremely variable, depending to a great extent on the native language of the speaker. For instance, since Japanese puts the verb at the end of the sentence, pidgin speakers of Japanese ancestry produced sentences like (2). (To make this material relatively easy to interpret, I've chosen examples that don't contain non-English words, and I've transcribed the sentences with English spelling—a convenient oversimplification.)

(2) *a* too-much money me think catch though
     "I think he earns a lot of money, though"
   b the poor people all potato eat
     "The poor people ate only potatoes"

By contrast, the Filipino languages characteristically put the verb before the subject, so Filipino speakers of pidgin produced sentences like (3).

(3) *a* work hard this people
     "These people work hard"
   b more plenty the Ilocano than the Tagalog
     "Ilocanos were more numerous than Tagalogs."

Interesting as this is, I want to go on to what happened next. What did the children do who were born in Hawaii in this pidgin-speaking environment? How did they end up speaking? As it turns out, the period from 1900 to 1920 saw the emergence of a new language, Hawaiian *Creole*, whose roots were in the pidgin, but which possessed its own grammatical properties. This language evidently developed as the response of children who grew up hearing pidgin spoken.

Let's see a little of what Hawaiian creole is like. In contrast to pidgin's extreme variability in word order, and its dependence on ethnic origin, creole is quite uniform from speaker to speaker in its basic word order: subject-verb-object. It never uses a word order with the verb at the end, like the pidgin sentences in (2). It sometimes uses a word order with the verb at the beginning, but only as a special option to highlight new information:

(4) no like play football, these guys
"These guys, they don't like to play football."

The language permits complicated syntactic constructions, including various kinds of subordinate clauses. Bickerton contrasts pidgin and creole versions of identical sentences to illustrate the difference.

(5) *a* Pidgin:
No, the men, ah–pau [finished] work–they go, make garden. Plant this, ah, cabbage, like that. Plant potato, like that. And then–all that one–all right, sit down. Make lilly bit story.

b Creole:
When work pau [is finished] da guys they stay go make [are going to make] garden for plant potato an' cabbage an' after little while they go sit down talk story ['shoot the breeze'].

Perhaps most interesting is that Hawaiian creole has a system of functional words, some of which can be seen in (5b). Some of these functional words have properties not found in any of the languages that contributed to pidgin. I'll give two cases.

First, the articles in creole are altogether consistent and meaningful. Where English uses the definite article "the," creole uses the equivalent "da." But where English uses the indefinite article "a," creole sometimes uses the equivalent "wan" (from "one"), and sometimes leaves it out. The choice isn't random or careless. "Wan" is always used when the speaker is referring to a specific item unknown to the listener, for example in (6).

(6) He get wan black book. That book no do any good.
"He has a black book. That book doesn't do any good."

On the other hand, if there is no specific reference, "wan" is omitted, as in (7).

(7) But nobody gone get job.
"But nobody will get a job."

Notice that in the English translation of (7) the speaker isn't referring to any particular job; this is why the creole sentence omits "wan." This difference between including or omitting the indefinite article is not present in English or any of the other parent languages of Hawaiian pidgin. It is, rather, an innovation in creole.

Another such case is found in the pair of sentences in (8). (Notice, by the way, that instead of the English past tense ending, creole uses the auxiliary verb "bin" to mark past time.)

(8) *a* John bin go Honolulu go see Mary.
b John bin go Honolulu for see Mary.

These are both translated into English as "John went to Honolulu to see Mary." But it turns out that they are different in a way not expressed in English. If the speaker says (8a), we know that John actually saw Mary; if (8b), we know that he failed to see Mary. The English sentence, in contrast, leaves the outcome open. So here again is a consistent grammatical difference between Creole and English (as well as the other parent languages).

As usual, these examples are only the smallest sampling of a rich and detailed study. But they are enough to raise the basic issue: Where did this language come from? We don't know how it happens that a community ends up speaking a uniform language, but sure enough, over a period of twenty years or so, a language with full grammatical properties appeared where there wasn't one before. This language has basic word order and vocabulary mostly derived from English, but its detailed grammatical properties are not those of English or of any of the other parent languages.

Let's think of it in terms of acquisition. The children who grew up speaking creole did not have parents who spoke creole—rather, they heard the rudimentary and highly variable pidgin. These children ended up speaking something different from what their parents, or any other adults, spoke. So we have here a situation much like the creation of home sign, except this time multiplied over an entire speech community.

Creole, of course, is much more elaborate than home sign, which, as we saw, is much simpler than even pidgin. But of course the children hearing pidgin have three things the home sign children lack.

First, they have access to the well-developed vocabulary of pidgin, while home sign children have to invent practically everything. Second, the children hearing pidgin have each other—there is a developing community of speakers of the more elaborated language. Third, the children hearing pidgin are also learning their parents' native language, so there is another fully fledged language in the environment (although in most cases one that has little to do with the developing creole). We don't really know how such a situation results in a uniform language developing in the course of one generation. That remains a mystery for the moment.

Still, the facts are incontrovertible. In one generation, the children growing up in pidgin-speaking homes have constructed uniform mental grammars that allow them to construct sentences far more complex than they ever heard from their parents. There simply is no adult model that accounts for what the children end up learning. Moreover, these mental grammars have properties that have evidently come from nowhere in the environment. So where could they have come from? We have no choice but to fall back on Universal Grammar.

The plot thickens. Bickerton points out startling similarities among the creole languages of the world, features that have developed independently in one language after another, without contact among them and without models in parent languages. As a consequence, he claims that the grammar of creole *is* Universal Grammar (he uses the term "bioprogram"). The idea is that children growing up hearing pidgin have essentially no useful grammatical input, so they simply adopt the mental grammar that is prespecified genetically. He bolsters this claim by pointing out that many of the grammatical constructions in creoles are found in child language. For instance, the treatment of negation in Hawaiian creole is not so far off Stage 2 of the acquisition of English negation that we saw in Chapter 8.

(9) Creole: no like play football, these guys
    Child language: I no want envelope

I don't think Bickerton's analysis is quite right here. Children exposed to English do eventually learn complex things like the English past tense, verbal auxiliaries, and negation. In Chapter 9 we examined learning by genetically impaired individuals and individuals past the critical period, and we found that these complex parts of language are just the ones that are most affected. We took this as evidence that one needs a learning capacity specialized for language in order to acquire them. Yet, on Bickerton's hypothesis, any complex principles that aren't found in creoles do not fall under Universal Grammar.

Alternatively, suppose that we go back to the idea that UG provides the child not with a complete basic mental grammar, as Bickerton claims, but with a menu of options for mental grammar, out of which the child eventually has to choose an option that is maximally tuned to the environmental input. Suppose in addition that this menu is like a lot of computer software menus: it has "default options" that are chosen if you don't tell it anything special. Then the story would go like this: children exposed to pidgin hear nothing that tells them how to select options in the menu of UG. Instead of doing nothing, they select the default options, which give them a mental grammar for creole languages. In addition, when learning other languages, children will often try the default options first before trying to find a better approximation to the language in the environment; this behavior will result in some of the kinds of systematic errors we find in normal language acquisition.*

However this story works out in the end, the crucial point for our larger picture is that children are hearing pidgin *as though it is a fully formed language*—that is, they have imposed organization on the environment that goes well beyond the organization actually present in the adult utterances from which they learn. This is a striking refutation of the view that children learn by imitating what they hear and somehow "soaking up" language from the environment. Again, it is strong substantiation of the Argument for Innate Knowledge—that the child brings powerful internal resources to language learning.

It also, by the way, provides more evidence for the critical period: the adults who speak pidgin to their children end up still speaking pidgin—they never acquire creole. They are just too old to acquire all the complex grammatical properties that their children have invented!

Teaching language to apes

No discussion of language acquisition would be complete without mentioning the most famous experiments in language learning: the attempts to teach language to chimpanzees and gorillas. In the 1950s,

---

* For the moment, Bickerton and I have agreed to disagree on this issue, but on the larger picture we are certainly in accord.

Keith Hayes tried to teach a chimp named Vicki to speak, with little success. Then a number of people had the idea that Vicki's problem was relatively superficial—that it had to do with limitations of the chimp's ability to control the vocal tract in a way appropriate for producing speech sounds. So several projects developed in which apes used the manual–visual modality instead.

Two of these projects involved artificial languages. Duane Rumbaugh and Susan Savage-Rumbaugh worked with a chimp named Lana, who was taught to communicate with a computer by pressing sequences of keys in response to sequences of symbols on a screen. (This research has more recently been extended to pygmy chimpanzees, with even greater success.) David Premack trained a chimp named Sarah to understand and construct "sentences" built out of different colored and shaped plastic chips. In these experiments the learning situation was highly controlled, and the "language" being taught was quite simple, having some basic word order but very little hierarchical structure of the sort found in our trees in Chapter 6.

The other projects were more "naturalistic." These are the ones I'll talk about here. The pioneering work was done by Allen and Beatrice Gardner, teaching a chimp named Washoe a version of sign language. In contrast to the Lana and Sarah projects, the language was not just used in teaching and experimental contexts. It was a medium of everyday communication between the chimp and her caretakers; Washoe was seeing signs and producing them all the time. This approach has been extended by Roger Fouts to a whole colony of chimps, who sign to each other; Francine Patterson has raised a pair of gorillas, Koko and Michael, using sign; and Herbert Terrace, attempting to replicate some of the Gardners' more ambitious claims, worked with a chimp appropriately named Nim Chimpsky.

Having described some of the characteristics of ASL, I can add something important about these projects: contrary to popular opinion, the apes were not taught ASL. What they were taught was a language whose vocabulary consisted of basic uninflected ASL signs, plus simplifications of ASL signs, plus signs the apes themselves made up. The grammar of this language was not ASL grammar, with its rich possibilities for simultaneous inflection and use of facial expression. Rather, the signs were strung together in English word order—but unlike Manual English, there were no translations of English functional words and inflections. In other words, what the apes were seeing was something like a three-year-old's English, or a pidgin English, translated word for word into signs. I've mentioned that children exposed to such a language don't buy it; typically, they spontaneously turn it into something more highly structured. Let's see what the apes did. (I should make clear that this is my own interpretation of the literature. There are many people who are much more enthusiastic, and many who are less.)

The animals learn most of their signs through explicit teaching. The total vocabulary after a few years of training often runs to several hundred signs. The signs include common objects and actions, the names of people and apes in the environment, a few properties like "hurt" and "dirty" (the latter often spontaneously used as a general-purpose insult), pronouns such as "me" and "you," the question words "what" and "where," and a few utility words like "yes" and "please."

It is pretty clear that the apes assign more or less the same meanings to these signs as people do. They use the signs copiously, and on most occasions their uses are interpretable. They use signs to indicate objects that are absent and that they want, so the signs are not just elicited by the here-and-now environment. When they make what appear to be errors, often there is an obvious reason for it. For example, Koko was taught the sign "straw" to mean a drinking straw. But she spontaneously used it as a label for plastic tubing, clear plastic hose, cigarettes, a pen, and a car radio antenna—all long thin objects for which she had no previous sign. So, like a child who at first calls all animals "doggie," Koko had interpreted the sign to refer to a larger class of objects than intended.

The apes often produce strings of signs that make novel sense. Two favorite anecdotes in the literature are Washoe's use of the signs "water bird" upon encountering a swan and Koko's "cookie rock" in response to a stale roll. Altogether common in the literature are utterances like "gimme drink" and "tickle me."

More generally, the apes' reliable use of signs suggests that (1) they have concepts (or thoughts) that are structured sufficiently similarly to ours to be recognizable; and (2) they are capable of attaching concepts to external symbols, in this case signs. The latter ability is a profound accomplishment, requiring considerable cognitive sophistication.

Let's next ask: do the apes have a mental grammar that allows them to combine signs in regimented fashion? The evidence seems to indicate that they don't. On one hand, there appear to be some rudiments of a basic word order. For example, the chimp Lucy clearly knew the difference between "Roger tickle Lucy" and "Lucy tickle Roger"—as shown by her response. This might be evidence for a preference for putting the actor of a sentence before the person acted upon, found even in home sign.

But on the other hand, the utterances of the chimps characteristically are full of multiple redundant repetitions. Things like "you me you out me" (Washoe), "please milk please me like drink apple bottle" (Koko), and "give orange me give eat orange me eat orange give me eat orange give me you" (Nim) are not exactly what you expect from a child learning to speak. Utterances like these are usually cited in the literature in greatly reduced form, so that what the chimp says looks more coherent than it actually is.

When children move from the two-word stage to three- or four-word utterances, they almost always add new information. Nim, for whom the best data are available on this score, typically did not. His most frequent two-sign utterances were "play me," "me Nim," "tickle me," and "eat Nim." His most frequent three-sign utterances were "play me Nim," "eat me Nim," "eat Nim eat," and "tickle me Nim." His most frequent four-sign utterances were "eat drink eat drink" and "eat Nim eat Nim." It's plain that not much is happening as the utterances grow longer.

Finally, since there are no functional words and no embedding in the input taught to the chimps, we might expect them not to acquire any. Still, the literature does not suggest that chimps improvise a grammatical use of space or simultaneous patterns of inflection, so characteristic of children exposed to Manual English. (A little of this behavior is reported for the gorilla Koko.) And human children, given the sort of input the chimp colony got, end up inventing creole languages.

So what are we to make of these results? A lot of people have taken the issue to be whether the apes have language or not, citing definitions and counter-definitions to support their position. I think this is a silly dispute, often driven by an interest either in reducing the distance between people and animals or in maintaining this distance at all costs. In an attempt to be less doctrinaire, let's ask: do the apes succeed in *communicating*? Undoubtedly yes. It even looks as if they succeed in communicating *symbolically*, which is pretty impressive. But, going beyond that, it does not look as though they are capable of constructing a mental grammar that regiments the symbols coherently. (Again, a matter of degree—maybe there is a little, but nothing at all near human capacity.) In short, Universal Grammar, or even something remotely like it, appears to be exclusively human.

I also have some caveats regarding the apes' acquisition of vocabulary. Remember the way children acquire vocabulary, once the great explosion starts: they are picking up on the order of ten words a day from hearing them in conversation, so that by the age of five they have a vocabulary on the order of ten thousand words. Nothing like this ever happens with the apes: their vocabulary peaks at five or six hundred, with continual teaching. It is possible that this is merely a quantitative difference, a big-brain effect, and that apes and children acquire vocabulary in essentially the same way.

On the other hand, there is a human activity that more closely resembles the apes' acquisition of vocabulary. Chinese is written with a system of characters, each of which represents a different word. In order to read and write Chinese, one must learn thousands of characters. Crucially, Chinese children must spend years and years being trained assiduously in order to master the characters. They don't just "pick them up" the way they pick up words. That is, the way apes learn words is actually much like the way people learn writing systems. It takes training and effort over years. We still see a big-brain effect: a Chinese child can learn a whole lot more characters than an ape can learn signs. But the learning is qualitatively similar.

If this comparison is correct, we have a further piece of evidence for a specialized language capacity. Human acquisition of vocabulary, which is quite robust even in genetically impaired individuals and late learners, does not appear to be a function of general-purpose learning. The apes can't do it. On the other hand, when the specialized capacity does not come into play (in learning to read and write and in the apes' learning of sign), symbols can still be learned—just not with the same facility.

Still, this leaves us with an embarrassing question: Why can apes learn to use symbols at all? It's as though evolution has provided them with a necessary precursor for language, but it's something they have no use for in their normal environment. Is it just a lucky accident? Or is it a by-product of some other cognitive capacity that is of more palpable survival value to the species? I don't think we know right now. Come back in ten or twenty years, when we might know more about the organization of concepts in humans and animals.

Assessment

We set out to look at language acquisition in unusual circumstances in order to help answer the question: What parts of language acquisition are due to general-purpose learning and what parts require a specialized device in the human brain? I would be the first to admit that none of the cases we have looked at is by itself conclusive. But put together, they make a rather impressive case for a substantial, though not total, specialization of the language capacity.

Over and over, inflection, nonstandard word order, and recursive embedding appear in normal language learners during the critical period—whether or not these features are present in the input. Over and over, these features are missing in language learners who are genetically impaired or past the critical period. In these less than optimal circumstances for learning, basic word order and rapid effortless vocabulary acquisition are retained; yet not even these are present in the apes. At the same time, the ability to construct a mental grammar that arranges signs into patterns appears to be distinct from the ability to use individual signs symbolically; this latter ability does appear in the apes. The evidence, therefore, points to a division of language acquisition into more and less specialized parts, some of which are uniquely human.

It is important to bear in mind that we cannot discover this differentiation of the language capacity without an understanding of the grammatical structure of language along the lines sketched in Part II. The subtle differences among the various cases of acquisition we have discussed depend on the details of phenomena such as word order, recursion, inflectional structure, and functional words like articles and auxiliary verbs. That is, it should be clear that the investigation of adult grammatical structures is essential for acquisition research: grammatical theory helps to determine what questions ought to be asked about learning.

More generally, let's think about the nature–nurture issue again. What we've seen is that nurture is maximally effective in language learning only when the proper elements of nature are in place—when a normal child is exposed to language during the critical period. If, for whatever reason, the proper elements of nature aren't in place, far more extensive nurture still doesn't produce performance at anywhere near the same level. What's more, the home sign and creole cases demonstrate that the child doesn't just copy the behavior of the people in the environment, but rather creates an internal system that can go well beyond the organization of the input. Nature places its own stamp on nurture.

11 Language and the brain

The frontiers of present-day brain science

Chapter 4 presented the functionalist approach to language in the brain: studying the abstract organization of the patterns of language, without worrying too much about how the brain actually encodes these patterns. Most linguists work within the functionalist approach, and all our discussion up to this point has been from the functionalist point of view.

But this still leaves a major mystery. How does the brain do it? What do the patterns of mental grammar look like in the neurons? How does an English speaker's brain differ from a French speaker's— or an ASL speaker's? When (from the functionalist point of view) speakers put together collections of mental patterns in Lego fashion to form long and intricately structured sentences, what are their neurons doing?

These sorts of questions pertain to the Argument for Mental Grammar. Similar questions arise for Argument for Innate Knowledge and its implications for language learning. What does Universal Grammar, the knowledge that a child brings to the language learning process, look like in terms of brain structure? When a child learns a language, how does the brain change? How do patterns of growth in brain structure over time account for the observed stages of language acquisition, and how does the brain spontaneously change by the end of the critical period so as to make language learning more difficult?

The past twenty or thirty years have seen remarkable advances in brain science, and from the media one might get the impression that a full understanding of how the brain works is not too far off. At the risk of seeming unduly pessimistic, though, I have the sense that the main lines of research in neuroscience, exciting as they are, are still not ready to approach the kinds of questions about language I've just posed. Let me try to summarize how far these approaches have gotten.

141

First the good news. It has become abundantly clear that the brain is not a big general-purpose device—its many functions are highly localized. Even vision, which on the face of it is a homogeneous undifferentiated process, proves to be broken up into numerous subfunctions (or *modules* in the sense of Chapter 4), each of which has its own area in the brain. There are separate brain areas devoted to the detection of the location, the shape, and the color of objects in the environment, all fed by the neurons of the optic nerve. There is even an area whose main function seems to be the recognition of familiar faces, a function whose purpose we'll discuss in Chapter 15.

It is also clear that these areas of the brain are not located where they are by chance. Though people vary to some extent in the precise location of particular brain areas, we find, for example, that the area for shape recognition is always in the temporal lobe, and that for location recognition is always in the parietal lobe—never the other way around. And brain areas with analogous functions are often found in analogous places in lower primates. So it looks as though this micro-differentiation of brain structure and function is genetically driven.

How are these areas identified? The most highly publicized current techniques are CAT (computerized axial tomography) scans, MRI (magnetic resonance imagery) scans, and PET (positron emission tomography) scans. CAT and MRI scans can provide exquisite images of details of brain anatomy; PET scans, while showing less detail, can detect what parts of the brain are most active while one is carrying out different tasks such as looking, listening, speaking, or doing mental arithmetic. PET scans reveal considerable differentiation even among apparently similar tasks: for example, counting aloud shows activity in different areas from counting to oneself. PET scans can also be used to show abnormalities in patterns of brain activity, for instance in schizophrenia.

Older techniques for detecting brain localization include EEG (electro-encephalogram) and, more gruesomely, electrical stimulation of different parts of a conscious patient's brain while it is open for an operation. (Since the brain itself doesn't have pain receptors, this doesn't hurt.) Animal experiments provide the further option of implanting electrodes in the brain, from which the activity of single neurons can be recorded while the animal is roaming around doing things.

But by far the most common approach to brain localization is to work with people who have sustained brain damage through injury, a stroke, a tumor, or a brain operation (to remove the focus of epileptic seizures, for instance). The area of damage can now be identified by means of a CAT scan or an MRI scan; in the old days it had to await an autopsy, which made research much more difficult. Numerous experimental techniques have been devised to discover what brain-damaged people can and cannot do.

Some of the deficits discovered by these techniques are fairly amazing. For instance, at the very back of the brain is the striate cortex, one of the first visual areas to receive input from the eyes. Damage to this region on one side of the brain produces blindness in the opposite half of the visual field. If people with such damage are shown things in such a way that they have to detect them with the blind part of the visual field, they will fervently deny that they are seeing anything. But suppose the experimenter says "Well, just for fun, imagine there *is* something there. Where do you think it might be? I know this is stupid, but would you point to it?" Under such prodding, they do surprisingly well. The recent discovery of this phenomenon of "blindsight" has stimulated a great deal of excitement among not only neuroscientists but philosophers as well, for it challenges our common-sense notions of what it means to see and to be conscious.

Much more widely known are the unfortunate people who, in order to control seizures, have undergone an operation that severs the corpus callosum, the large bundle of fibers that connects the left and right hemispheres of the cortex. If such people are shown a salacious picture in the left-hand visual field, they will blush or giggle appropriately. But if asked what they saw, they will honestly say "Nothing," for the language areas of the brain, in the left hemisphere, can't get information from the areas in the right hemisphere responsible for the left visual field. How are we to understand the behavior of such people? Do they have two independent minds, or two independent seats of consciousness? Or is the right hemisphere unconscious? It's hard to know what to say, and reputable people come down on all different sides of the issues.

I'd like to add that many popularizations of brain science focus almost exclusively on the asymmetry of the left and right hemispheres, speaking of the left hemisphere as "analytic" and the right as "holistic" and even "emotional." While there is some truth to this, at the same time each hemisphere is heavily broken down into further specializations, of which some are asymmetrical and some are not. For instance, language is usually concentrated in the left hemisphere, face recognition in the right. But low-level visual processes, tactile sensation, and motor control are divided pretty much symmetrically between the two hemispheres. And in addition to the left–right asymmetry, neuroscientists talk about differences of "style" between the top and bottom of the brain, and between the front and the back. So the highly publicized left–right distinction is only one of many.

Such a picture of brain localization is, of course, altogether congenial to the overall view we have reached in studying language from the functionalist approach. If the brain in general is made up of a lot of specialized modules, and if these specialties develop under genetic control, then it is hardly outrageous to use the Argument for Innate Knowledge as evidence for a genetically determined specialization for language.

On the other hand, establishing that language (or any other function) is specialized in the brain only gets us down to a certain fairly crude level of detail. It doesn't tell us how those functions *work*. Imagine someone explaining how a TV set works: "There are a number of specialized devices in the set. There is an area that tunes in the signal from the antenna and responds to your changing the channel. It sends a signal to another area, which splits the signal into sound and picture. The sound signal goes to another area, which. . ." We couldn't be blamed for complaining, "This is helpful up to a point, but *how* does the first area tune in a signal, *how* does the next area split the signal? How do they work?"

This is about the way I feel about brain localization studies. How does the specialized linguistic part of the brain combine speech sounds into syllables? How does it combine adjectives and nouns into noun phrases? How do the neurons store the word "banana"—its phonological structure and the fact that it is a noun? What do nouns have in common in the way they are stored in the brain that makes them different from verbs? And so forth. The fact that brain functions are localized may tell us that nouns and verbs are stored somewhere different in the brain from, say, smells and tastes—or even that nouns and verbs are stored in different places from each other. But that doesn't help us much on the question of how nouns and verbs work neurally within their specialized areas, or of how the neurons bring nouns and verbs together to produce and understand sentences.

Another active area of brain research concerns the chemical substances called neurotransmitters, which affect different types of neurons, leading to overall changes in mood, attention, and body control. A well-known case is the interaction of the neurotransmitter dopamine with the basal ganglia that control voluntary movement; a disruption or depletion of dopamine leads to the movement disorders of Parkinson's disease. This sort of research, while it is extremely exciting and of great medical importance, is also at too coarse a scale for our purposes. We need to know more than whether the speech centers are generally stimulated or inhibited. The operation of mental grammar has to involve the fine structure within the speech areas of the brain.

What about research on the fine structure of the nervous system? A lot is known about how an individual neuron works: what goes on when a neuron fires, how neurons communicate with each other through their synaptic connections, and how a neuron can change its pattern of behavior in reaction to new patterns of input (that is, the neural basis of learning). But again, while this research is fascinating, it does not immediately help us with the question of how the neurons accomplish language behavior, other than to rule out certain oversimplistic hypotheses. Any facet of language has to involve more than a single neuron and its synapses. It's not as though there's a particular cell for the word "icecream" that fires whenever you hear the word or think of it, or that there's a single cell for "noun" that fires whenever you use a noun. The problem is how larger assemblies of cells are wired up to perform these functions. So this kind of research is *too* fine-scale for our purposes.

To develop a neural account of mental grammar, we'll have to understand the combinatorial behavior of assemblies of neurons— how each one of a group of neurons (how many? hundreds? thousands? millions?) is reacting to the others and to inputs presented to the system as a whole. Such work is in its infancy. To understand a system of a couple of dozen interacting neurons in detail is, for now, a real *tour de force*. Larger systems of so-called "neural networks" are being extensively modeled on computers (this line of research is also called "connectionism" or "parallel distributed processing"). But on one hand these models leave out many properties of real neurons, and on the other hand they don't approach the richness of language that has been described under the functionalist approach.

This is not to denigrate the many important advances made by neuroscience over the past decades. It is just that there still seems to be a long way to go before we will be able to answer the kinds of questions about the brain that are raised by the study of the structure and learning of language. That should not discourage us from asking such questions, or from keeping our eyes open for hints from neuroscience for where answers might come from.

Language deficits due to brain damage

With all these caveats in place, let me turn to a brief survey of what *is* known about language and the brain, and what sorts of conclusions might be drawn.

The study of language deficits due to brain damage has a long history. In fact, the localization of language in the brain was one of the earliest examples of localization to be discovered, and it served as a major impetus to other brain research.

In 1864, the French surgeon Paul Broca showed that patients with a particular set of linguistic deficits proved upon autopsy to have damage to a particular area in the left frontal lobe. He also pointed out that corresponding right-hemisphere damage showed little effect on speech. The area in question has come to be known as *Broca's area*, and the set of symptoms as *Broca's aphasia*. Broca's aphasics seem to understand what is said to them, but their speech is slow, effortful, and poorly articulated. They have evident difficulty in finding words. Here are two representative quotes from Broca's aphasics (which in the transcripts I have available do not record the problems in pronunciation):

> (1) *a* Me . . . build–ing . . . chairs, no, no cab–in–nets. One,
> saw . . . then, cutting wood . . . working . . .
> *b* Cookie jar . . . fall over . . . chair . . . water . . . empty
> . . . ov . . . ov . . . [Examiner: "overflow"] Yeah.

Notice that these quotes are not just slowed-down sentences. They are missing a great deal of the grammatical tissue that holds normal speech together—things like articles, auxiliary verbs, and tenses. For this reason Broca's aphasia is also called *agrammatism*. (I should add that sometimes Broca's aphasics can still swear fluently, and they can often sing.)

A quite different set of symptoms was identified by Karl Wernicke in 1874. In people with *Wernicke's aphasia*, Broca's area is intact, but there is damage in the left temporal lobe, in an area now called *Wernicke's area*. The speech of Wernicke's aphasics is altogether fluent—if anything, it tends to come out in a big rush. Taken a few words at a time it often makes a little sense, but the larger parts don't fit at all, and there are often insertions of nonsense words:

> (2) *a* [Examiner: "What kind of work have you done?] We,

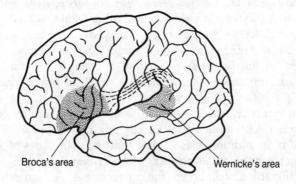

Figure 11.1 *The areas of the left hemisphere relevant to language*

> the kids, all of us, and I, we were working for a long
> time in the ... you know ... it's the kind of space, I
> mean place rear to the spedwan ... [Examiner:
> "Excuse me, but I wanted to know what work you
> have been doing."] If you had said that, we had said
> that, poomer, near the fortunate, forpunate, tamppoo,
> all around the fourth of martz. Oh, I get all confused.
> b Well, this is ... mother is away here working out
> o'here to get her better, but when she's working, the
> two boys looking in the other part. One their small
> tile into her time here. She's working another time
> because she's getting, too.

Not only don't Wernicke's aphasics make much sense, they don't
seem to understand much of what you say to them. For instance, for
the most part they don't follow instructions well. By contrast with
Broca's aphasics, who are painfully aware of their deficits, Wernicke's
aphasics often seem unaware that they aren't making sense, and they
become irritated at people who can't understand them.

There are many other sorts of language deficits due to brain
damage. *Anomic aphasics* have word-finding deficits, more extensive
versions of the experiences we all have occasionally in not being able
to think of a word or a name. *Conduction aphasics* have relatively
fluent meaningful speech, but with many errors of pronunciation;
and, oddly, they have great difficulty repeating sentences spoken to
them. A whole class of deficits involves reading: there are patients

who can speak but not read, read but not write, write but not read (even what they've just written!), and other combinations. One of the strangest afflictions (for my taste) is *deep dyslexia*: if a deep dyslexic is asked to read the word "apple," he may say "fruit" or "flower"—something related but not the same. The word seems to get in and influence what comes out, but the person doesn't (and possibly can't) check whether the response is correct.

In practice, these symptoms are rarely entirely "clean": a random stroke seldom affects exactly one area and spares everything around it. In addition, it isn't clear that the boundaries of any of the areas in the brain are altogether "clean" either. But, along with most of the literature, we'll accept the conventional idealizations for now.

What has gone wrong in these aphasias? One widespread approach seeks to view aphasia as a disorder of general conceptual thinking. There are indeed afflictions of *dementia* that result in generalized diminutions of cognitive functions, usually as a result of widespread brain deterioration due for instance to Alzheimer's disease. These may simultaneously affect naming, ability to pantomime, purposeful movement, memory, and reasoning. But aphasias are not like this: they often leave the nonlinguistic abilities intact. And, conversely, the ability to produce grammatical sentences is often spared in the face of other substantial cognitive loss due to brain damage. This points to language ability being quite distinct from general-purpose cognitive functioning.*

Wernicke himself proposed a different account of aphasia. He observed that Wernicke's area is near the area of the brain involved in hearing, and that Broca's area is adjacent to the area that controls motor movements of the vocal tract. He suggested, therefore, that Wernicke's area stores the auditory memories of words, and Broca's area stores the memories for how to pronounce them. This nicely explains the fact that Wernicke's aphasics can articulate language but can't understand it (even their own), and that the reverse is true of Broca's aphasics.

However, while Wernicke's account acknowledges the specialization of language ability, it is still inadequate. Language doesn't just consist of knowledge of the sounds of words and how to pronounce them. Rather, auditory and motor abilities are only the most superficial part of language. Most of the interest is in the abstract

---

* Notice that this evidence for the specialization of the language capacity parallels the evidence drawn from the different varieties of genetic brain impairment discussed in Chapter 9.

phonological and syntactic patterns that organize both perception and production. Wernicke's theory has nothing useful to say about how these abilities are manifested in the brain, and how they could be disrupted.*

A serious difficulty with Wernicke's approach was discovered in the 1970s. Up to that time, it had been thought that Broca's aphasics understand what is said to them, and just have trouble speaking. So Broca's aphasia was viewed purely as a problem with production. It turns out, though, that most Broca's aphasics have problems understanding language as well. Their difficulties, in fact, turn on just the sorts of things they most typically leave out in their speech: the parts of language that signal grammatical structure.

Here's one kind of experiment that reveals this comprehension deficit. Suppose we show Broca's aphasics pictures of a boy hitting a girl and of a girl hitting a boy. Then we ask them: "Which of these pictures goes with the sentence I'm now going to say to you?" If we say (3a), they get the right answer, but if we say (3b), they choose randomly.

(3) *a* The boy hit the girl.
  b The boy was hit by the girl.

Apparently, the "was" and "by" of the passive sentence (3b), both functional words, are causing them difficulty.

Similarly, Broca's aphasics have trouble telling the difference between sentences (4a) and (4b). The reason, evidently, is that they cannot take account of the functional word "the," so both sentences sound to them like (4c).

(4) *a* He showed her baby the pictures. (Who saw the
                                   pictures? The baby did)
  b He showed her the baby pictures. (She did)
  c He showed her baby pictures. (ambiguous)

(Incidentally, notice that Broca's aphasics are not simply *ignoring* functional words; if they did, they would always guess that (3b) means the same as (3a). So there is some more subtle story here.)

Since Broca's aphasia usually affects both comprehension and

---

* You can't blame Wernicke; hardly anything was known about the psychology of language in 1874. In the light of what is now known about language, though, it is hard today to condone explaining aphasia by means of Wernicke's hypothesis, as was done in a recent public television series on the brain.

production, it looks as though it is a deficit in a part of the mental grammar that is shared between the two—in the processing of phonological or syntactic structure. By contrast, Wernicke's aphasia appears to be a disruption of the linkage between language and thought—also in both comprehension and production. Returning to our functional diagram of the crude organization of language, we can place these aphasias approximately in the regions designated in Figure 11.2.

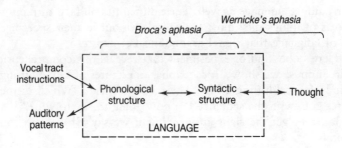

Figure 11.2 *The areas of linguistic information affected by Broca's and Wernicke's aphasias*

There have been lots of fascinating experiments that attempt to pin this down further—to develop theories about *exactly* what part of mental grammar is disrupted in Broca's aphasia. None of these theories has yet proven entirely satisfactory, though we have learned a lot about Broca's aphasia from them. It would take us too far afield here to explain the various theories and how they differ. However, given that Broca's aphasics have both phonological and syntactic problems—and that more specific deficits in either phonology or syntax are not so frequently attested—it may not make sense to seek a single grammatical problem in Broca's aphasia. Rather, some researchers are coming to the conclusion that Broca's aphasia is a general deficit in the ability to process fine details of linguistic structure. In addition, it may be that phonological and syntactic abilities are closely interspersed in Broca's area (in adjacent layers of cortical tissue, say), so that a lesion to one almost inevitably affects the other as well.

In any event, even for the intensively studied Broca's aphasia, it's still hard to draw a clear relation between the deficit we observe, the affected brain area, and the functional organization of grammar.

So much the worse for the other aphasias, which have received considerably less attention from neurolinguists.

Aphasia in ASL

In one of the most spectacular findings of the last ten years, it has turned out that precise analogues of Broca's and Wernicke's aphasias occur in brain-damaged speakers of ASL—and parallel brain areas are affected! An ASL Broca's aphasic signs slowly and leaves out all the grammatical inflections of location and style of movement; an ASL Wernicke's aphasic signs fluently but confusingly, and shows obvious comprehension problems. Not only that: sign language aphasics can produce and comprehend pantomime despite their language deficits, and they're fine at using their hands for purposes other than language.

And not only *that*. There exist *right*-hemisphere deficits that impair one's understanding of space, typically producing a so-called *left neglect*. People with these deficits fail to see things in the left half of their visual field, fail to draw the left-hand side of pictures, and fail to dress the left-hand side of their bodies. But if they happen to be ASL speakers, they still use the left side of the space in front of them *just for the purpose of signing ASL syntax*. Another kind of right-hemisphere damage can lead to loss of the ability to produce facial expressions. But despite such damage, ASL speakers can produce the aspects of facial expression that are relevant to ASL grammar, using the very same muscles.

In each of these cases, the differential character of the deficit shows that it is not a case of motor paralysis: the muscles can still be activated. What is damaged is the part of the brain that organizes the use of the muscles into coherent actions. And it turns out that the part of the brain organizing *ASL* action is not the same as the part that organizes ordinary action.

You can see why these results are so exciting. They confirm just about all the main points we made about sign language on the basis of the functionalist approach, but now adding evidence in terms of brain damage.

1. ASL is a language, not a collection of pantomimes and facial expressions. And it is localized in the language areas of the brain, in a different place from pantomimes and facial expressions.

2. The use of space in ASL is grammatical, not just a collection of pointing gestures. And the use of space for pointing at things out in the world is localized in a different place in the brain from the grammatical use of space for ASL.
3. The grammar of ASL is, with only a few exceptions, entirely parallel to the grammar for spoken languages. And brain damage to English and ASL speakers produces parallel deficits.
4. The fact that signed and spoken grammars have similar organization shows that mental grammar is abstract—it does not have directly to do with auditory and vocal tract function. The existence of sign language aphasias shows vividly that Wernicke was wrong about the function of the language areas—they have to do with abstract *linguistic* function, not especially with the auditory–vocal channel.

All the research on aphasia, both spoken and signed, is remarkable—I can't stress enough how hard it is to work with brain-damaged subjects and to obtain reliable experimental results. Yet this research suffers from some of the same limitations as the rest of neuroscience: even if we can identify a particular deficit in function as due to damage in a particular brain area, this doesn't tell us how that brain area works. We don't know how the neurons are wired up to do what they do. Ultimately, that's what we have to understand in order to explain how language (or anything else) works in the brain.

Brain variation and plasticity

What I've said so far about the brain localization of language applies most reliably to right-handed adults who have no left-handers in their families. With other groups—children, left-handers, and right-handers with left-handed relatives—the probable severity of aphasia from damage to the "language" areas in the left hemisphere is lower, and the probable recovery from such aphasias is better.*

What's the difference? There are three possibilities: In children, etc., either (1) language is encoded more diffusely in the left hemisphere; or (2) language is encoded to some degree in the right

---

* Some researchers also include women among the "exceptions" to the generalizations about brain localization of language; but the evidence is less conclusive.

hemisphere as well as the left; or (3) some combination of these two. Which of these is correct, and what are the consequences for our main question of nature vs. nurture in the language capacity?

As a baseline, it is hard to believe that right-handers without left-handed relatives experience anything different in the environment from left-handers or from right-handers with left-handed relatives—at least, anything that is relevant to a difference in brain localization of language. So there is evidently some genetic input involved in these differences.

In addition, even newborns (for the most part) exhibit an asymmetry in raw size between the two hemispheres, with noticeable enlargement of the language areas on the left side. This might lead us at first to guess that hemispheric size alone is responsible for language being situated on the left. However, these asymmetries have turned up in apes as well, so they probably don't have to do entirely with language—the localization of language on the left seems to follow from more general considerations.

How much language is found in the right hemisphere? One of the best tests has been the patients mentioned earlier whose corpus callosum has been severed, so that the hemispheres cannot communicate. As a result, any task to be performed with the left hand has to be understood by the right hemisphere alone, and any verbal response based on what the left visual field has seen has to be produced by the right hemisphere alone. The linguistic capacity of the right hemisphere has turned out to be quite variable. Some of these people show virtually no verbal responsiveness in the right hemisphere, some can understand but not produce language, and some can even speak or write a few words. But at best they show hardly any capability for understanding grammatical structure, suggesting again that the left hemisphere is the seat of the language specialization.

Ah, well (says my imaginary critic), *but what about children? Don't they recover from aphasia better than adults? Doesn't this show that the brain is more adaptable than you say?*

It does show that the brains of children, who are still within the critical period, are more adaptable—but it certainly isn't *nurture* that makes them more adaptable. Rather, the loss of brain plasticity as children grow up seems to be part of the biological pattern of brain development, a factor of *nature*. Moreover, the way brain-damaged children recover is not dictated by the way they are treated. The best we can do for them is give them an environment that is rich and motivating enough to stimulate nature to take its own course. That is, proper treatment may result in better recovery, but the method of

treatment doesn't itself determine which areas of the brain compen-
sate for the damage; that too is a factor of nature.

*But what about those children who, for some reason, have
had their whole left hemisphere surgically removed? They
still learn to talk.*

Children missing a left hemisphere develop language that may
seem fine to a naive observer, but under more probing examination
they turn out to show some odd little deficits—for instance, an
inability to do rhymes and some difficulty with tests like the ones that
Broca's aphasics have trouble with (such as examples given earlier in
this chapter). So the right hemisphere can take over language pretty
well, but not entirely.

The hypothesis that most appeals to me at the moment is that
the brain, like most of the body, is genetically coded to be essentially
symmetrical, even in the language areas. However, this is overlaid
genetically with relatively small asymmetries here and there between
the hemispheres, which make each hemisphere slightly better than the
other at performing certain tasks. In particular, the left hemisphere
has a small advantage for language. In a normal brain, this advantage
comes to be magnified to a full-blown asymmetry, either just because
the left hemisphere learns more language, or even possibly because it
actively inhibits language learning in the other hemisphere.

What happens to the right-hemisphere "language area" then? It
doesn't atrophy. Rather, adjacent areas use it as extra workspace for
their own specialized functions. Strikingly, just this sort of co-
optation appears to take place in the congenitally deaf, who prove to
have greater than normal sensitivity to certain kinds of visual inputs,
especially the detection of motion in peripheral vision. It has been
suggested that, in these people, the areas normally devoted to
auditory processing, lacking normal input, come to be taken over by
the visual system; the larger number of neurons they use for visual
processing accounts for their greater sensitivity.*

In a child who is missing the left hemisphere, though, the right
hemisphere's language area is not inhibited by the left, and it is the
only part of the brain available to process language. As a result, it
develops to its full potential as a language device, instead of being co-
opted for other purposes at which the right hemisphere excels. Under
these conditions, it does pretty well, but not *quite* as well as the left

---

* These suggestions have been confirmed by animal experimentation, where it is
possible to insert electrodes in the brain to investigate the sensitivities of different brain
areas. In animals deprived of auditory stimuli from birth, visual inputs do indeed give
rise to neural firing in the normal auditory regions of the brain.

hemisphere. For a less extreme case, left-handers perhaps have less inherent asymmetry between the hemispheres, so less inhibition of right-hemisphere language function takes place.

Of course, all this talk about hemispheres is much too crude. Language isn't spread all over the left hemisphere, it's centered in particular places. I'm going through this material anyway, because it's representative of the level at which the relation of language and the brain is often discussed. Unfortunately, it doesn't help us much with the deeper problem of exactly how the brain accomplishes language perception and production, and how mental grammar is encoded in the neurons.

Still, even at this level, we come up with a story about the brain altogether compatible with the results from the organization of adult language and from the study of language acquisition. There are brain specializations for language, especially for grammatical structure. Of course, it takes the right kind of environment for these specializations to develop properly. But consider that language develops in *this* part of the brain and not *that* one (even in signed instead of spoken language!), and that language learners extract just the right kind of stuff from the environment to construct a mental grammar. These facts strongly indicate that the role of the environment is essentially to nourish the natural development of a complex "mental organ" that is part of our genetic heritage.

PART IV
Mental capacities other than language

12 The argument for the construction of experience

Overview of Part IV

At the beginning of the book, I posed the question: What does human nature have to be like in order to account for the fact that we can all speak and understand a language? At the risk of beating a dead horse, let's review the two Fundamental Arguments, elaborating a little bit in terms of what we've found out in Parts II and III.

> **The Argument for Mental Grammar:**
> The expressive variety of language use implies that a language user's brain contains a set of unconscious grammatical principles.

Our mental grammars make it possible to understand and construct the unlimited repertoire of sentences in our language. Mental grammar is encoded in a special-purpose component of the brain, which converts information between thought and the sensorimotor encoding of overt signals (vocal output/auditory input for spoken language, manual output/visual input for sign).

> **The Argument for Innate Knowledge:**
> The way children learn to talk implies that the human brain contains a genetically determined specialization for language.

In order to learn a language, children must construct a mental grammar on the basis of an interaction between input from the environment (nurture) and their own innate resources (nature).

The innate resources available for language learning include Universal Grammar, a highly specific menu of possibilities for grammatical organization. As a result, the apparently wide differences among languages of the world—even sign languages—actually turn out to be relatively constrained variations on a theme.

159

Universal Grammar actively structures learning. Children instinctively apply its principles to whatever reasonably appropriate input they receive, constructing a mental grammar that gives them a language-like repertoire—even when the input itself is not so well structured, as in the creation of home sign and creoles.

Universal Grammar is a species-specific adaptation, like an upright stance and an opposable thumb—and sonar in bats, for that matter. It is not just an automatic consequence of having a big brain; it is a consequence of having a particular part in the brain (whose location is known, but whose organization is as yet not).

* * *

As we have worked through the material supporting these conclusions, I have constantly raised the question: If the human mind has to be like this in order to account for our use of language, what broader conclusions can we draw for human nature?

Of course, it's logically possible that there are *no* broader conclusions—that nothing else in the brain works the way language does. But there are some immediate reasons to suspect that this is not the case. We have already spoken of the specialized nature of activities such as motor control and face recognition, which are localized at predictable positions in the brain. And the critical period for language learning, which seems to be a biological consequence of the brain's development, is paralleled by critical periods for learning in other animals.

In addition, the language capacity must have evolved from other capacities in the brains of our precursors. If language were completely unique among the mental faculties, it would be hard to explain how it could have come about. If, on the other hand, language shares the general character of other faculties of the mind, its evolution may still be tough to explain, but at least language looks like a possible natural outcome of the evolutionary process. (I know: in the absence of a satisfying account of the evolution of language, this argument rings rather hollow. But I would like to set the stage properly for an explanation to emerge someday.)

If language is of a piece with other biological capabilities of the brain, we should expect to find analogues to the two Fundamental Arguments in other domains of human activity and experience. This last part of the book is devoted to providing evidence that this is indeed the case. But first I want to add an important point to our characterization of language.

The argument for the construction of experience: The experience of spoken language is actively constructed by the hearer's mental grammar

Let's recall our discussion in Chapter 5, when we were beginning to establish the nature of phonological representation. As pointed out there, we have no difficulty intuitively segmenting the speech stream into words. However, this segmentation can't be reliably measured in the physical sound waves produced by the vocal tract and detected by the ears. That is, although words are *psychologically* (or *experientially*) distinguishable, they are not entirely *physically* distinguishable.

This point has not played a major role in linguistic theorizing, so I have left it aside until now. Having turned to the larger question of human nature, it is time to raise it again, for it is a special case of a much more general issue that for centuries has been central to psychology and to the philosophy of mind: *How is our experience related to physical reality?*

To make this a little bit more concrete, let's return to the communicative situation depicted in earlier chapters, but cast it from the point of view of Sam, the person hearing the utterance. Figure 12.1 shows what Sam actually has access to.

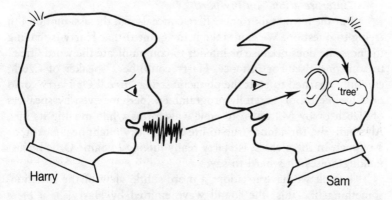

Figure 12.1 *A communicative act: What Sam can actually observe*

Sam can see Harry moving his mouth, and he can hear the noises that are coming out, and he can understand these noises as the word "tree."

But Figure 12.2 shows what Sam *perceives* to be going on.

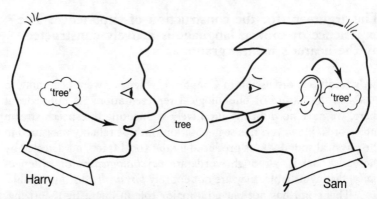

Figure 12.2 *The natural communicative stance: What Sam perceives*

With only the sound wave as evidence, Sam *perceives* Harry as having a thought about a tree and uttering a word to express this thought. That is, in some sense Sam constructs an interpretation of the situation that goes beyond the evidence available to him.

My imaginary skeptic objects:

This is absurd. When people talk to me, it's obvious that they're thinking about what they say. That's not just an "interpretation" on my part!

But the term "talk to me" here conceals just the assumption I'm trying to question. We can't take it for granted that Harry is making the noise he does because he intends to communicate the word "tree" to someone else. For instance, Harry could be a speaker of Czech, carefully coached to emit the phonetic string "tree." Or Harry could be a lifelike robot, carefully programmed (perhaps even by speakers of Czech or by Martians) to emit waveforms while moving its lips. Alternatively, for a more true-to-life case, Harry might be a parrot, or a puppet. In these cases, is Harry really *talking to* Sam? Or is he just making noises? It's hard to say.

I think we have to adopt a more subtle view of the situation, something like this: the sound wave emitted by Harry, *as a mere physical event*, isn't a word or sentence. But it *counts as* a word or sentence to Sam, whose brain automatically and unconsciously converts it into an internal phonological structure and associates it with a thought or an idea.

Of course, we don't *experience* spoken words and sentences as noises that it is up to us to interpret. We experience them more like Figure 12.2: the words come out of the speaker's mouth and are transmitted to us. That is, the way we experience language depends on the mental representations we unconsciously construct in response to the physical signals striking our sense organs. Moreover, we are not (normally) aware of these processes of interpretation: it's impossible to turn them off and hear spoken language as mere sounds.

Do children have to learn to adopt this attitude toward the language they hear? Do they have to figure out that the noises coming out of people's mouths are intended as communications of thoughts? My guess is that they don't. They're not always wondering if you're lying to them or if you're a robot (the fabled innocence of a child!); they instinctively (i.e. innately) adopt the same basic assumptions as adults, and the possibilities of defective communication are learned only later as conscious strategies.

This point is important enough that I'm going to enshrine it as a third Fundamental Argument:

> **The experience of spoken language is actively constructed by the hearer's mental grammar.**

To put it bluntly, a sound wave on its own is meaningless: it is meaningful only to a hearer equipped with the proper mental grammar.

My critic breaks in:

Your position is awfully surreal. You're claiming that the reality of language as we hear it is a product of our perceptual machinery interacting with an otherwise meaningless sound wave. Doesn't that make what we hear completely subjective?

Well, actually it makes it just subjective enough. For a bottom line, think what happens if someone speaks (or signs) to you in a language you don't know. You have no way of mapping such signals into thoughts or even words, so they just aren't meaningful to you. As far as getting a message across goes, the speaker might as well be talking to a zucchini.

But suppose I do understand the language. If you're right, what's to prevent me from hearing any old thing I want?

My reply has two sides. On one hand, our mental grammars are pretty much the same (if we are all speakers of English), so we all unconsciously assign pretty much the same structure to a given sound wave. We can't help all experiencing just about the same sounds and meaning. But why are our mental grammars pretty much the same?

Because we are all born with the same Universal Grammar; and Universal Grammar, interacting with the sound waves produced by English speakers, always comes up with the same answers—namely, the mental grammar of English. That's why, among speakers of the same language, we can treat what a speaker says as more or less "objective": we usually all come up with the same interpretation.

On the other hand, it's true that people *don't* always hear exactly what the speaker intended. Drawing on one of our examples from Chapter 6, suppose Harry asks Sam to find "the man in the chair with a broken leg," not noticing that the phrase is ambiguous. What Harry has in mind is a man in a broken-legged chair. But Sam, also not noticing that the phrase is ambiguous, looks for a seated broken-legged man. In this case the natural communicative stance of Figure 12.2 has subtly failed.

For a more radical case, think of the last time you got into an argument with your significant other. Didn't each of you think, "I'm being perfectly clear, but YOU are deliberately misinterpreting what I said"? Beyond a certain point—especially when understanding the speaker involves more than pure literal interpretation, and especially when the passions are aroused—what we experience the speaker as saying *can* be to some degree subjective. But to some degree only: even under the most extreme of (mis)interpretations, we'll never think that someone who utters "Please don't try to kiss me" is saying "Napoleon probably had big feet." That is, our mental grammars allow a certain amount of variability, but not too much; so the process of interpretation, while it is not entirely definitive, is far from arbitrary.

The point of the Argument for the Construction of Experience, then, is that the act of understanding spoken language isn't just a passive taking in of information. It involves a great deal of unconscious activity: organizing (or reorganizing) the input signal in accordance with the patterns of mental grammar. Without mental grammar, there's no language perception—just noise.

With this piece in place, we're ready to venture out into the world of other mental capacities and see how much they're like language.

13 Music and vision

To start expanding our sights, let's try to find analogues to the three Fundamental Arguments in two other human activities: listening to music and seeing the external world. Discussion of either of these could easily fill a book like this one, so I will necessarily be extremely sketchy.

Music

Like language, music is a uniquely human activity. To be sure, people differ radically in their musical talent, but nearly everyone learns lots of nursery rhymes, folk songs, and popular tunes, and nearly everyone derives some sort of aesthetic pleasure from the experience. So in thinking about music, we'll leave aside the Beethovens and Beatles of the world and concentrate on the more mundane commonalities of musical experience.

Although music is often spoken of as a kind of language, it is certainly not within the same space of possibilities as English, French, Zulu, and ASL. Music communicates something, perhaps emotional states, and it is sometimes symbolic, for instance when the Wedding March is played to symbolize weddings. But music shares few of the grammatical and expressive possibilities found in all standard languages, including signed languages. Music has no words, no syllables, no nouns or verbs, and no plurals or tenses; it has no way to name people, objects, or actions, no way to count, no way to say whether something is true or false, and no way to ask questions or give instructions. Consequently, it seems appropriate to treat music as a form of communication, but not as a *language* in the technical sense that we have been using here.

In order to understand the effect music has on us, we have to ask a very basic question: Why should it be that a sequence of notes coheres into a melody, makes sense as music? Not every collection of notes sounds like music. If we play a 33 rpm record at 78 rpm or fast-forward through a CD, it just sounds like a lot of tinkling—it doesn't make any musical sense. If we turn a piece of sheet music upside down and try to play it on the piano, it doesn't make any musical sense either. Why not?

Our first guess might be that it's because we're not used to hearing things like that. But, recalling our discussion of language, such a response sounds suspiciously facile. The problem goes deeper than merely being used to things.

Imagine we're listening for the very first time to some tune, say "Happy Birthday," and let's compare this experience with hearing the same tune played upside down and backwards. Even on the first hearing, we will surely recognize the former tune as a coherent tune, and we'll probably be able to hum along after hearing it a couple of times. But the latter (let's call it "Yadhtrib Yppah") will sound odd, like a bunch of senseless notes, and it will be pretty tough to hum along with (see Figure 13.1). What accounts for these radically different reactions?

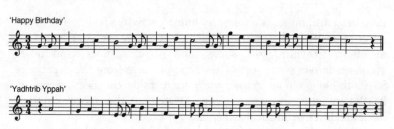

Figure 13.1 *A simple tune loses coherence if played upside down and backwards*

The difference is that "Happy Birthday" conforms to *patterns* of music that we are familiar with, and "Yadhtrib Yppah" doesn't: its rhythm feels all irregular, its melody doesn't seem to go anywhere, and its ending doesn't sound like an ending. But what are these patterns? They can't be memories of specific pieces of music we've heard, because by hypothesis we've never heard either of these particular tunes. Rather, the patterns are *commonalities* we've extracted from pieces we've heard.

Knowing these patterns enables us to do other things too. For instance, even on a first hearing of "Happy Birthday," we may well be able to notice it if the performer plays wrong notes. Why? Because (some) wrong notes violate the melodic or harmonic patterns that we associate with this style of music. Or consider listening to a jazz arrangement of a familiar tune, in which each of the players takes a chorus. They don't play the literal notes of the tune—it wouldn't be jazz if they did. Rather, they play something that is related to the tune in harmony, rhythm, and melodic structure. We can recognize these relationships (to a greater or lesser degree, depending on the style of jazz they're playing). How? Evidently by intuitively extracting and comparing the patterns of the original tune and the solo choruses.

What does "intuitively" mean here? It means that we don't carry out these comparisons *consciously*. All we consciously register is "Oh, yes, it fits" or "Something odd is going on." Without some study of music theory, the patterns themselves are unconscious.

The analogy to language ought to be obvious. Our ability to make sense of music in a certain style—to hear it as more than a sequence of notes—comes from having in our heads a collection of musical patterns that we use to organize the music we hear. This collection of patterns is general, in that it doesn't depend on knowing any specific tune, and it can be applied to an indefinitely large number of new tunes in the same style. On the other hand, the tune "Yadhtrib Yppah" intuitively sounds odd because it doesn't conform to these patterns (just as its *title* intuitively sounds odd because it doesn't conform to the phonological patterns of English). To push the parallel, I'll call this collection of patterns a *musical grammar*. So here we have an analogue to the Argument for Mental Grammar: our ability to make sense of new pieces of music in a familiar style implies that we have an unconscious musical grammar that organizes our understanding of music in this style.

As usual, my critic objects:

How can there be a musical grammar—rules that music must obey? The essence of great music is that it is always breaking the rules.

There are three answers. First, notice that this objection assumes that indeed there *are* rules to be broken—conventions or patterns that previous music conforms to. Second, with a few notorious exceptions, great music doesn't usually break previous conventions *very much*. All it takes is a little judicious stretching and bending of conventions to create a striking impression. And conversely, merely breaking rules doesn't make music great, as witness our poor hapless tune "Yadhtrib Yppah." Third, a new and striking piece leads listeners to extract new patterns unconsciously, and thus alter their musical grammar, preparing them to understand pieces in the new style more readily. That is, listening to music that breaks the rules leads listeners to construct new rules.

But if we each have a mental grammar for music, how did we get it? Surely not through teaching: a person doesn't have to be able to read music or play an instrument to appreciate music. It's possible for children to just "pick it up" from hearing tunes and singing songs.

Do children even have to "pick it up"? It's often said that an appreciation of music is "instinctive," that music is a "universal language" that everyone can appreciate. If that were true, we would have, with no further ado, an analogue to the Argument for Innate Knowledge—we could simply take it for granted that musical grammar is innate, and that would be the end of it.

Actually, it isn't quite that easy. Musical styles aren't as universal as a lot of people think. For instance, people who have been exposed only to American popular music will be hard put to understand what is going on in Indian ragas, or ceremonial Japanese *gagaku*, or Bulgarian folk dances. They may have a pleasant (or unpleasant!) overall impression. But everything will sound more or less strange. Not only won't they be able to hum along with the music, they may not even be able to tap their foot to it. They won't be able to tell whether mistakes are being made, and they won't be able to tell what parts of the music are variations on what other parts. The patterns in these styles of music just aren't available in their brains. It takes a certain amount of exposure to music in an unfamiliar style before it starts making sense. So there has to be some learning—or constructing of unconscious patterns—involved in getting to know a musical style.

Moreover, there exist ways of organizing patterns of notes that don't seem to be learnable in this intuitive fashion. One such is so-called "serial" or "twelve-tone" music, the technique of composition pioneered by Arnold Schoenberg and taken up by a wide range of composers during this century. This music can be tough to understand. Even composers who use this technique often admit they can't hear twelve-tone organization intuitively. And it's not a matter of just having sufficient exposure: from the experience of acquaintances, I can attest that children who grow up hearing lots of this music in their household still don't have a much easier time with it than the general public. In short, not every conceivable kind of musical pattern is accessible to intuitive learning.*

This suggests that although musical grammar is not *all* innate, it

* This does not necessarily mean that twelve-tone music is *bad* music. What makes something artistically successful is to a certain degree independent of its intuitive accessibility. There are great works that use twelve-tone techniques, bad works, and lots in between—just as in any other artistic medium.

is not all learned either. Rather, there is some innate "grain" to our ability to construct musical grammars: we can extract some sorts of musical patterns readily on the basis of experience, but not others. As a consequence, some musical styles are more accessible (or more easily learnable) than others. Hence we have an analogue to the Argument for Innate Knowledge: just as our ability to learn language requires innate resources that form the basis of learning, our unconscious ability to construct musical grammars requires some underlying innate resources that go beyond just an ability to "soak up" sequences of sounds.

Let me dignify these innate resources by calling them *Universal Musical Grammar*. As in the case of language (recall Chapter 3), we can ask two questions:

1. How much of musical grammar for any particular style is due to Universal Musical Grammar, and how much to learning? This can be determined by looking at what the musical styles of the world have in common, and how they can differ.
2. How much of Universal Musical Grammar comes from a brain specialization for music, and how much of it comes from general-purpose processes of perception? This can be determined by comparing the elements necessary for musical understanding to the elements necessary for other kinds of understanding, and by studying such phenomena as brain localization of musical ability.

For now, the answers to these questions are a good deal less definitive than the parallels for language. At the moment it seems likely that there are fewer dimensions of variation among musical styles than among languages—that is, musical grammar is somewhat more "universal" than linguistic grammar. In other words, there is probably less to learn in order to become familiar with a new musical style than there is for a new language.

It also appears that much of musical ability is based on more general properties of auditory and rhythmic processing, but still there are elements that are special to music, such as the organization of musical scales. There have been studies documenting brain localization; the consensus seems to be that the right hemisphere is involved in musical perception, and that in experienced musicians the left hemisphere becomes involved as well. Cases have also been documented of brain damage that affects musical ability, leaving language and general intelligence intact.

So the overall picture is that there is a partly specialized Universal Musical Grammar, which, like language, is a species-specific adaptation. An adaptation for what?—That's not so clear. It's easy to see what evolutionary advantage is conferred by having language, but it's hard to imagine how music does any good for our survival as a species. I consider this a real puzzle: Why should there be such a thing as music among our abilities?

In fact, music presents a double puzzle for evolution. First, there is the more general puzzle of why human nature should at all include such a thing as aesthetic pleasure, which we can experience in response both to natural phenomena such as landscapes and bird song and to human creations such as literature, art, music, dance, and food. Aesthetic pleasure doesn't enhance survival of the species, it only makes us feel good. But we undeniably have aesthetic experiences, and they are a primary reason behind our sense that it diminishes us to view people as mere machines.

The second and more specific puzzle is why there should be such an aesthetic object as *music*. All our other sources of aesthetic pleasure make use of materials already present in experience: the visual arts make use of visual perception, literature (including poetry and drama) makes use of language and our understanding of social situations, dance makes use of our preexisting sense of movement, and artistic preparation of food makes use of the preexisting sense of taste. Initially we might think that music just uses preexisting materials from auditory perception. But in fact, as I pointed out a moment ago, it's more specialized than that. Not any old collection of sounds can be made into music (except perhaps music of the John Cage sort). So why should the somewhat specialized principles of Universal Musical Grammar be present in our genetic heritage, when their only apparent use is for organizing aesthetic objects?

Having no coherent answer to these puzzles, I'll go on to the Argument for the Construction of Experience. This one is easy. We speak of music as happy or sad, dignified or poignant or sensuous. But where are these feelings? Music can't have feelings, it's nothing but sound waves! Rather, it's clear that the feelings are emotional responses evoked *in us* by the sound waves. That is, the emotional content that we experience in music must be constructed by our minds—it's not out there in the physical signal that strikes our ears. (Just as Sam's experience of the word "tree" in Chapter 12 is a product of his perceptual processes.)

Some of this emotional content may be fairly immediate and primitive. Fast loud music is often exciting and soft slow music is often soothing, probably because of rather simple effects on the autonomic nervous system. (Note well, though, that even these "simple" effects are actually not so simple: it still takes substantial brain processing to convert speed and volume into autonomic effects.) On the other hand, in order to experience the music of Haydn as witty, we need a rather sophisticated grasp of the conventional melodic, harmonic, and rhythmic patterns in Haydn's style, so that we can appreciate how he uses these patterns to make jokes.

But in either of these cases, we experience *in the music* some character of excitement or wit that in fact comes from *within us*, that is actively but unconsciously constructed by our brains, using principles of auditory perception and musical grammar. That's the point of the Argument for the Construction of Experience.

We see, then, that language is not splendidly isolated among human mental capacities. All its basic characteristics are mirrored in our ability to understand music.

Vision

Next I'd like to show that vision, too, is governed by a mental grammar. What could this mean? Don't we just see things out there? I'll try to make clear what the problem is, drawing on a long and rich tradition of research on visual perception.

Remember in Chapter 2, when we had Harry looking at a tree, and we represented what he saw by drawing a little tree inside a cloud in his head? Here it is again.

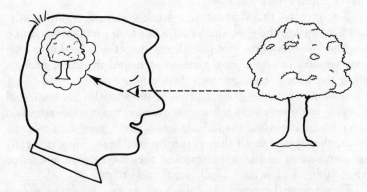

Figure 13.2 *The way we think about Harry seeing a tree*

This is the way we normally think about seeing: we think of producing inside our heads an image of the thing being seen. But let's think about it more closely. If we cut open our brains, we don't find any little images in there, any more than we find consonants and vowels.

And if there were little images in there, what good would they do? Who would look at them? There's no little person inside the head who sees the images. If there were, who would look at the images inside *that* person's head?

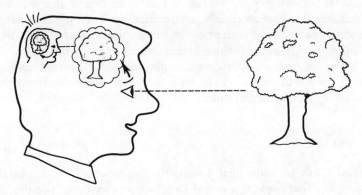

Figure 13.3 *Who looks at the image of a tree inside Harry's head?*

We might be tempted to answer that the brain *interprets* the images in the head. However, the brain can't interpret the images by *seeing* them—it doesn't have visual organs.

We have to think about the process somewhat differently. When light strikes the eyes, the lenses focus it to produce images on the retinas. But nobody looks at those images either. Rather, the retinas convert the light into patterns of neural impulses, and it's nothing but neural impulses from there on out.

Some areas of the brain reproduce the spatial arrangement of the neural impulses coming from the retinas; these areas are often said to have "retinotopic maps." But again, these maps aren't images as such; they're not at all like pictures in the head. They're merely more patterns of neural impulses, and they have to be processed further to arrive at what I'll call *visual understanding*.

To see what I mean by visual understanding, let's start with a very simple example, Figure 13.4.

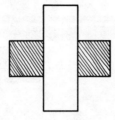

Figure 13.4 *Does the shaded rectangle go behind the white rectangle?*

This looks like a white vertical rectangle in front of a shaded horizontal rectangle. But think carefully about the physical basis for this perception. There is indeed a white vertical rectangle, but there's no single shaded horizontal rectangle behind it—only two shaded rectangles on opposite sides of it. Nevertheless, our brains construct an experienced configuration in which the two shaded rectangles are unified behind the white rectangle—in a place where the eye can provide no evidence.

Moreover, the brain constructs the *simplest possible* way of unifying the two shaded rectangles. It connects them with a part that is bounded by straight lines and homogeneously shaded, as in Figure 13.5:

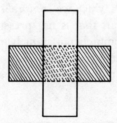

Figure 13.5 *The way we see Figure 13.4*

Wouldn't it be a little surprising if I removed the white rectangle and revealed one of the things in Figure 13.6?

Of course, *actually* there's nothing at all behind the white rectangle except the page. It's only a drawing. Yet our brains construct the "unseen" part completely reliably and with no effort—we don't *guess* that the shaded rectangle goes behind the white one, we *see* it, as if directly.

Figure 13.6 *Two ways we don't see Figure 13.4*

Of course I see it! I'm used to seeing things behind other things, and that's what they look like.

Right. But seeing a fence behind a tree trunk doesn't look exactly like Figure 13.4, and seeing a car behind a flagpole doesn't look exactly like Figure 13.4, and seeing a belt behind a belt-loop doesn't look exactly like Figure 13.4. All of these are instances of a common *pattern* of one object partially occluding the view of another object. The pattern occurs in indefinitely many different ways in daily experience.

In order for us to use this pattern to understand Figure 13.4, it has to be there somewhere in our brains. And it has to be different from a visual image (or a retinotopic map), because it is more general than any image can be—it applies to vast numbers of different situations. It is a tool with which we *comprehend* visual situations. In addition, it contains a part that is not present in any of the visual situations it helps us comprehend, namely the "virtual contours" indicated by the dotted lines in Figure 13.5.

Let's look at some more examples of patterns.

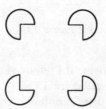

Figure 13.7 *Is there a square in the middle?*

Everybody sees Figure 13.7 as four circles, with a sort of "invisible square" in front that occludes part of each one. Of course, there's no real invisible square there, just blank paper, but, still, that's the way it looks. How is it that we see Figure 13.7 this way? It isn't as though we're are "used to" seeing invisible squares! And again, we can't see Figure 13.7 just any way we want to—it's invariably interpreted like the left-hand configuration in Figure 13.8, not like the other possibilities.

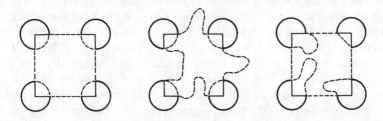

Figure 13.8 *The way we see Figure 13.7, plus two ways we don't see it*

What appears to be going on—very roughly—is that the brain unconsciously finds the simplest way to construct an interpretation of the visual field out of known patterns. In Figure 13.7, it's apparently simpler to see the "Pac-Man" shapes as occluded circles, and the occlusions adding up to a square—even an invisible square—than to see four isolated "Pac-Men." But to do this, the brain must be making choices among possible interpretations, rating them against known patterns.

Another example. It's possible to see Figure 13.9 in two different ways: (1) as a black square with a white disk in front of it; or (2) as a black square with a circular hole in it, through which can be seen the white background behind the square.

Figure 13.9 *A black square with a disk on it, or a black square with a white hole in the middle*

Now notice that even though there are are two ways of seeing Figure 13.9, it produces only one pattern on your retinas. This again shows that seeing involves more that just recording the patterns of light: it requires interpreting the patterns in principled ways.

In this case the principle is, very roughly, that a contour (or boundary) in the visual field has to separate the inside of a region from the outside background in a consistent way. (For convenience, I'll call this the Contour Principle.) For instance, in Figure 13.9 the square contour is understood as separating the inside of the square region from the outside background. But the circular contour can be understood in two ways. It can be understood as separating the inside of a disk from the outside background, in which case the disk's background is the square region. Or it can be understood as separating the inside of the square region from the outside background, in which case the round region is seen as a hole in the square, as part of the background that also surrounds the square. In other words, the Contour Principle allows two consistent analyses of the visual field.

This same principle accounts for the strangeness of some of the "impossible figures" that appeared in Chapter 4. Figure 13.10 is one of them, the "snakes."

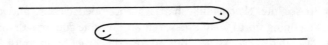

Figure 13.10 *"Snakes": an impossible figure*

Intuitively, the oddness here has to do with insides and outsides: somehow the inside of the top snake merges indistinguishably into the outside of the bottom snake, and vice versa, violating the Contour Principle. In other words, a very general principle accounts for both the ambiguity of Figure 13.9 and the anomaly of Figure 13.10.

So what? What do these silly illusions have to do with the real world?

Here's what: as far as we can tell, the processes responsible for these unusual perceptual experiences are exactly the same as those responsible for perception of the ordinary world. It's not as though we turn on a special set of processes when we're doing a psychological experiment. So if we unconsciously apply principles such as the Contour Principle in the sorts of situations I've just illustrated, we must be doing so in ordinary seeing as well.

It should be clear that I'm going through these examples in order to construct a visual analogue of the Argument for Mental Grammar. Our being able to comprehend an unlimited number of visual situations depends on our having in our brains a set of unconscious patterns and principles that can analyze a visual image and create an interpretation. We can call this set of patterns and principles a visual grammar—though it will probably bear little substantive resemblance to a linguistic grammar. (I don't care much whether we actually use the term "grammar," which some readers may find strained. The point is that the principles in the brain abstract away from particular visual images and help to organize what we see.)

Skipping the Argument for Innate Knowledge for a moment, it is not hard to see how the Argument for the Construction of Experience applies to visual understanding. The "invisible contours" in Figures 13.4 and 13.7, the visual ambiguity in Figure 13.9, and the strangeness of Figure 13.10 are certainly part of our visual experience. But there is no sense in which they are actually in the physical world—any more than words are physically present in an acoustic signal. Yet we can't help experiencing these figures the way we do: unconscious processes in the visual system make use of stored visual patterns and principles to construct an optimal understanding of the optical signal presented to the eyes. Every time we see something behind something else, and every time we see something standing out against its background, we are making use of principles of visual understanding illustrated here. And many more such principles, which I don't have space to mention here, have been studied in great detail by experimental psychologists.

Now let's go back to the Argument for Innate Knowledge. How do we acquire the patterns and principles of visual understanding? As usual, the right balance must be found between learning from the environment and using innate resources that make that learning possible.

Now environmental input certainly plays an important role in learning to identify particular kinds of objects. Someone who has never seen a car won't be immediately able to tell a Fiat from a Volkswagen, and someone who has never looked under the hood of a car won't be able to tell a generator from a carburetor. To draw on a parallel with language, this is sort of like learning a "visual vocabulary." We must carry around in our heads representations of thousands of objects whose appearance we are familiar with.

But recall that, in the case of language, learning a vocabulary is not sufficient for learning the language. Many principles of mental grammar are abstract; they determine how the vocabulary can be constructed from smaller parts such as distinctive features, and how items of the vocabulary can be combined into larger utterances. In the case of vision, the parallel questions are. What are the abstract pieces available for constructing items in the visual vocabulary? And how can individual items be combined in order to understand the full configuration of objects in the visual field (including, for instance, objects behind others)?

The evidence that has accumulated suggests that an overwhelming proportion of the basic principles of visual perception (for instance, the Contour Principle) are innate. For one thing, the visual system is scattered over numerous highly specialized areas or modules in the brain. It is unlikely that such differentiation in the brain is the result of learning, especially since (1) it is quite consistent across individuals and (2) the specialized areas are paralleled in other species such as monkeys. Rather, this points to a genetic predisposition for the brain to develop in a certain way.

Evidence has also arisen from infant studies. Infants' visual acuity isn't very good. And they don't have very much visual vocabulary. *But*—to the extent that they can be tested, infants as young as a few hours show command of some of the principles of visual perception. For example, suppose we show an infant Figure 13.9, and then gradually change it in one of the two ways shown in Figure 13.11.

The infant won't react very strongly to the change in Figure 13.11a: it just looks as though the circle moves to the left a little bit. But there will be a stronger reaction to the change in Figure 13.11b, which violates the integrity of the shapes: half of the square and half of the circle have moved together. (The strength of reaction is measured in terms of how long the infant looks at the display and how hard the infant sucks on a pressure-sensitive nipple.) That is, as early as we can measure it, infants are already making use of principles of visual understanding.

To be sure, as I've mentioned a couple of times before, it's necessary to have visual input in order for the visual system to develop properly. If nothing else, the neurons of the visual system require stimulation in order to acquire and tune their connections. But such stimulation is more like nourishment than like teaching. The baby comes to see the world in the way it does because of the brain's genetic disposition to develop in a certain way in response to visual stimulation.

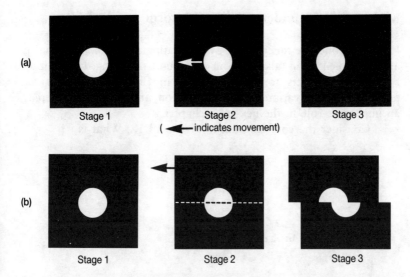

Figure 13.11 *Infants find the change in part a. unremarkable, but are surprised by the change in part b.*

To sum up, we now have musical and visual analogies to the three Fundamental Arguments for the nature of language.

The Argument for Mental Grammar: In each of these domains, our ability to make sense of novel stimuli is supported by a set of abstract patterns that are specialized for that domain.

The Argument for Innate Knowledge: In each of these domains, we learn the patterns we do in part because our brains are genetically programmed with substantial aspects of these patterns in advance. Learning is not "soaking up" of patterns, but rather active tuning and elaboration of the innate specialized mental "proto-patterns." That is, a great deal of nature lies behind learning through nurture.

The Argument for the Construction of Experience: Our experience and understanding of stimuli in each domain is actively constructed by our minds, making essential use of the abstract mental patterns specific to that domain.

Making visual understanding conform to ideal forms

I want to conclude this chapter by illustrating a phenomenon that is absolutely central in talking about visual understanding. I bring it up because it connects to our discussion in Chapter 12 about the possible extent of variation in interpretation, and because it will play an important role in the next two chapters.

Consider the configuration in Figure 13.12. What is it?

Figure 13.12 *An A or an H?*

Seen in the context of Figure 13.13a, it's the one that's not an A; in the context of Figure 13.13b, it's the one that's not an H.

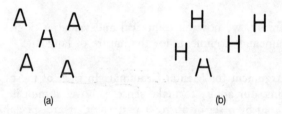

Figure 13.13 *a. It's not an A b. It's not an H*

But in the context of Figure 13.14, it's a funny H in the first word and a funny A in the second word.

TAE CAT

Figure 13.14 *It's either an A or an H, given the proper context*

So, depending on the context, it can be an A or not an A, an H or not an H. How can this be?

For a very rough approximation—which is all we'll need here—it seems that elements of the visual vocabulary, such as letters of the alphabet, are stored in the brain in terms of sets of criteria. For example, the criteria for a capital A are two slanted sides that meet at the top, plus a horizontal crossbar that joins the two sides in the vicinity of their midpoints. A configuration that meets these criteria is seen as an "ideal" or "stereotypical" A.

However, these criteria are not entirely rigid. Figures 13.15a and 13.15b push the crossbar up and down. Figure 13.15c has a crossbar, but it's not horizontal. Figure 13.15d has slanted sides, but they don't meet at the top (it's the same as Figure 13.12). Figure 13.15e doesn't have slanted sides; the sides meet at the top by virtue of another crossbar. All of these are acceptable as capital A's, especially if we put them between a C and a T.

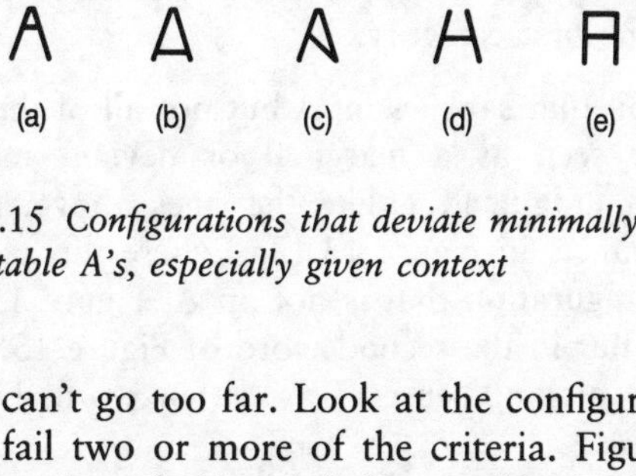

Figure 13.15 *Configurations that deviate minimally from an ideal A are acceptable A's, especially given context*

Still, we can't go too far. Look at the configurations in Figure 13.16, which fail two or more of the criteria. Figures 13.16a and 13.16b have nonslanted sides and the crossbar in the wrong place; Figure 13.16c has sides that don't meet and a nonhorizontal crossbar. These are unlikely to be seen as capital A's, even if they are put between a C and a T. (Try it!) Figure 13.16d has nonslanted sides that don't meet, so it falls under an alternative set of ideal criteria, namely those for an H. As a result, it definitely can't be seen as an A.

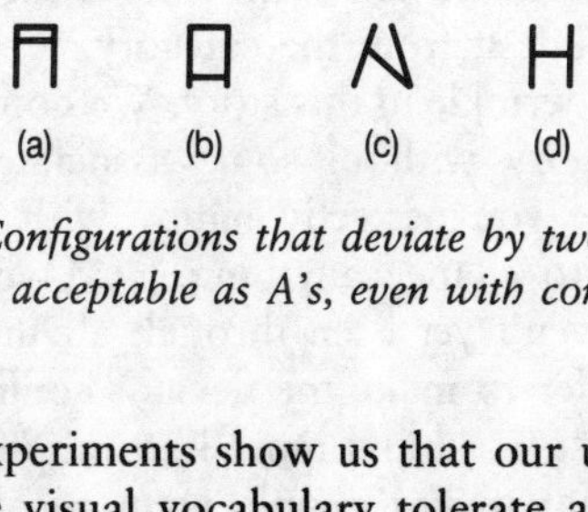

Figure 13.16 *Configurations that deviate by two criteria from an ideal A are not acceptable as A's, even with context*

These little experiments show us that our unconscious criteria for elements of the visual vocabulary tolerate a certain amount of deviation, but not too much. The way deviations are tolerated in these examples is altogether typical:

1. A configuration that meets all the criteria for some category is seen as an "ideal" or stereotypical example of the category, independent of context. For instance, an ideal capital A will still look like a capital A if put someplace where it makes no sense, say between a T and an E—or even between a cat and a mouse!

2. A configuration that violates too many criteria is seen as not belonging to the category, no matter in what context. For instance, no amount of context can make the configurations in Figure 13.16 look like capital A's.

Corollary: A configuration that not only violates several criteria for a category but also satisfies the ideal criteria for another category (for example, Figure 13.16d) is seen especially readily as not belonging to the first category.

3. A configuration that satisfies most but not all of the criteria for a category can be seen as a marginal or deviant member of the category. Such a judgment, unlike the ones above, *is* sensitive to context. For instance, in Figure 13.13a, where the context involves choosing the configuration that is not an A, Figure 13.12 is judged not to be an A. But in the second word of Figure 13.14, where the context demands making sense of a written word, Figure 13.12 *is* judged to be an A.

Corollary: A configuration that "falls in the cracks" between the criteria of two categories can be seen as belonging to either one, depending on the context, as seen in Figure 13.14.

In other words, context can affect the way we see things—but not all the time. Context plays a role just when the things we're looking at *almost* satisfy the "ideal" criteria of some category; in such a situation, different contexts can either coerce the configuration into the category or exclude it from the category.

There is a final wrinkle in this story. We don't tolerate marginal members of a category without some associated cognitive stress. Suppose I ask, "Are you perfectly happy with Figure 13.14 as it is—would you like to change anything?" (Maybe we also have to suppose that we haven't yet been through all this discussion.) You would probably prefer to make the deviant configuration more like an ideal H in the first word and more like an ideal A in the second. (It's this impulse that makes people want to straighten a picture hanging crookedly on the wall.) That is, ideal configurations in some sense make us happier than marginal ones.

It stands to reason that our perceptual systems have to be equipped to deal with marginal members of a category. The world out there isn't populated exclusively by things that conform completely to our ideals. Things are always going to be falling in the cracks, and if we couldn't deal with them, we'd be in trouble.

On the other hand, the specific way we respond to a marginal configuration is not so self-evident: we are more sensitive to context, and we often experience a certain degree of uneasiness and/or a desire to "improve" the configuration toward the ideal. Unless we work through an analysis of the sort we've just done, these aspects of the response are largely unconscious.

I think it is an important fact about human nature that we have this particular complex way of fitting the things we perceive into categories (and it is a fact that has eluded most philosophers and psychologists). It's not clear that we had to be built this way, but so it is. In the context of innocuous examples like Figure 13.12, it doesn't seem very important, but as we'll see, its effects in our lives are pervasive.

14 Language as a window on thought

The study of the relation between language and its meaning is traditionally called *semantics*. I have not talked much about semantic issues so far in discussing the structure of language, partly because there is less consensus on how these issues are to be framed. This chapter will sketch one of many possible approaches to questions of meaning, one that connects with our concerns with human nature, and especially with the three Fundamental Arguments.

Meaning as an internal organization

It is common to think of the meaning of a word as an objective fact, recorded in the dictionary. On this view, a word's meaning is determined by the people who write dictionaries—or alternatively, by a somewhat vague entity called "the culture," whose consensus is simply *recorded* by the people who write dictionaries.

For the purpose of figuring out how the human mind works, it is more useful to think about meaning another way. The question I want to focus on is:

> What kind of information is stored in people's heads that enables them (1) to create and produce novel sentences that express their thoughts, (2) to understand someone else's use of novel sentences, and (3) to use this understanding as a basis for reasoning and action?

That is, how are the meanings of words and sentences encoded and used *in the brain*?

This focus parallels the tack we have taken on language in general. In Chapter 2, we compared the idea of a rule of grammar as an objective or cultural fact, enforced by outside authorities such as schoolteachers, to the idea of a rule of *mental* grammar—the encoding of a pattern of sentence construction that each of us carries around unconsciously. Our interest has been in the latter notion. In turning to semantics, we will likewise be interested in the *internal* organization that allows us to use language meaningfully.

The diagrams of the language faculty in Parts II and III contained a component on the right-hand end tentatively called "thought," which I identified with the meaning or message that language conveys. We will now ask about the mental organization of this component, in much the way that previous chapters have looked at the organization of phonological and syntactic structure. We begin in a somewhat roundabout way, by establishing what thought is *not*; we will then be prepared for a more positive characterization.

Meaning is neither syntactic structure nor visual images

Chapters 4 and 6 argued that language and thought, while related, are distinct forms of mental information. Let's now review and amplify those arguments.

The basic reason for keeping language and meaning separate is that pretty much anything we can say in one language can be translated into any other, preserving the thought that the original language conveys. This means that thoughts can't be embalmed in the form of any single language—they must be neutral as to what language they are to be expressed in. For instance, the same thought can be expressed in English, where the verb precedes the direct object, and in Japanese, where the verb follows the direct object; hence the form of the thought must be neutral as to word order.

To be fair, there are two classes of exceptions to the blanket assertion that translation is always possible. First, one language may have words for different things from another language, so that a simple word-for-word translation can't be done. (A case frequently cited is the alleged existence in Eskimo languages of words for many different kinds of snow, but no word for just plain snow.) Such gaps can usually be remedied by coining new words or borrowing words from one language to the other. A notable instance has occurred in the revival of Hebrew as a spoken language in Israel. Quite naturally, the ancient language lacked words for all sorts of concepts of modern science and technology, and they have been coined and borrowed wholesale.

The other class of problems in translation is a little tougher. One language may, as a matter of its grammatical structure, make it necessary to express certain things that another language leaves open.

For instance, French requires its speakers to specify their social relation to the person they're speaking to, by choosing the proper second-person pronoun (familiar "tu" versus formal "vous"). Because this distinction is absent in English, translations from French to English lose specificity, and translations from English to French must make choices that the English speaker never had in mind. Similarly, the third-person pronouns of English require us to specify the gender of the individual we're talking about ("he," "she," or "it"); whereas in Finnish or ASL, a single third-person pronoun suffices for all genders. Again, mismatches in translation inevitably occur.*

Taking these considerations into account, we can revise the basic point slightly: if one is allowed to borrow vocabulary freely, any sentence of any language can be translated into any other language, with a few minor exceptions due to differences in grammatical structure. Moreover, these remaining differences can be explained to speakers of the language being translated into, in the fashion that I have just explained the difference between French and English. So differences in grammar do not reflect differences in the character of thought; the form of thought must be distinct from the linguistic garb in which it is clothed.

A second reason for keeping language separate from thought is that the syntactic structure of language is built out of things like nouns and verbs, prepositional phrases and tenses. But thought isn't built out of such units—thought concerns things like objects, actions, properties, and times. As we saw in Chapter 6, there isn't as tight a match between the units of syntax and of thought as we were taught in school. For instance, nouns don't all pertain to objects, since "earthquake" and "concert" describe actions or events. So object nouns like "chair" and event nouns like "earthquake," which are not distinguished in syntax, must be radically distinguished in thought.

We have also pointed out sentences that are grammatically correct but express an anomalous meaning, for instance "My toothbrush is pregnant." These contrast with sentences that express a

---

* During the 1940s, the linguist Benjamin Lee Whorf cited such mismatches of translation to argue that our way of thinking is to a large extent shaped by the grammatical structure of the particular language we speak—the so-called *Whorf Hypothesis*. It has since been established that Whorf's contrast between English and Hopi, which formed the basis for the most radical form of the Hypothesis, was considerably overblown (as was his account of the Eskimo words for snow). Current consensus is that differences in thought that can be conditioned by differences of grammatical structure are relatively superficial.

legitimate thought but are grammatically anomalous, for instance "What did Beth eat cereal and for breakfast?" (i.e. "Beth ate cereal and something else for breakfast. What was that other thing?") Only if language and thought are separate can this distinction be made.

My imaginary skeptic is getting a little nervous:

When I think, I think in English (or Chinese, or whatever).
So how can thought be different from language?

My response is that the language we hear in our heads while thinking is a *conscious manifestation* of the thought—not the thought itself, which isn't present to consciousness.

We certainly have enough precedent by now for talking about completely unconscious parts of the mind. Still, it may seem counterintuitive that thought is unconscious. Two examples may help for now. First, consider the experience of bilinguals who can "think in two languages." We would like to be able to say their thoughts are the same, no matter which language they are "thinking in." This is possible only if the form of thought is *neither* of the languages, and therefore something of which they are not conscious.

Second, consider the experience of suddenly arriving at a conclusion "intuitively." Surely thought has been taking place—it's just that we didn't have any awareness of it, and that's why we call it "intuitive." Only if thought is unconscious is such an experience possible.

When we don't think "in a language," we often experience our thought as visual images, "pictures in the head." Could visual images instead be the form of thought? I don't think this is possible either. For one thing, recall that in Chapter 13 we found the notion of "pictures in the head" problematic: Who looks at them? For another, back in Chapter 2 we talked about the sorts of things that can't be conveyed in a visual image. How could visual images clearly distinguish the thoughts expressed by sentences like "There's a bird in the tree," "A bird was in the tree yesterday," and "Birds like that tree"? What visual images convey the thoughts expressed by words such as "justice," "if," "tomorrow," or, for that matter, "thought"?

In fact, even simple visualizable words present a problem. For instance, the visual image that goes with "dog" is of one particular dog—so how can it be the thought that encompasses the appearance of collies, dachshunds, St. Bernards, and chihuahuas?

From these simple examples, we can see that visual images aren't adequate as a vehicle of thought. Rather, like things we say to ourselves "in our minds," they're a way that thought can manifest itself in consciousness. Again, I urge the idea that thought itself is completely unconscious.

I'll use the term *conceptual structure* for the form in which thoughts are couched. Like all the other kinds of mental information we've discussed, conceptual structure ultimately amounts to patterns of neural firings in the brain. But again we'll discuss it in functionalist terms, paying attention to the way it is organized rather than to the biological hardware, about which little is known.

Applying the Fundamental Arguments to conceptual structure

Having shown that thought is a distinct part of the mind from language, I next want to apply analogues of the Fundamental Arguments to thought, in order to demonstrate again that language is only one example of a much broader organization in human nature.

Let's begin with the Argument for Mental Grammar. A dictionary can record the meanings of words, but it can't record the meanings of *sentences*—there are too many to list. Similarly, we can store the meanings of words in our heads, but not the meanings of all the sentences we can speak and understand. As we saw in Chapter 2, it's easy to construct more English sentences than there are neurons in the brain. Since all (or at least most) of these sentences express different thoughts, there must be an indefinitely large number of possible thoughts as well. Of course, no one thinks *all* of these thoughts, any more than anyone says all of those inane example sentences in Chapter 2. But we all have the *potential* for thinking them.

In other words, the expressive variety found in language implies a corresponding expressive variety in the thoughts expressed by language. But as with language, this infinity of potential thoughts must be encompassed in a finite brain. Again, the only way this is possible is for us to store in our heads a finite number of "pieces of thought" or "simple concepts" plus a set of patterns for putting them together into more and more complex thoughts. I'll call these "simple concepts" *conceptual primitives* and I'll call the patterns that combine them *conceptual grammar* (not to bias the issue with terminology!).

What might this grammar of thought be like? For a first approximation, we might suppose that each word of the language is associated in the brain with a conceptual primitive, and that, corresponding to the syntactic patterns that build words into sentences, there are conceptual patterns that build primitive concepts into complex thoughts. On this approach, translation between languages is easy to account for: equivalent words in different languages can be thought of as associated with the same conceptual primitive.

But in fact we can push the Argument for Mental Grammar further. Consider the similarities among word meanings. Words like "committee," "herd," and "bouquet" all describe collections of entities; words like "long," "wide," and "narrow" all pick out linear dimensions of objects; words like "push," "yank," and "squeeze" all refer to actions of one entity exerting force on another. How can we (i.e. our brains) encode these relationships among words?

To answer this question, let's draw a parallel to phonological structure. How do we encode the fact that "green" rhymes with "clean," or "cuff" rhymes with "enough"? It's not because of similarities in their spelling: children can appreciate rhymes long before they can read, and the examples I've just given aren't similar in their spelling anyway. What makes words rhyme is that they have certain parts of their phonological structure in common—the end, of course.

Similarly, the only way anyone has thought of to describe relationships among the meanings of words is to suppose that related words share part of their conceptual structure. For instance, in the meanings of "committee," "herd," and "bouquet" the part that describes a plurality of entities is the same, and the part that describes what those entities are (people vs. animals vs. flowers) is different. (There are a lot of radically different theories about what these parts are like, but at this broad level everyone resorts to the same answer.)

In order for different word meanings to be able to share parts of their structure, the meanings of individual words must be built up out of smaller parts. So, just as phonological grammar governs how the pronunciations of words can be put together, conceptual grammar must govern how the meanings of words are assembled from smaller conceptual primitives.

But this leads us to an analogue of the Argument for Innate Knowledge. Where do the word meanings in our heads come from? Obviously, input from the environment is needed: children have to learn the meanings of words. As we noticed in Chapter 8, children learn about ten words a day between the ages of two and five. But how do they do it?

For the most part, not in terms of other words. Parents don't go around *defining* words for their children. Instead, in many cases parents point to things while naming them ("This is a *dog*. Can you say 'dog'?"). But this is not enough: words like "thought" and "from" don't submit to pointing. No one says "Here's *from*, Amy! Can you say 'from'?" So how does the child learn these meanings?

In fact, even a word such as "dog" presents problems to the learner—for much the same reason that a visual image of a dog doesn't suffice to encode the thought. When the parent points to a particular dog, how is the child supposed to know that the noise "dog" stands for all kinds of other dogs that look different? What's more, this thing the parent is pointing to is an *animal* and a *pet* as well as a dog. How is the child supposed to get the idea that the noise "dog" pertains to this thing's dogginess rather than its animality or pethood?

I'm trying to give, very sketchily, a sense of how formidable a job it is for a child to acquire the meanings of words. And in fact, the Paradox of Language Acquisition applies here in spades. If there is disagreement and uncertainty among linguists about the structure of mental grammar for phonology and syntax, it's nothing compared to the disagreements on the structure of concepts, including word meanings. Yet every child acquires tens of thousands of words without much apparent effort. Again, I see no choice but to draw two conclusions:

1. Children do not just "soak up" concepts from the environment, but rather actively construct them.
2. Children bring well-articulated innate machinery to the task of constructing concepts and associating them with words—machinery that is not at our disposal when we reflect consciously on words and their meanings.

By analogy with language, I'll call this innate machinery the *Universal Grammar of concepts*.

Let me be a bit clearer about what I have in mind. When I speak of an innate basis for concepts, I don't necessarily mean that any *particular* concepts are innate: rather, what's innate—what human nature gives us—are the building blocks from which the infinite variety of possible concepts can be constructed.

And I use the term "building blocks" advisedly. We often imagine thought as a kind of amorphous process from which clarity eventually emerges. In fact, thought just *seems* amorphous because, as I've stressed before, it's mostly unconscious. We don't experience all the work going on beneath awareness. As I'll try to show in the next three sections, within this apparent fog is a richly organized texture of discrete pieces and patterns in concepts. That is, concepts are more like a Lego set than like modeling clay. We can't construct thoughts in just any old shape: there is a selection of different kinds of basic pieces that can fit together only in certain ways and not others.

Our skeptical friend:

How can you say my thought is restricted by the way basic parts fit together? I can think any damn way I want!

But notice: "wanting to think a certain way" is also a thought, and so it's built out of the very same collection of parts. We can *want* to think only in the way we're built to think! As the philosopher and psychologist Jerry Fodor has put it, "*From in here* it looks as though we're fit to think whatever thoughts there are to think . . . . It *would*, of course, precisely because we *are* in here. But there is surely good reason to suppose that this is hubris bred of an epistemological illusion. No doubt spiders think that webs exhaust the options."

So far, then, we have constructed analogues to the first two Fundamental Arguments. The third, the Argument for the Construction of Experience, will arise in due time. But first we have other business. We have just shown that there *must be* innate parts underlying our concepts. This is rather unsatisfying unless we can show what at least some of these innate parts *are*. So the rest of this chapter will be devoted to working out some elementary aspects of conceptual structure that can plausibly be called innate.

Figure–ground organization in spatial location

Since we don't have direct intuitions about the form of thought, we have to use indirect means to get at it. An approach that has proven productive in the past couple of decades is to examine the grammatical form of the language that expresses thought. This section and the next will present two brief examples of conceptual organization revealed by the syntactic form of language.

The first is the way we express the spatial relations between objects. Take a simple sentence like "The cat sat on the mat." Example (1) gives its syntactic structure.

(1)

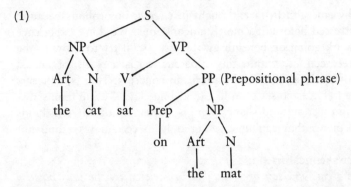

The two objects being described, the cat and the mat, are expressed asymmetrically: "the cat" is subject of the sentence, near the top of the tree, but "the mat" is way down inside the prepositional phrase.

The meaning of the sentence reflects this asymmetry. This is how the meaning is put together.

1. The mat is conceptualized as a *reference object* or *landmark*.
2. The reference object helps to define a *region* of space. This region of space is expressed by the prepositional phrase "on the mat": it is the region in contact with the upper surface of the mat. If we use different prepositions, we get different regions based on the same reference object, for instance "under the mat," "beyond the mat," and "off the mat."
3. The verb of the sentence uses this region of space to locate a *figural object*, namely the cat. In the present example, the verb "sat" also indicates the posture of the figural object and the past time of the situation in question.

So the basic analysis of the thought expressed by "the cat sat on the mat" is something like (2).

(2)

the cat	**sat**	**on**	**the mat**
figural object	location of figural object in region		reference object
	+		
	posture of figural object		region
	+		
	past time		

In other words, "the cat" and "the mat" play quite different roles in the meaning of the sentence.

To see the asymmetry more clearly, let's reverse the roles, giving us the sentence "The mat lay under the cat." This sentence sounds distinctly odd, even though the physical situation it depicts is exactly the same; and certainly the grammar is impeccable. Why should this be?

Toward answering this question, let's look at a situation in which we *can* reverse the roles of the figural and reference objects. Both the sentences in (3) are conceivable descriptions of Figure 14.1.

Figure 14.1 *An ambiguity of figural and reference objects*

(3) *a* The star is inside the circle.
   b The circle lies around the star.

Still, even here there is an asymmetry in the concepts expressed by these two sentences. We can see this by using them as answers to questions.

(4) *a* Where is the star?   It's inside the circle.
                           The circle lies around it. (???)
   b Where is the circle? It lies around the star.
                           The star is inside it. (???)

That is, sentence (3a) is a much better way of saying where the circle is, and sentence (3b) is a much better way of saying where the star is. This difference is explained by the analysis in (2), which says that the reference object (the object of the preposition) is being used to help locate the figural object (the subject of the sentence), not the other way around.

We can now see why our previous example, "The mat lay under the cat," sounds odd. It's telling us how to find the mat by using the cat as a point of reference; but it's hard to imagine circumstances in which we would want to do this.

For an even more striking case pointed out by the linguist Leonard Talmy, we are used to thinking of "next to" as totally symmetrical: if X is next to Y, it stands to reason that Y is next to X. Yet—"The bike is next to the house" is fine, but its reverse, "The house is next to the bike," sounds odd again. The reason is that we normally use relatively large immovable objects as landmarks for locating small movable objects, but not the other way around. (Notice that if the house we're looking for happens to be a toy "Monopoly" house, so it *is* relatively small and movable, "The house is next to the bike" suddenly sounds fine after all.)

Now the asymmetries in these sentences don't have anything to do with the syntactic structure of English. English syntax just says that the subject NP comes first, the NP that's object of the PP follows the preposition, and so forth. It doesn't specify what those NPs refer to in the world. And, as Figure 14.1 makes clear, these asymmetries don't have to do with the physical world either. Rather, they have to do with the way we *conceptually organize* the world we perceive: how we use objects to find other objects.

These examples also show that we locate objects not in terms of absolute space, but always in terms of figures placed against a background. This background is a region of space whose organization is determined by reference objects. In other words, the organization of our thought parallels the figure–ground organization of the visual field.

This conceptual organization, and the grammatical organization that goes with it, is replicated in language after language of the world. Thus we have good reason to believe it is part of the innate Universal Grammar of concepts—the way we "instinctively" put together the pieces of the world we perceive.

The same organization in abstract domains of thought

I originally became interested in this way of studying the organization of thought through the research of the linguist Jeffrey Gruber in the mid 1960s. Gruber showed that many grammatical patterns used to describe physical objects in space—including the pattern we just discussed—also appear in expressions that describe nonspatial domains.

To see what I mean, compare the groups of sentences in (5) through (8). The first example, (5a), exhibits the figure–ground organization we have just talked about; the whole set illustrates some larger grammatical and conceptual patterns within which this particular pattern is situated. Notice especially the parallels among these groups indicated by the italicized words.

(5) *Spatial location and motion*
    a The messenger *is in* Istanbul.   (Location)
    b The messenger *went from* Paris *to* Istanbul.
                                    (Change of location)
    c The gang *kept* the messenger *in* Istanbul.
                                      (Caused stasis)

(6) *Possession*
    a The money *is* Fred's.   (Possession)
    b The inheritance finally *went to* Fred.
                                     (Change of possession)
    c Fred *kept* the money.   (Caused stasis)

(7) *Ascription of properties*
    a The light *is* red.   (Simple property)
    b The light *went/changed from* green *to* red.
                                     (Change of property)
    c The cop *kept* the light red.   (Caused stasis)

(8) *Scheduling activities*
    a The meeting *is on* Monday.   (Simple schedule)
    b The meeting was *changed from* Tuesday *to* Monday.
                                     (Change of schedule)
    c The chairman *kept* the meeting *on* Monday.
                                      (Caused stasis)

Each of these groups contains one sentence with the verb "be," one with the verb "go" or "change," and one with the verb "keep." When "be" appears with a preposition (as in (5a) and (8a)), the very same preposition can appear with "keep"; if "be" appears without a preposition (as in (6a) and (7a)), so does "keep." On the other hand, "go" and "change" characteristically appear along with the prepositions "from" and "to."

Why should this be? What do these groups have to do with one another? Changing possession doesn't necessarily have anything to do with changing location: for instance, when we sell a house or some stocks, they certainly don't move. A thing's color doesn't have anything at all to do with where it is or who owns it. And setting the appointed time for a meeting or trip bears no apparent relationship at all to the other three.

On the other hand, on a more abstract level, we can find a sense in which the meanings of the four groups of sentences are parallel.

1. The "be" sentences all describe some state of affairs in which some characteristic is ascribed to the subject of the sentence: location in a region in (5), belonging to someone in (6), having a property in (7), and having an appointed time in (8).

2. The "go/change" sentences all describe a change involving the subject of the sentence, in which it ends up having the characteristic ascribed by the corresponding "be" sentence. The subject's characteristic at the beginning of the change is described by the phrase following "from," and at the end of the change by the phrase following "to."

3. The "keep" sentences all describe the subject of the sentence making the object of the sentence have the characteristic ascribed by the corresponding "be" sentence, and this characteristic persists over a period of time.

In other words, the linguistic parallelism among these sets reveals an underlying conceptual parallelism. So maybe it isn't such an accident after all that we use many of the same words in (5)–(8).

The idea behind the conceptual parallelism goes roughly like this: The characteristics that things can be conceived to have fall into broad families or "semantic fields" such as the headings in (5)–(8). Within such a family, there are simple characteristics expressed by "be" sentences, such as being in a particular location, belonging to a particular person, being of a particular color, or being scheduled at a particular time. But in addition, the conceptual system allows us to build complex concepts, among which are (1) a change from one characteristic to another (the "go/change" sentences) and (2) something making something else have a particular characteristic over a period of time (the "keep" sentences). Because the same abstract system appears in many (and possibly all) semantic fields, we are likely to find the same words used as we switch from one field to the another, as seen in (5)–(8).

In fact, almost any time we find a characteristic that varies along a one-dimensional range of values, we find that it is expressed in terms of the linear opposites "up" and "down" or "high" and "low." Numbers (and hence prices, weights, and temperatures) go up and down, military ranks go up and down, pitches on the musical scale go up and down, and so does one's mood. Time concepts, though, are an interesting exception to this generalization: in just about every language, they are expressed by terms that also apply to space, sure enough; but instead of "up" and "down," they use a front-to-back continuum—for example, "before" and "after" in English.

It's not that these ways of talking are creative, novel metaphors that make our speech more colorful. In most cases, including (5)–(8), they are the *only* ways we have of expressing these concepts in English—and similar patterns appear in language after language. This suggests that thought has a set of precise underlying patterns that are applied to pretty much any semantic field we can think about. Such an underlying "grain" to thought is just the kind of thing we should expect as part of the Universal Grammar of concepts: it's the basic machinery that permits complex thought to be formulated at all. In other words, the linguistic parallelisms shown in (5)–(8) lead us to substantive theories of the innate basis behind conceptual structure.

These examples also bear on the third Fundamental Argument, the Argument for the Construction of Experience. Consider the semantic field of the scheduling of activities. What can it mean to say "The meeting was changed from Tuesday to Monday"? This sentence, unlike "The cat sat on the mat," points to nothing perceptible. It describes something that takes place only in people's minds, changing their future behavior. In fact, the idea of named time periods like "Monday" is a purely conceptual invention—what's *perceptually* so special about the boundaries of Monday? Yet we indubitably experience reality as containing Mondays and schedules.

Even more compelling is the case of possession. If something belongs to you, it doesn't belong to me; and our behavior is strongly constrained by this knowledge. Who owns what is an important part of reality as we experience it. Yet it is often impossible to tell who owns something simply by looking at it—consider finding something accidentally left on the street, and wondering whose it is. Rather, the notion of possession is deeply conceptual.

The point is that these concepts, like the virtual visual boundaries and the musical emotions discussed in Chapter 13, are constructed by our minds. Nevertheless, this doesn't make them fictional or senseless—they are part of the way the world is *for us*, and for all human beings. All cultures have some notion of naming time periods, setting schedules in advance, and so forth; all cultures have some notion of possession or property rights. On the other hand, some alien being with a different evolutionary history might well construe the world quite differently. Who knows?

The pitfalls of definitions

So far I have stressed aspects of the Universal Grammar of concepts that lead to precision and articulation in our thought. Now we have to turn to the downside: reasons why our concepts are always inherently *im*precise.

To start with an innocuous example, let's examine the verb "defrost" in the sentence "Harry defrosted the roast." For a first approximation, it means something like "Harry made the roast change from a frozen state to an unfrozen one." That is, the word "defrost" packages a complex concept which, as we can see from the paraphrase, is built up partly from the sorts of pieces we discussed in the previous section, "to *make* (or *cause*) something to *change from* having one property *to* having another." This paraphrase would normally be a fairly adequate definition, good enough that someone who happened not to know the word could get the idea.

But let's look more closely at the "make" or "cause" part of this. To do so, we need a little terminology: I'll call Harry the *Agent*, the roast the *Patient*, and the roast's getting unfrozen the *Effect*. I want to show you that the concept of an Agent causing an Effect on a Patient is itself made up of a number of criteria, combined into an ideal—much like the "capital A" discussed in Chapter 13.

At least three criteria are involved in the ideal act of causation (or making something happen). First, the Agent (Harry) performs the act *deliberately*, desiring the Effect (the roast's getting unfrozen) to take place. Second, the Agent is *directly* involved in the Effect's taking place. Third, the Effect must actually take place. This last is essential. No matter what Harry did to the roast, if it remained frozen we can't say he defrosted it, but only that he *tried* to defrost it.

However, the other two criteria are not absolutely essential. Consider the following scenarios, which deviate more and more from the ideal. In each case, does Harry defrost the roast?

> (9) *a* Harry, wishing the roast to be unfrozen, takes the roast out of the freezer, puts it on the counter and leaves it there for several hours. The roast becomes unfrozen.
> *(Deliberate and direct)*

    b Harry, not knowing the roast is still in the freezer, unplugs the freezer and goes to work. The roast becomes unfrozen.
    (Not deliberate, relatively direct)
    c Harry, wishing the roast in Sam's freezer to be unfrozen, sabotages the electric company, blowing out all the electricity in town. The roast becomes unfrozen.
    (Deliberate, indirect)
    d Harry, not knowing there is a roast in Sam's freezer, sabotages the electric company, blowing out all the electricity in town. The roast becomes unfrozen.
    (Not deliberate, indirect)

I think you'll agree that Harry certainly defrosted the roast in the first case, and that it's very odd, if not incorrect, to say Harry defrosted the roast in the last case. In (9b) we'd probably qualify the statement by saying he *accidentally* defrosted the roast; in (9c) I'd say he did it, but in an awfully strange way.

There are further complexities. For instance, if Harry took the roast out of the freezer, but immediately afterward it was struck by lightning and became unfrozen *that* way, it's hard to say Harry defrosted it. And doubtless you can dream up other bizarre scenarios.

The point is that everyone agrees on their judgment of the ideal situation. As we move away from the ideal, there is a broad gray area or penumbra of cases that "sort of" fall under the concept, and about which people may disagree somewhat. Then, as we move still further away from the ideal, everyone is in agreement again that the situation does not fall under the concept.

As in the case of the "capital A" in Chapter 13, if we try to imagine an act of defrosting a roast, we tend to think of the ideal case, something pretty much like (9a). That is, the ideal has some sort of cognitive priority. And nonideal cases result in a certain degree of cognitive stress. That's why we may feel uncomfortable (or even snicker) about calling penumbral cases like (9b) and (9c) "defrosting."

In the case of the concept of defrosting, the existence of a gray area is harmless enough. Why bother worrying about it? But there are other cases where it has more serious consequences. Consider these four scenarios.

(10) *a* Chris, wishing Pat's death, plunges a knife into Pat's heart. Pat dies.

b Chris, who has never before seen or heard of Pat, stumbles. The knife Chris is carrying is plunged into Pat's heart. Pat dies.

c Chris, wishing Pat's death, decides to trip Sandy, who happens to be carrying a knife. The knife plunges into Pat's heart. Pat dies.

d Chris, who has never before seen or heard of Pat, stumbles and bumps into Sandy. The knife Sandy is carrying plunges into Pat's heart. Pat dies.

Did Chris kill Pat? My own judgments are parallel to those for "defrost": yes in (10a), no in (10d), yes, but with qualifications, in (10b) and (10c).* That is, (10b,c) are not ideal instances of the concept of killing, but they count because they fall in the penumbra of the concept.

As with defrosting, we can also think of cases that involve deviance in the Effect. Suppose Chris mortally wounds Pat, but before Pat expires, lightning strikes and incinerates them both. Did Chris kill Pat? (Well, no, but . . .)

This time the imprecision of the concept is more crucial. The legal system has to decide what to do to Chris. If Chris's action was killing, punishment is necessary; if not, Chris is off the hook. But actions in the world don't come neatly dividing into killings and nonkillings: the gray area of the concept shades smoothly from pretty much ideal acts of killing to things that are pretty clearly not killing. And, as with the "capital A," it is just in these penumbral cases that context plays an important role. For instance, does the legal system presume guilt or does it presume innocence? What is Chris's past history? And even, do you like Chris? These factors will play a far stronger role in a case like (10b) than in the crystal-clear ideal case (10a).

In fact, the legal system recognizes variations from the ideal by making distinctions between, say, murder and manslaughter, which carry different penalties. But that doesn't solve the problem entirely, since each of these is itself an ideal, and has its own gray area. As a result, the very same problems arise, albeit on a finer scale. That is, the difficulties can't be eliminated entirely by creating more precise definitions; at best they can be confined to a smaller range of cases. This problem is constantly confronted by judges and by legal

---

* If (10d) is not clear enough, consider a case where Chris, an innocent bystander, fails to arrest the fall of the stumbling Sandy, whose knife, as a consequence, plunges into Pat's heart—or still more inadvertent and indirect cases, which I leave to the reader's imagination.

theorists; it is recognized as an inherent difficulty in interpreting any kind of written legal document.

One last complication in the concept of killing. Just as defrosting presumes that the roast starts out frozen, killing presumes that the Patient is alive before the act takes place—otherwise the Patient couldn't die. This presumption plays a role in the bitter dispute over abortion, for one central issue is whether a ten-week human fetus is a living being.

Those opposed to abortion claim that it is, and indeed that it is an ideal case of a living being; hence for them an abortion is to be seen as a plain and simple case of killing.* Those favoring the legality of abortion take the position that the issue is a matter of degree, since a fertilized egg is pretty clearly not a living being, and an eight-and-a-half-month fetus pretty clearly is. Such a position accords better with common sense, but it is rhetorically weaker *because it submits to the cognitive stress induced by nonideal instances of a concept*. As a result, the rhetoric on this side of the argument typically avoids the issue of fetal life altogether and focuses on the conflicting ideal of maintaining personal autonomy for the woman carrying the fetus. The dispute between alternative ideals is analogous to disputing whether the funny figure at the end of Chapter 13 is an A or an H. Who's right?

Most participants on both sides of the debate acknowledge the agony involved in deciding on their position, a mark of a penumbral instance of a concept and of conflicting ideals. And the cognitive stress is a hell of a lot greater because the decision involves human life and dignity rather than mere shapes on a page. Yet the situation seems to require drawing a sharp line; in order to do so, each side finds it necessary to downplay some of the conflicting criteria and to treat abortion as if it were an ideal instance.

I can't give you the solution. I just want you to notice that this situation and many others like it follow inevitably from the very

---

* Although everything in anti-abortion rhetoric (to start with, its use of the term "prolife") treats abortion as an ideal case of killing, surely there is implicit acknowledgment that it is in the gray area. Only the most rabid opponents of abortion advocate a murder penalty for women undergoing abortions and for doctors performing them. And many acknowledge the context-sensitivity characteristic of a penumbral case, for instance in the willingness to permit abortion in pregnancies due to incest or rape (as if that affected whether the fetus is alive or not). Moreover, no one to my knowledge has suggested that it should be possible to take out life insurance on a ten-week fetus. I *thought* no one would ever try to take an income tax deduction for an "unborn child"—too bizarre—but I recently saw in the paper that someone did. (It was, by the way, denied.)

nature of human concepts. They are not going to go away by our being more precise about language or about facts of science. Maybe we can mitigate them somewhat by openly acknowledging the existence of the gray area, and by accepting the cognitive stress of penumbral cases instead of getting angry. Or maybe not.

* * *

Turning back to our main concern, I've tried to show that the way our concepts work unconsciously is not the way we normally think of them. We're brought up to think that words have precise meanings, and that any imprecision is a mark of "sloppy thinking." In fact, though, aside from their social importance, the examples I've raised here are typical. Just about any word we choose turns out to raise similar problems of definition. Some degree of imprecision is unavoidable. Part of the Universal Grammar of concepts—the way we inherently understand the world—is that our concepts include not only ideal examples, but also context-sensitive gray areas around the ideals.

> *But wait!* (says our friend) *That implies that words don't have strict and precise definitions. You're suggesting that everything we say is mired in dependence on context, or even that language has no determinate meaning. Surely we don't want be forced to such a desperate conclusion.*

I don't think the situation is that bad: After all, I *am* claiming that language has meaning. It is just that meaning comes with inherent uncertainty around the edges—but, on the other hand, the uncertainty is around the edges only. In these gray areas, context is indeed crucial, but there are plenty of clear cases where it plays less of a role. And yes, we do have to give up the idea that words have strict and precise definitions. But definitions with the proper context-sensitivity can still be worked out in terms of sets of criteria, some of which are essential, and others of which can be relinquished in nonideal cases. That's the way our thoughts are constructed.

Why do we *think* that words have strict and precise meanings? In all likelihood, because the word "meaning" expresses a concept too, and like all concepts, when we contemplate it consciously, we imagine it in terms of an ideal—one in which everything is clean and clear. But why should "meaning" be better off than any other word? Why shouldn't it have lots of fuzz around the edges too?

As with other aspects of our unconscious that we've discussed here, the idea that meaning is inherently imprecise may take a bit of getting used to, but I think we can learn to live with it. Recognizing the organization of this imprecision in conceptual grammar may even help us think more clearly sometimes.

Conclusions

Our goal in this final part of the book has been to show that the characteristics of the human mind revealed by language apply to other aspects of the mind as well—that language is but one example of a broader human nature. We have now seen that our capacity for thought, the part of us we often consider most human, is governed by underlying principles a lot like those for language.

1. Our thoughts are built out of a finite set of unconscious patterns which give us the potential for thinking an infinite number of thoughts of indefinite complexity.
2. These patterns in turn are constructed from an innate Universal Grammar of concepts, some details of which we have been able to work out here: figure–ground organization, the extension of figure–ground organization to abstract concepts, and the organization of criteria into ideals with context-sensitive gray areas around the fringes.
3. Our way of understanding the world—including our way of *learning* about the world—is a consequence of this unconscious organization; this often comes in conflict with our conscious sense of how we *should* understand the world.

Unlike language, music, or vision, though, we have not been able to show that there are specialized brain areas for conceptual thought. I assume that this awaits a more mature neuroscience.

15 Social organization

Introduction

The question of nature vs. nurture is nowhere as pointed as in issues of culture and society. The most commonly invoked environmental influence on the child, after the parents, is the "culture" or the "social context." And even the parents are often said merely to be passing on to the child the culture's perceptions, customs, and values.

Yet the child's social context is ultimately determined by the way other people behave; and the way other people behave is conditioned by *their* having assimilated the culture. So a little reflection leads us to questions of a form by now familiar:

1. What is the organization in people's heads that enables them to behave socially and to understand others' behavior as part of a social context? What knowledge are they "passing on" to the child?
2. How is this organization acquired by the child? That is, what is the human "capacity for culture"?

In this chapter I'm going to suggest that our cultural knowledge, like the rest of our way of dealing with the world, is constructed by the child from a combination of environmental input and a fairly substantial innate endowment. That is, this aspect of the mind is like language too.

This material is admittedly more speculative than the rest of the book. I'm taking the risk of presenting it anyway, because the approach to human nature we've developed here has fascinating implications for our view of society and culture.

The capacity for culture compared to the capacity for language

Let's begin by comparing cultural knowledge with the knowledge of language as we have come to understand it here.

Just as the child obviously starts life unable to speak and ends up speaking a language, the child starts life with little or no social or cultural capability, and ends up being socialized. And just as children raised in different linguistic environments end up speaking different languages, children raised in different cultural environments end up with different cultural behavior.

In the case of language, this learning has turned out to be based on a very rich innate ability, which reaches fruition by virtue of exposure to a linguistic environment. In fact, it is the innate capacity, Universal Grammar, that enables the child to *make sense* of the linguistic environment. Children can learn different languages in the environment precisely because Universal Grammar provides the child with a menu of possibilities. On the basis of this menu, the child constructs a set of patterns, or a mental grammar, that is tuned to the examples presented in the linguistic environment. Couldn't social/cultural learning be the same way, with a rich innate component that supports the child's acquisition of the local culture?

It is often assumed that cultures are infinitely variable: for any putative "universal" of culture, an exception can be found. But languages, too, are infinitely variable. The menu of Universal Grammar permits an amazing amount of variation among languages: languages using a range of exotic sounds; languages with different ordering between the verb and the direct object; languages where questions move wh-words to the front, to the end, to second position, or not at all; languages where the verb can be elaborated radically with prefixes and suffixes to include the subject, the object, the manner of action, and how sure the speaker is of the assertion; and even languages that use the manual/visual modality instead of the vocal/auditory. Yet there are universals; it is just that they do not yield themselves up to superficial examination. For the most part they appear at a more abstract level of organization. Moreover, the fact that many features of language are drawn from a menu allows for variation and nonuniversality—but still not for *arbitrary* variation.

Similar considerations might well apply to cultural variation: the innate capacity for culture might provide rather abstract universals that do not appear on immediate examination of any particular culture. It might provide a menu with sufficient possibilities that the differences among cultures would appear overwhelming, yet still not permit arbitrary variation. In the course of this chapter some areas of cultural knowledge will be suggested in which this view appears altogether plausible.

Our imaginary skeptic makes a final appearance:
*The notion of a structured "human nature" underlying our
ability to function in a culture implies a rigid determinism
that I for one find unwelcome: it undermines our sense of
human freedom and creativity.*

In the case of language, though, does Universal Grammar
restrict our freedom? No: on the contrary, it is what *permits* us our
freedom. Without it, children couldn't internally construct the
patterns of mental grammar that make possible the infinite variety
and richness of linguistic expressions.

We might also return to the biological analogies of Part I. The
physical structure of the human hand—and the brain mechanisms
necessary to control it—are genetically determined. Everyone
acknowledges that the hand is a marvelous instrument produced by
evolution, permitting us a range of creative action unavailable to
other animals. Yet it certainly has its limitations. We're never going
to be able to perform tasks that require us to voluntarily bend the
fingers back to the wrist, or tasks that require speed and strength
beyond that of our muscles and bones. This too is determinism, but it
is hardly unwelcome or rigid. It's just a fact of life.

And again, couldn't the same be true of cultural knowledge?
Couldn't it be the case that our cultural richness is the product of a
range of cognitive possibilities provided to us by our genetic heritage?
Indeed, we might well have limitations on how we can deal with
social organization, but is that necessarily bad for us? And even if it *is*
bad for us—maybe it's just an unfortunate fact, just like the fact that
we can't smell as well as dogs, or see ultraviolet light as well as bees,
or construct sentences like "What did Beth eat cheese and for
breakfast?". We can't let the fact that we are a lot smarter than other
animals allow us to think we can do *everything*.

How would an innate capacity for culture be transmitted?
Recall the steps in the Genetic Hypothesis of Chapter 3. Our
linguistic behavior consists of producing and understanding utterances. This behavior is governed by a repertoire of patterns, namely
mental grammar. Mental grammar, in turn, is acquired through the
interaction of Universal Grammar with environmental input. What is
under genetic control is not linguistic behavior, nor mental grammar,
nor Universal Grammar, but the *physical brain structures* that make
Universal Grammar and the learning process possible. Similarly, it is
unlikely that there is a gene for a social behavior—say altruism or
aggression. What the genes can control at best is the construction of

brain structures that make learning of patterns of altruism or aggression possible.

The source of such genes, whatever they do, must be evolution. Can you give an evolutionary explanation for the features of cultural knowledge that you claim to be innate—a reason why these particular features of behavior could have enhanced the survival of individuals possessing them?

I wouldn't want to deny that searching for evolutionary explanations often leads to insight. But, taking my cue from the case of language, I'm more concerned with first finding out what the organization in our heads is like. For instance, it's unlikely that we can explain on evolutionary grounds exactly why adverbs (of all things) enhance individual survival. But that doesn't prevent us from accepting the existence of adverbs in our mental grammars and studying their properties. Similarly for concepts of social organization: there may be features that are accidental (and just don't *hurt* individuals); and there may be features that *do* enhance survival, but in a way we can't figure out until we see the larger structure of the system. In such cases, looking for an immediate evolutionary explanation may get in the way of seeing what's going on.*

Anyway, what gives you the idea that you can study other cultures systematically? Any description of another culture is unavoidably ethnocentric, an imposition of your own cultural and theoretical prejudices.

But what about language? Any description of another *language* is unavoidably ethnocentric too, an imposition of our own linguistic and theoretical prejudices. So what? Any description of *anything* is inevitably tainted by the point of view of the describer.

In the case of linguistic descriptions, usually the best accounts are provided by native speakers who have been trained as linguists. But not always: sometimes our own cultural assumptions can prevent us from noticing phenomena in our language (or culture) that are obvious to someone with a different point of view. Does that mean

---

* Many important arguments for the evolution of innate cultural knowledge have arisen in the discipline of *sociobiology*, a term coined by the noted biologist E.O. Wilson. However, some sociobiologists have looked for evidence of innate racial differences, or differences between homosexuals and heterosexuals, or other differences that invite invidious discrimination. Such a line of investigation has not been carried out on other species, and my impression is that the evidence is typically pretty flimsy. These efforts have indeed been roundly criticized, but unfortunately in such a way as to unfairly dismiss the entire sociobiological enterprise. As in the case of language, I'm interested more in characterizing the mental characteristics of the species as a whole.

we should stop doing science? I hope not: it just means we have to proceed with sensitivity and an awareness of our own fallibility. In particular, in dealing with another language or culture, it is important to respect the point of view of those we are observing and analyzing.

To sum up: many of the basic observations about culture and cultural learning apply equally to language. Given what we know about language, it is possible to acknowledge the diversity of culture and to acknowledge that cultural knowledge must be learned, and yet come to believe (1) that there is an innate human "capacity for culture," (2) that it might well be highly structured, and (3) that we should be able to study it scientifically through cross-cultural investigation.

Applying the Fundamental Arguments

In a view of social organization that parallels the view of language developed here, the basic premise is that in order for people to comprehend social interactions and participate in a culture, they need an appropriate cognitive organization. That is, the way people can act within a society depends on the way they can internally represent the social context.

It's not hard to construct analogues of the Fundamental Arguments for the case of social organization. First, the Argument for Mental Grammar: In the course of our lives we engage in vast numbers of social interactions, no two of which are exactly alike. Our ability to interact so creatively surely can't be encoded just as some large repertoire of memorized scripts, which we rattle off word-for-word and gesture-for-gesture in response to our counterparts—who, coincidentally, have memorized exactly the same repertoire. Such a position is absurd—not only because it presents us as robots, but also simply because the number of scripts necessary couldn't fit into our brains.

So, as usual, we fall back on the position that what we *have* memorized is a finite set of patterns or principles that enable us to perceive and assess a potentially unlimited number of novel social situations and to act (more or less) appropriately. However, we tend to take much of our social knowledge for granted; we don't notice how rich and complex it is. Thus it's quite likely that the patterns and principles involved are largely unconscious (though perhaps not as unconscious as those for language).

The question then arises of where these patterns in our heads came from. Are they explicitly taught to children? Considerations like those for language suggest that not all of them can be taught. (1) Children often "pick up" the mores of their peers' subculture without any explicit teaching—and often to the dismay of their parents! (2) To the extent that the parents' cultural knowledge is unconscious, they can't formulate it explicitly enough to teach it to their children. Rather, children learn partly just by observing the example of others. (3) But if children are learning by example rather than through transmission of rules, then they themselves must be internally constructing the patterns involved in social and cultural understanding.

These are highly abbreviated versions of the preliminaries to the Argument for Innate Knowledge. As in the case of language, the conclusion is that children come innately equipped with a substantive head start on learning culture, which enables them to assimilate quickly and effortlessly into their social/cultural environment. Most of the rest of this chapter will be devoted to this Argument, so I will put off any details for the moment.

Turning to the Argument for the Construction of Experience, consider a typical social concept such as marriage. Unlike rocks and trees, such things as marriages exist only because there are people with minds that can grasp the concept of marriage; the rights and obligations that go with marriage are all in people's heads. A couple can go through all the motions of being married without being married; and, unfortunately, the converse is true as well. That is, the institution of marriage is distinct from any particular physical manifestations—other than a ceremony at which some culturally sanctioned authority says "I now pronounce you man and wife" or its cultural equivalent. But in turn, this ceremony consists just of language and/or other culturally sanctioned ritual acts, and it presupposes that everyone understands these acts in the same way. In short, our experience of marriages is a consequence of our conceptual possibilities. The same is true of any social contract such as gaining ownership of a house, conferring an academic degree or a military rank, or voting for a president. It counts as such only because people *understand* that it counts as such. In other words, our experience of the social environment is constructed by virtue of our social knowledge.

We now turn to the task of substantiating the Argument for Innate Knowledge.

Brain specializations for social perception

One of the important things to know in a social encounter is who the other person is. This might seem just to be a matter of ordinary visual perception—we see who we're talking to, and that's that. But evidently the task of identifying individuals is so important that evolution has come up with special-purpose modules, which piggyback on ordinary perception to give us finer discrimination on this particular topic. One such system is the specialization of vision for face recognition, mentioned in Chapter 11; another is the specialization of hearing for voice recognition, mentioned in Chapter 5.

But identifying other people isn't the only important issue in social interaction. As you may remember, we talked in Chapter 5 about how the auditory system factors incoming signals, dividing them into what the speaker is saying (the linguistic system), who the speaker is (voice recognition), and the speaker's emotional tone. This last module is another part of social interaction: it's important to know whether the person speaking is friendly, threatening, indifferent, surprised, frightened, sexually receptive, or whatever. Our auditory systems are amazingly good at picking up these elements of tone. (In fact, some of the impact of music undoubtedly comes from this auditory subsystem, picking out in the musical signal those aspects of emotional tone to which it is so acutely tuned.)

The visual system has a parallel specialization that helps us read emotional tone from people's facial expressions, gestures, and posture—what's sometimes called "body language." This system is sensitive enough that we can read emotions into extremely attenuated signals like those in Figure 15.1.

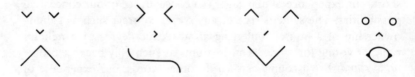

Figure 15.1 *Some scribbles that are perceived as faces expressing emotion*

These four modules in perception—visual and auditory identification of individuals, and visual and auditory detection of emotional tone—turn out to be associated with separate brain localizations, so that a stroke can impair a person's ability at one of them, leaving the others spared. As usual, this suggests an innate brain specialization.

Where do auditory and visual signals of emotional tone come from? They come from motor activities of other people. People are constantly signaling emotional tone, whether consciously or (more often) unconsciously. In order to produce such overt signals, there must be brain activities that convert emotional tone into motor patterns—smiles, frowns, raises of the eyebrows, openness or aggressiveness or sensuality in the posture, and so forth.

Again, there is suggestive evidence that a great deal of this is innate. Many facial expressions and much of body language are immediately interpretable cross-culturally without effort. And certain types of brain damage leave their victims with an emotionally "flat" appearance, unable to produce the outward manifestations of emotional tone. Moreover, as Charles Darwin pointed out over a century ago, many of these expressions of emotional tone can be traced to mammalian antecedents.

As with language, the fact that there is an innate component to perception and production of emotional tone does not preclude there being a culturally determined component as well. Such a component would have to be learned by someone growing up in (or entering) a community, and would result in "misreading" of the tone of someone from a different culture. Again, as with language, the proper question to ask is not, Is It Nature Or Is It Nurture? but rather, What combination of nature and nurture is responsible for the effects we observe? To sum up: we have a purchase on the Argument for Innate Knowledge in this domain: there is indeed evidence that the patterns and principles we use to make sense of social interactions are in part unlearned, and that they are encoded in specialized modules of the brain.

We also have further evidence for the Argument for the Construction of Experience. Consider the "faces" in Figure 15.1, in which we can't help seeing emotions. There aren't any emotions there, they're just scribblings I made, to which our perceptual systems happen to be attuned. Similarly, if some of the effect of music comes from the auditory system's specialization for detecting emotional tone, we are being "misled" by our perception: the music has no emotions, it's just a sequence of sound waves. These are both cases of our experience being shaped by our perceptual systems, even when the physical world contains nothing like what we perceive.

Three concepts at the basis of social understanding

Fascinating though these aspects of our social interaction are, I'd like to go beyond them and explore some of the more abstract concepts that lie behind our understanding of social interactions. These aspects of social knowledge piggyback not on the perceptual and motor systems, but rather on the system of conceptual structure we discussed in Chapter 14.

Perhaps the most obvious of these is *kinship*. In every culture, each individual is in a special relationship with his or her parents, children, spouse(s), and siblings. Many aspects of this relationship arise clearly from our mammalian heritage, in which the parents (or mother alone, depending on the species) must take care of the young for some period of time. Evolution has evidently provided us, like other mammals, with patterns of perception and behavior that make this care possible and basically pleasurable.

Humans have a more elaborate form of the basic mammalian pattern, in that kinship bonds are extended to more distant relatives as well. And in many cultures there are elaborate customs, obligations, and rights associated with being in particular kin relations. For example, every culture has an incest taboo, but its precise extent varies from culture to culture—with which extended kin sexual relations are forbidden and with which they are permitted or even encouraged.

Although we have perceptual cues for who is in our immediate family (the people we live with), we don't have any such cue for more distant relatives—we rely on someone *telling* us we're related, and miraculously we come to feel the bonds of kinship. Consider, too, the bonds often felt by an adopted child toward a newly discovered biological parent whom he or she has never met before. Such examples show that the bond of kinship is not just *per*ceptual, but *con*ceptual as well. When we conceive of being kin to someone, we feel and behave differently toward them.

A second fundamental social concept is *group membership*. Among birds and mammals it is common to find collections of unrelated individuals of a species living together as a flock or herd, sharing resources and participating in common defense against predators. But in some species, especially primates, it goes further:

the group is not just a convenient aggregate of individuals, but a semi-permanent collection of individuals who know each other. What does this mean? It means that any individual of the species will be recognized by group members as "in the group" or "out of the group," and in many species the latter will be met with some form of hostility. For a new individual to *join* the group is a long and touchy process.

In addition, in many primate societies—for example, chimpanzees and vervet monkeys—a group defends a *common territory* against other groups. The territory isn't just the aggregate of the members' territories, it is the group's, and the members range fairly freely within it.

As in kinship, we can see the primate concept of a social group at the core of a richer human realization. We conceive of ourselves as members of a vast number of different groups—all at once. We distinguish ourselves from each other by groupings of nationality, race, religion, social class, profession, political beliefs, and many more. I'll take up some of the ramifications of group membership in the next section. For now, it's important only to notice how pervasive group membership is in our social organization, how important it is to us to belong to the groups we belong to, and—whatever the group may be—how differently we treat people conceived of as "in the group" from people conceived of as "out of the group."

A third parameter of social organization in many animal societies is *dominance*, a relation between two individuals whereby one (the subordinate one) regularly defers to the other (the dominant one) in matters of food choice, sexual selection, grooming partners, and so forth. Dominance is often based on size and aggressiveness, but it doesn't have to be. For instance, it can depend on kinship relations: in many species, the children of highly ranked mothers often inherit high rank. This means that dominance can't be a purely perceptual relation—it too needs a conceptual basis.

In animal societies, dominance relations often fall into a linear order: if A is dominant to B, and B is dominant to C, then A is also dominant to C; and every individual in the group has a distinct place in the "pecking order." Such dominance hierarchies characteristically remain stable over time, but subordinate individuals may mount challenges which, if successful, rearrange the pattern.

In human societies, dominance relations are pervasive too. Like group membership, they can be organized along many different dimensions: think of relations like parent-to-child, teacher-to-student, boss-to-worker, ruler-to-subject, celebrity-to-fan, and in many societies, including many sectors of our own, husband-to-wife. It seems to me that when larger-scale human dominance hierarchies develop, they differ from animal hierarchies in tending to be pyramidal rather than linear: we often find a top person dominant to a number of relatively equal subordinates, each of whom is dominant to further subordinates, and so on. But the basic notion of a stable asymmetrical relationship based on deference of one individual toward the other bears a strong resemblance to the animal model.

Of course, relationships among particular individuals can't be innate. We have to learn who is kin to us, what groups there are to belong to and who belongs to them, whom we are dominant and subordinate to, and under what circumstances. And we have to learn how our culture codifies these relationships—for instance, what being someone's kin entitles us to do or prohibits us from doing with them. The idea, though, is that these three kinds of relationships (and possibly others) are very abstract skeletons that help us structure how to behave toward other people and what to expect from them. In other words, the Arguments for Mental Grammar and for Innate Knowledge are invoked again: as with language, culture-particular facts are backed up by an innate framework.

I've stressed that kinship, group membership, and dominance are not consistently perceptual—that is, they're not driven entirely by the environment. Rather, it's only because we can *conceive* of such relationships that they are functional elements of society. This point may be hard to see, because these relationships seem so obvious and natural. My sense, though, is that they are just about as obvious and natural as *words*—and words, as we've seen, require a lot of mental machinery, including an innate notion of phonological structure. That is, without the *concepts* of kin, social grouping, and dominance, we would be able to see our social world only in terms of unstructured aggregates of people, more like zebra herds—or perhaps the crowds of faceless interchangeable people on the subway. (Arguments for Innate Knowledge and for the Construction of Experience again.)

It does not appear to be the size of our brain that makes these concepts of social relations possible. Lots of animals with smaller brains have similar concepts. Rather, what allows us to have these concepts is a certain kind of structure in our brains, a structure shared with other social mammals. What the *size* of our brain seems to give us is the ability to have a lot more of the same: the vast elaboration of kinship, group membership, and dominance in humans as compared to animals.

More about group membership

I want to give a sense of how powerful the concept of a social group is in our lives. First consider that every society has lots of rituals and ceremonies, most of which involve an element of confirming group membership. I'm thinking not only of religious rituals, but also of club initiations, school assemblies, dedications of buildings, coronations, inaugurations, and investitures. Even public sports events are a kind of ceremony, and they too confirm the spectators' allegiance to their team's school, city, or country—as well as their allegiance to the larger political units both teams belong to (that's why the national anthem is played), and even their allegiance to the informal social group of "sports fans." This inevitable link between public occasions and a sense of group solidarity may be strange and "irrational," but it's present in any culture I've ever heard of.

The social group is also the unit over which we define *codes of conduct*. A code of conduct may be as informal as the fads practiced by a teenage clique or the sense of professional ethics in science; it may be as formal as a company's bylaws or a nation's legal system. In any case, a code of conduct specifies certain classes of behavior by members of the group as desirable or undesirable. The code gives the group (or its authority figures) the license to punish (or otherwise sanction) a group member who engages in undesirable or impermissible behavior. Part of the "social contract" is that if we admit to doing something wrong, we thereby acknowledge that it's acceptable for the group to punish us. And one of the worst punishments that a group can impose is expulsion—evidently belonging to the group matters a lot. (Try this framework out with any social group you can think of.)

When I say that the social group is the unit over which a code of conduct is defined, I mean that the code is understood to be a code *for members of this group.* The users of a code of conduct implicitly or explicitly acknowledge that it does not necessarily apply to other groups, which have codes of their own. (It may apply in part to visitors within the group, though.) And if a group has a formal initiation or induction ceremony, the ceremony inevitably invokes the group's code of conduct ("I swear that I will uphold, etc., etc.").

Of course, part of "learning" a particular culture or subculture is learning the details of its code of conduct. But we don't have to learn *that there is such a thing as a code of conduct.* The concept of a code of conduct associated with a group is another of these skeletal notions around which we structure our social existence.

Next, remember that, in the case of many animals, a basic premise of group membership is friendliness toward members of the group and hostility to nonmembers. I am inclined to think this is a fundamental attitude in the human case as well: we basically think better of people—and treat them better—if we think of them as belonging to a group with which we identify. The group in question may be citizens of our country, alumni of our college, or members of our profession, religion, or club. It doesn't matter: we tend to react positively upon discovering the bonds of group membership.

On the darker side, chauvinism and prejudice consist precisely of displaying automatic hostility toward someone just because they belong to a group other than the one we identify with. Not only that, group displays of hostility toward another group—from football games to pogroms—serve to reinforce the sense of group membership.

If I'm right that we have inherited this underlying stance from our primate ancestors, then it ought to be absolutely crucial to us to know whether someone we haven't encountered before is a member of our group or not. How friendly should we be, and how friendly should we expect them to be? And in fact, social groups everywhere invent all kinds of things to make their members perceptually identifiable: uniforms, badges, funny hair styles, ripped blue jeans, you name it. Or a group may adopt a particular vocabulary or style of speech, anywhere from legalese to Valleyspeak. In fact, it has been suggested that dialect differences among speakers of a language develop and persist in part to mark group membership, along both regional and class lines.

Still, visual or auditory appearance isn't everything. Rather, the criteria for group membership form an ideal (in the sense developed in Chapters 13 and 14), from which there may be all sorts of deviations. Do you look like members of the group look? Do you do the things that members of the group do? Do you talk the way members of the group talk?

From what we've seen with other concepts, we might expect individuals who deviate from the ideal group member to produce cognitive stress in other members of the group. What astounds me is how fierce this cognitive stress can be, especially in the presence of other social stresses—and how important people find it to "improve" the composition of the group toward the ideal (parallel to "improving" the defective capital A in Chapter 13). Such pressures toward group uniformity are at the bottom of racism, religious intolerance,

homophobia, and the strong movements to repress minority languages and customs throughout the world.

As I mentioned earlier, for many primates the concept of group
membership includes defending a common territory. Again, in the
human case this aspect of the concept can surface in virulent form. In
the ideal, the group is not only racially, religiously, and linguistically
homogeneous: it also has its own territory, occupied only by
members of the group. I don't have to give examples of the pressures
toward this ideal. The first page of the newspaper shows, day after
day, year after miserable year, what a driving force it continues to be
all over the world.

At smaller scales of social grouping, we find the very same
patterns of behavior. To pick a random example, take your
professional identity—say, as a linguist. (Feel free to substitute your
own field.) The ideal linguist was trained in a Ph.D. program in
linguistics (i.e. has the right ancestry), goes to linguistics conferences
(i.e. observes the customs), does research on problems that everyone
else recognizes as the problems of linguistics (i.e. lives in the right
intellectual territory), and so forth. Someone with a Ph.D. in, say,
philosophy or computer science who tries to break into the field is
viewed with suspicion; someone with a Ph.D. in linguistics who
works on problems not traditionally recognized as linguistic risks
losing touch with the community. More generally, interdisciplinary
endeavors are always touchy undertakings—until those who straddle
the boundaries form their *own* group (say, cognitive science) and
thereby redefine the boundaries. Does this sound familiar?

If I'm right about the concept of group membership, then, this
concept appears to be a major source of gratuitous tension and
hostility in the world. Is it really that bleak? What keeps people from
always trying to wipe each other out?

One factor is an aspect of human social understanding that isn't
present even in the higher primates: what psychologists call a theory
of mind and common language calls empathy. Humans (but not
chimps) can imagine the thoughts of others, and can imagine how
they would feel and act in a comparable situation.* This ability
obviously acts as a brake on inflicting harm. We're less reluctant to
cause pain if we can imagine how it feels.

We can see the importance of this inhibition by noticing that

---

* This difference between us and primates is no longer just a matter of speculation.
Chimps do engage in some behavior that we might recognize as motivated by empathy,
but it is strictly limited, as documented by observers such as Jane Goodall.

people need to get around it when they commit aggression. They do everything they can to think of the other group as subhuman, as animals—precisely in order to suppress empathy. This applies to trivial situations like football games as well as to more serious ones such as slavery and war. Alternatively, it helps not to perceive the other person at all: it's often been remarked how much easier it is on the conscience to kill people by dropping bombs on them than by shooting them point-blank. If they can't be seen, empathy can be disengaged.

The theory of human concepts developed in Chapter 14 does provide an alternative to insisting on group homogeneity: to learn to accept the cognitive stress that comes with the gray areas of concepts, in this case group members who don't conform to the ideal. As we have seen, there's nothing inherently wrong with boundaries that are less than sharp—it's just our own distress with them that makes them intolerable. (Argument for the Construction of Experience again.) And indeed, I think we can see genuine progress over the past several hundred years toward the alternative ideal of accepting as peers a broader diversity of individuals—though not without a great deal of horrendous backsliding as well.

Final thoughts

By digging just a little beneath the surface, we have found that our social/cultural knowledge shares many of the properties of linguistic knowledge. According to this view, social behavior and experience are governed in part by unconscious patterns and principles which are not entirely based on perception. Like the patterns of our language, social patterns are learned (or, better, internally con-structed) by each of us as an attunement to our social environment. However, they are not just the result of "molding." Despite the great diversity among cultures, the patterns of cultural knowledge are elaborations of an innate cognitive specialization whose character is revealed (1) in parallels to our primate cousins and (2) in abstract universals of culture at all scales from families and cliques to nations.

Let's now return to the question that motivates this book: Is there a "human nature"? The picture that has emerged is that our "human nature" consists in having a collection of innate brain specializations or modules, each of which confers on us certain kinds of cognitive powers: the ability to learn a language, to learn to appreciate music, to come to understand the visual world, to construct concrete and abstract thoughts, to learn to function in a social environment, and no doubt more.

The most powerful evidence for this view comes from the study of language and of vision. But once we recognize the symptoms, we see them in every human activity. And so it becomes a scientific question to determine what innate specializations we have, and what their details are; we might think of this undertaking as a sort of "mental anatomy."

We can't take it for granted that people will always operate—or will always *want* to operate—in the most "rational" way possible. After all, much of our behavior, starting from the principles behind our use of language, is "irrational," in the sense that we can't explain it consciously. Nevertheless, such "intuitive" behavior is governed by an unconscious logic of its own, a logic that can be studied scientifically.

I suspect a lot more of our behavior is this way than we usually would like to think. For example: From time to time, I used to read predictions of a future in which we would be spared the trouble of eating meals. We'd only have to take a few pills in order to meet our needs for nutrition. Why is this vision so awful, so chilling? It's irrational to want to spend hours cooking and shopping and eating, when we could live so much more efficiently—isn't it?

Maybe we should trust our "irrational" intuitions a little more. The question is not what's mechanically efficient, but what we as human beings need in order to thrive. Maybe food fills more than a chemical need. For instance, maybe people need to experience the taste of food and the effort of chewing. In fact we can go beyond this: every culture has ceremonies around food and drink, and communal eating and drinking are signs of social solidarity, allegiance, and affection. We demonstrate hospitality by offering food; we drink toasts to honor people. This suggests that eating also fulfills a *social* need, one that couldn't be met by everyone taking pills in their own bathrooms. And it's the prospect of *this* need going unfulfilled that upsets us so much.

I'm just making this up. But it's an interesting possibility, one that flows from this way of looking at human nature.

A real-world example along the same lines comes from contemporary architecture and city planning, where the postwar philosophy of "rationality" and "efficiency" churned out ugly impersonal buildings that turned out invariably to create feelings of alienation among their inhabitants. More recent practice recognizes and respects the need within human nature for beauty, for structured open space, and for places to congregate, and the result has been environments in which people take delight, in which they feel more human.

Another current myth of "rationality," one with far greater impact, is the belief that people's only basic need is to look out for their own survival.* This is the fundamental assumption behind the economic philosophy of the "free market": the idea that the main thing people need in order to thrive—and therefore what the optimal society needs—is a state of unlimited competition, with minimal social regulation.

I take issue with this assumption. Is it really the case that we need only unlimited opportunity to look out for our own survival? Like the need to eat food, this is a claim about human nature that's more subtle than it may initially seem. Even our very cursory look at social understanding suggests that people need more than the opportunity to further themselves economically. For instance, they need to feel allegiance to a group, and they expect this group to have a code of conduct, part of whose function is to protect its members from each other's aggression. And this includes economic as well as physical aggression: there are always codes about stealing, for example. At some level, free-market philosophy would deny such economic protection to those who are so unfortunate as to lose the competition.

Moreover, as the psychologist Alan Fiske has pointed out, contemporary Western society is quite unusual in the degree to which it stresses market competition as a way to distribute goods and services. Most other societies rely far more heavily on other modes, such as communal sharing within the group, equal distribution among individuals, or distribution according to seniority. Perhaps these modes are easier to implement in smaller groups, where everyone can know everyone else personally—but still it's clear that these modes exist as socially viable alternatives to the free market. In fact, even in Western society, we obviously don't apply the free-market model everyplace. We aren't usually in economic competition for food and clothing with our own children, for example. So economic freedom, though it is quite possibly a human need, is not necessarily the predominant one, nor is it necessarily the one that *should* predominate in a society.

This analysis may be wrong; but I hope at least to have shown

---

* In the sociobiological literature, this has been extended to looking out for members of one's own gene pool, to explain why people like to take care of their families.

that the assumptions behind the free market are not as obviously true as we are often told. The larger point I want to make is that analyzing the structure of social concepts, using the approach developed and justified for the analysis of language, can lead us to different ways of viewing important situations in our lives. Like my discomfort with nourishing myself on pills, I can begin to pinpoint my discomfort with free-market philosophy.

Very speculatively, what other "irrational" needs might we find in human nature—things that are essential if we are to thrive? One such need came up in Chapter 13 in connection with music: we seem to need to experience beauty. It isn't just that we take pleasure in beautiful things; we actively seek them out. There isn't a culture that doesn't create all kinds of artistic artifacts—art, poetry, music, and dance. Why do we waste our time with all this? The "efficient" society would make do without, wouldn't it? But in fact maybe it's not a waste after all, at a deeper psychological level.

Perhaps our most fundamental need beyond food, shelter, sex, and social interaction is for a sense of dignity and self-esteem. Dignity and self-esteem can't be seen or touched, but they are real to us nevertheless—just as real as virtual boundaries in visual perception (Argument for the Construction of Experience).

One way to increase self-esteem is the "free-market" way: to achieve physical or social or economic dominance at the expense of others. But surely we can think of other ways. Think of the sense of self-esteem that comes from doing fulfilling work that exercises our creativity and craftsmanship. Or the feeling that comes from belonging to a group and feeling secure in it. Or—following the ethical traditions of all the great religions—from the exercise of selflessness as opposed to selfishness. And who knows what other routes there may be?

Again, these are "irrational" intuitions. For now, we have no idea how to characterize them scientifically. But the fact that they appear as enduring values of so many cultures suggests that they are rooted in the unconscious structure of human nature—something we should respect, even though we don't "rationally" understand it.

I don't want to claim that following the dictates of human nature is always the right way to go. We've seen here quite a few cases where human nature seems to bias us toward positions that I, for one, don't like: pressure for ethnic purity, hostility toward people who don't belong to our group, quite possibly dominance of men over women. Just because these are "natural" positions doesn't mean they're morally correct.

I'm claiming, rather, that human nature has a rich and complicated organization that is largely inaccessible to conscious introspection. It reveals itself only upon careful study. If we are trying to develop social policy, it pays to attend to what such study can reveal, instead of relying on oversimplified truisms about what people want or need.

Science is often thought of as being in opposition to human values—"the triumph of reason over superstition." I'm suggesting that in fact science need not and should not ignore human values: they are a vital aspect of our experience and ought to be studied as an essential part of human psychology. No doubt some of our most fervently held values *will* prove to be mere superstitions, but others will be recognized as deeply grounded in our heredity, for better or for worse.

Further reading

Preface

Noam Chomsky, *Syntactic Structures*. The Hague: Mouton, 1957.

Noam Chomsky, Review of B.F. Skinner's *Verbal Behavior*. *Language* 35, (1959), 26–58. Reprinted in Jerry A. Fodor and Jerrold J. Katz, eds, *The Structure of Language*. Englewood Cliffs, NJ: Prentice Hall.

Chapter 1

The use of psychological "evidence" to justify repression

Stephen Jay Gould, *The Mismeasure of Man*. New York: W.W. Norton, 1981.

Animal thought and communication

Donald Griffin, *The Question of Animal Awareness*, revised and enlarged edition. New York: Rockefeller University Press, 1981.

Wolfgang Köhler, *The Mentality of Apes*. London: Routledge & Kegan Paul, 1927.

Brain size in animals

Harry J. Jerison, *Evolution of the Brain and Intelligence*. New York: Academic Press, 1973.

Chapter 2

The need for a mental grammar

Noam Chomsky, *Language and Mind*. New York: Harcourt, Brace & World, 1968.

223

Noam Chomsky, *Reflections on Language*. New York: Pantheon, 1975.

Chapter 3

The need for an innate Universal Grammar
Chomsky, references for Chapter 2

Mother-child dialogue
David McNeill, "Developmental Psycholinguistics." In Frank Smith and George Miller, eds, *The Genesis of Language*, 15–84. Cambridge, MA: MIT Press, 1966.

History of prescriptive (school) grammar
Albert C. Baugh, *A History of the English Language*, second edition. New York: Appleton-Century-Crofts, 1957. [See especially Chapter 9, "The Appeal to Authority."]

Expletive infixation
John McCarthy, "Prosodic Structure and Expletive Infixation." *Language* 58 (1982), 574–90.

The child's construction of mental grammar
see references for Chapter 8

The use of the term "knowledge" (knowing that and knowing how)
Gilbert Ryle, *The Concept of Mind*. Chicago: University of Chicago Press, 1949.

Development of the brain after birth
Carla J. Shatz, "The Developing Brain." *Scientific American*, September 1992, 61–7.

Evolution of language
Derek Bickerton, *Language and Species*. Chicago: University of Chicago Press, 1990.

Steven Pinker and Paul Bloom: "Natural Language and Natural Selection." *Behavioral and Brain Sciences* 13 (December 1990), 707–26. [See also commentaries following

the article and Pinker and Bloom's reply.] Reprinted in
Jerome H. Barkow, Leda Cosmides, and John Tooby, eds,
The Adapted Mind. New York: Oxford University Press.

Chapter 4

Formats of information and their interconnections

Ray Jackendoff, *Languages of the Mind*, Chapter 1.
Cambridge, MA: MIT Press, 1992.

Functionalism

Douglas Hofstadter, *Gödel, Escher, Bach.* New York: Basic
Books, 1979.

Zenon Pylyshyn, *Computation and Cognition.* Cambridge,
MA: MIT Press, 1984.

Visual illusions

Richard Gregory, *Eye and Brain*, fourth edition. Princeton,
NJ: Princeton University Press, 1990.

Roger Shepard, *Mind Sights.* New York: W.H. Freeman,
1990.

Modularity Hypothesis

Jerry Fodor, *The Modularity of Mind.* Cambridge, MA: MIT
Press, 1983.

Howard Gardner, *Frames of Mind.* New York: Basic Books,
1983.

Ray Jackendoff, *Consciousness and the Computational Mind*,
Chapter 12. Cambridge, MA: MIT Press, 1987.

Marvin Minsky, *The Society of Mind.* New York: Simon &
Schuster, 1985.

Chapter 5

General discussion (three standard introductory texts)

Adrian Akmajian, Richard Demers, Michael Harnish, and
Ann Farmer, *Linguistics: An Introduction to Language and
Communication*, third edition. Cambridge, MA: MIT Press,
1990. See especially Chapters 3 and 4.

Victoria Fromkin and Robert Rodman, *An Introduction to Language*, fifth edition. New York: Harcourt Brace Jovanovich, 1993. See especially Chapters 5 and 6.

William O'Grady, Michael Dobrovolsky, and Mark Aronoff, *Contemporary Linguistics: An Introduction*, second edition. New York: St. Martin's Press, 1993. See especially Chapters 2 and 3.

Relationship of the speech signal to phonological representation

Peter B. Denes and Elliot N. Pinson, *The Speech Chain*, second edition. New York: W.H. Freeman, 1993.

Early discussions of distinctive features

Roman Jakobson and Morris Halle, *Fundamentals of Language*. The Hague: Mouton, 1956.

N.S. Trubetzkoy, *Principles of Phonology*. Berkeley, CA: University of California Press, 1969. [German original, *Grundzüge der Phonologie*, published 1939.]

Distinctive features in phonological rules

Morris Halle, "Knowledge Unlearned and Untaught." In Morris Halle, Joan Bresnan, and George A. Miller, eds, *Linguistic Theory and Psychological Reality*, 294–303. Cambridge, MA: MIT Press, 1978. [Much of my discussion in this chapter is borrowed from here.]

Voice recognition and tone of voice (affect) recognition

Nancy L. Etcoff, "Asymmetries in Recognition of Emotion." In F. Boller and J. Grafman, eds, *Handbook of Neuropsychology*, vol. 3, 363–82. New York: Elsevier Science Publishers, 1989.

Filtering view of perception

Ulric Neisser, *Cognitive Psychology*. Englewood Cliffs, NJ: Prentice Hall, 1967.

Chapter 6

General reading (the textbooks cited in Chapter 5)

Akmajian *et al.*, Chapter 5.

Fromkin and Rodman, Chapter 3.

O'Grady *et al.*, Chapter 5.

The relation of syntactic categories to categories of meaning

> Ray Jackendoff, *Semantics and Cognition*, Chapter 3. Cambridge, MA: MIT Press, 1983.

Changes in the significance of "deep" or "underlying" structure over the history of generative grammar

> Frederick J. Newmeyer, *Linguistic Theory in America: The First Quarter-Century of Transformational Generative Grammar*. New York: Academic Press, 1980.

Experiments on the detection of traces

> *Journal of Psycholinguistic Research* 18.1: Special Issue on Sentence Processing, David A. Swinney and Janet D. Fodor, eds, January 1989.

Early work on constraints on long-distance dependencies

> Noam Chomsky, *Language and Mind*, Chapter 2. New York: Harcourt, Brace & World, 1968.

> John Robert Ross, *Constraints on Variables in Syntax*. Doctoral dissertation, Massachusetts Institute of Technology, 1967. Published as *Infinite Syntax!* Hillsdale, NJ: Erlbaum.

Other approaches to syntax within the generative tradition

> Joan Bresnan, ed., *The Mental Representation of Grammatical Relations*. Cambridge, MA: MIT Press, 1982.

> Gerald Gazdar, Ewan Klein, Geoffrey Pullum, and Ivan Sag, *Generalized Phrase Structure Grammar*. Cambridge, MA: Harvard University Press, 1985.

> James McCawley, *The Syntactic Phenomena of English* (2 volumes). Chicago: University of Chicago Press, 1988.

> David M. Perlmutter, ed., *Studies in Relational Grammar, Vol. 1*. Chicago: University of Chicago Press, 1983.

> The above are approaches that trace their ancestry to Chomskian generative grammar. Numerous other approaches on the market have arisen more explicitly in opposition to Chomsky's approach. Among them are:

> William Foley and Robert van Valin, *Functional Syntax and Universal Grammar*. Cambridge: Cambridge University Press, 1984.

George Lakoff, *Women, Fire, and Dangerous Things.*
Chicago: University of Chicago Press, 1987.

Ronald Langacker, *Foundations of Cognitive Grammar, Vol.
1.* Stanford, CA: Stanford University Press, 1986.

Chapter 7

General reading

David M. Perlmutter, "The Language of the Deaf." *New
York Review of Books,* March 28, 1991, 65–71.

Oliver Sacks, *Seeing Voices.* New York: HarperPerennial,
1990.

Jerome D. Schein, *Speaking the Language of Sign: The Art
and Science of Signing.* Garden City, NY: Doubleday, 1984.

The grammar of ASL

Charlotte Baker and Robbin Battison, eds, *Sign Language
and the Deaf Community: Essays in Honor of William C.
Stokoe.* National Association of the Deaf, 1980.

Susan D. Fischer and Patricia Siple, eds, *Theoretical Issues in
Sign Language Research, Volume 1.* Chicago: University of
Chicago Press, 1990.

Edward S. Klima and Ursula Bellugi, *The Signs of Language.*
Cambridge, MA: Harvard University Press, 1979.

William Stokoe, *Sign Language Structure: An Outline of the
Visual Communication System of the American Deaf.* Silver
Spring, MD: Linstok Press. [Original publication 1960]

*Deaf culture, the American Deaf community, and the experience
of Deafness*

Harlan Lane, *When the Mind Hears: A History of the Deaf.*
New York: Random House, 1984.

Harlan Lane, *The Mask of Benevolence: Disabling the Deaf
Community.* New York: Alfred A. Knopf, 1992. [Includes a
discussion of the disadvantages of "mainstreaming" and
cochlear implants.]

Carol Padden and Tom Humphries, *Deaf in America: Voices*

From a Culture. Cambridge, MA: Harvard University Press, 1988.

Martha's Vineyard Sign

Nora Ellen Groce, *Everyone Here Spoke Sign Language: Hereditary Deafness in Martha's Vineyard*. Cambridge, MA: Harvard University Press, 1985.

Chapter 8

General reading

Jean Aitchison, *The Articulate Mammal: An Introduction to Psycholinguistics*, second edition. New York: Universe Books, 1983. Excerpted in Virginia P. Clark, Paul A. Eschholz, and Alfred F. Rosa, eds, *Language: Introductory Readings*, fourth edition, 90–110. New York: St. Martin's Press, 1985.

Jill G. de Villiers and Peter A. de Villiers, *Language Acquisition*. Cambridge, MA, Harvard University Press, 1978.

Henry Gleitman, *Psychology*, third edition, Chapter 9 (by Lila R. Gleitman and Henry Gleitman). New York: W.W. Norton, 1991.

Breyne Arlene Moskowitz, "The Acquisition of Language." In Clark *et al.*, *Language: Introductory Readings*, 45–72. [Originally published in *Scientific American*, 1978]

Steven Pinker, "Language Acquisition." In Dan Osherson and Howard Lasnik, eds, *Language: An Invitation to Cognitive Science*, Vol. 1, 199–241. Cambridge, MA: MIT Press, 1990.

Father–child dialogue

Martin Braine, "The Acquisition of Language in Infant and Child." In C.E. Reed, ed., *The Learning of Language*. New York: Appleton-Century-Crofts, 1971.

The child's phonological errors

Clara Levelt, "Consonant Harmony: A Reanalysis in Terms of Vowel–Consonant Interaction." To appear in *Amsterdam Series in Child Language Development*.

Neil Smith, *The Acquisition of Phonology: A Case Study*. Cambridge, Cambridge University Press, 1973.

The experiments with Big Bird and Cookie Monster

Kathy Hirsh-Pasek and Roberta M. Golinkoff, "Language Comprehension: A New Look at Some Old Themes." In N. Krasnegor, D. Rumbaugh, M. Studdert-Kennedy, and R. Schiefenbusch, eds, *Biological and Behavioral Aspects of Language Acquisition*, 301–20. Hillsdale, NJ: Erlbaum.

The experiment with "DAX"

Nancy Katz, Erica Baker, and John Macnamara, "What's in a Name? A Study of How Children Learn Common and Proper Names." *Child Development* 45 (1974), 469–73.

John Macnamara, *Names for Things*. Cambridge, MA: MIT Press, 1982 [Explores in considerable detail the philosophical and psychological implications of the child's learning of proper and common nouns, with reference to the Argument for Innate Knowledge.]

The experiment with "wugs"

Jean Berko, "The Child's Learning of English Morphology." *Word* 14 (1958), 150–77.

The learning of questions and negated sentences

Edward S. Klima and Ursula Bellugi, "Syntactic Regularities in the Speech of Children." In J. Lyons and R.J. Wales, eds, *Psycholinguistics Papers*, 189–219. Edinburgh: Edinburgh University Press, 1966.

Stages of learning the past tense

Steven Pinker and Alan Prince, "On Language and Connectionism: Analysis of a Parallel Distributed Processing Model of Language Acquisition." *Cognition* 28 (1988), 73–193.

Learning of more complex aspects of syntax

Stephen Crain, "Language Acquisition in the Absence of Experience." *Behavioral and Brain Sciences* 14 (1991), 597–650. [See also commentaries following this article, and Crain's reply.]

Chapter 9

Genetically impaired language learners

Myrna Gopnik and M.B. Crago, "Familial Aggregation of a Development Language Disorder." *Cognition* 39 (1990), 1–50.

Turner's and Williams Syndromes

Ursula Bellugi, Paul P. Want, and Terry L. Jernigan, "Williams Syndrome: An Unusual Neuropsychological Profile." In S. Broman and J. Grafman, eds, *Atypical Cognitive Deficits in Developmental Disorders: Implications for Brain Function.* Hillsdale, NJ: Erlbaum, 1993.

Jeni Yamada and Susan Curtiss, "The Relationship between Language and Cognition in a Case of Turner's Syndrome." In *UCLA Working Papers in Linguistics*, vol. 3. Los Angeles: UCLA Department of Linguistics, 1981.

Critical period

Eric Lenneberg, *Biological Foundations of Language.* New York: John Wiley & Sons, 1967.

Elissa Newport, "Maturational Constraints on Language Learning." *Cognitive Science* 14 (1990), 11–28.

James Hurford, "The Evolution of the Critical Period for Language Acquisition." *Cognition* 40 (1991), 159–201.

Critical periods in animals

James Gould and Peter Marler, "Learning by Instinct." *Scientific American*, January 1987, 79–85.

Konrad Lorenz, *King Solomon's Ring.* New York: Thomas Y. Crowell, 1952.

Torsten N. Wiesel and David H. Hubel, "Single Cell Responses in Striate Cortex of Kitten Deprived of Vision in One Eye." *Journal of Neurophysiology* 26 (1963), 1003–17.

Genie

Susan Curtiss, *Genie: A Linguistic Study of a Modern-Day "Wild Child."* New York: Academic Press, 1977.

Victoria Fromkin, Stephen Krashen, Susan Curtiss, David Rigler, and Marilyn Rigler, "The Development of Language in Genie: A Case of Language Acquisition Beyond the 'Critical Period.' " *Brain and Language* 1 (1974), 81–107. Reprinted in Clark *et al.*, *Language: Introductory Readings* (see Chapter 8 references).

Russ Rymer, *Genie: An Abused Child's Flight from Silence.* New York: HarperCollins, 1993.

Victor

Jean-Marc-Gaspard Itard, *The Wild Boy of Aveyron.* (Translated by George and Muriel Humphrey.) New York: Appleton-Century-Crofts, 1962.

Isabelle

Roger Brown, *Words and Things*. New York: Free Press, 1958.

Chelsea

Susan Curtiss, "Language as a Cognitive System: Its Independence and Selective Vulnerability." In C. Otero, ed., *Noam Chomsky: Critical Assessments*, vol. 4. London: Routledge, 1994. Revised version to appear in *Brain and Language*.

Late learners of ASL and second languages

Elissa Newport, "Maturational Constraints on Language Learning." *Cognitive Science* 14 (1990), 11–28.

David Birdsong, "Ultimate Attainment in Second Language Acquisition." *Language* 68 (1992), 706–55.

Chapter 10

Home sign

Susan Goldin-Meadow and Carolyn Mylander, "Beyond the Input Given: The Child's Role in the Acquisition of Language." *Language* 66 (1990), 323–55.

Susan Goldin-Meadow, Cynthia Butcher, Carolyn Mylander, and Mark Dodge, "Nouns and Verbs in a Self-Styled Gesture System: What's in a Name?" To appear in *Cognitive Psychology*.

Creoles

Derek Bickerton, *The Roots of Language*. Ann Arbor, MI: Karoma Publishers, 1981.

Derek Bickerton, "Creole Languages." In Clark *et al.*, *Language: Introductory Readings* (see references for Chapter 8), 134–50. [A shorter exposition of Bickerton's analysis.]

Ape sign language

Eugene Linden, *Apes, Men, and Language*. New York: Penguin Books, 1974.

Francine Patterson and Eugene Linden, *The Education of Koko*. New York: Holt, Rinehart & Winston, 1981.

Carolyn Ristau and D. Robbins, "Language in the Great Apes: A Critical Review." In J.S. Rosenblatt, ed., *Advances in the Study of Behavior*, vol. 12, 142–255. New York: Academic Press, 1982.

Mark Seidenberg and Laura Petitto, "Signing Behavior in Apes: A Critical Review." *Cognition* 7 (1978), 177–215.

Herbert Terrace, *Nim*. New York: Knopf, 1979.

Chapter 11

The current situation in neuroscience

Scientific American, September 1992. [Special issue devoted to the brain]

Blindsight

Lawrence Weiskrantz, *Blindsight: A Case Study and Implications*. Oxford: Oxford University Press, 1986.

Lawrence Weiskrantz, "Some Contributions of Neuropsychology of Vision and Memory to the Problem of Consciousness." In Anthony Marcel and Eduardo Bisiach, eds, *Consciousness in Contemporary Science*, 183–99. Oxford: Oxford University Press, 1988.

Other deficits due to brain damage

Oliver Sacks, *The Man Who Mistook His Wife for a Hat*. New York: Summit Books, 1985.

Aphasias

Howard Gardner, "The Loss of Language." In Clark *et al.*,
Language: Introductory Readings (see references for Chapter
8), 184–95.

Jeannine Heny, "Brain and Language." In Clark *et al.*,
Language: Introductory Readings (see references for Chapter
8), 159–83. [These two articles are the sources for the quotes
from Broca's and Wernicke's aphasics.]

Edgar Zurif, "Language and the Brain." In Dan Osherson
and Howard Lasnik, *Language: An Invitation to Cognitive
Science*, vol. 1, 177–98. Cambridge, MA.: MIT Press.

Edgar Zurif and David Swinney, "The Neuropsychology of
Language." In M.A. Gernsbacher, ed., *Handbook of
Psycholinguistics*. New York: Academic Press, 1993.

ASL aphasias

Ursula Bellugi, Howard Poizner, and Edward S. Klima,
"Language, Modality, and the Brain." *Trends in
Neurosciences* 12 (1989), 380–88.

Ursula Bellugi, David Corina, Freda Norman, Edward Klima,
and Judy Reilly, "Differential Specialization for Linguistic
Facial Expression in Left and Right Lesioned Deaf Signers."
Paper presented at Academy of Aphasia Annual Meeting,
Santa Fe, New Mexico, October, 1989.

Brain plasticity

Maureen Dennis, "Language Acquisition in a Single
Hemisphere: Semantic Organization." In David Caplan, ed.,
Biological Studies of Mental Processes, 159–85. Cambridge,
MA: MIT Press, 1980.

Eric Lenneberg, *Biological Foundations of Language*. New
York: John Wiley & Sons, 1967.

Helen Neville, "Intermodal Competition and Compensation
in Development: Evidence from Studies of the Visual System
in Congenitally Deaf Adults." In *The Development and
Neural Bases of Higher Cognitive Functions* (vol. 608 of the
Annals of the New York Academy of Sciences) (1990), 71–91.
[This presents the evidence that the auditory areas of congenitally
deaf individuals are "taken over" by visual functions.]

Sidney J. Segalowitz, ed., *Language Functions and Brain Organization*. New York: Academic Press, 1983. [See especially Chapter 15, "Individual Differences in Hemispheric Representation of Language."

Chapter 12

Ray Jackendoff, *Consciousness and the Computational Mind*. Cambridge, MA: MIT Press, 1987.

Ray Jackendoff, *Languages of the Mind*, especially Chapter 8, "The Problem of Reality." Cambridge, MA: MIT Press, 1992.

Kurt Koffka, *Principles of Gestalt Psychology*. New York: Harcourt, Brace & World, 1935.

Chapter 13

Music

Leonard Bernstein, *The Unanswered Question*. Cambridge, MA: Harvard University Press, 1976.

Diana Deutsch, ed., *The Psychology of Music*. New York: Academic Press, 1982.

Carol L. Krumhansl, *Cognitive Foundations of Musical Pitch*. New York: Oxford University Press, 1990.

Fred Lerdahl and Ray Jackendoff, *A Generative Theory of Tonal Music*. Cambridge, MA: MIT Press, 1982.
[For a general idea of experimental research going on in the perception of music, browse through the journal *Music Perception*.]

Vision

Richard Gregory, *Eye and Brain*, fourth edition. Princeton, NJ: Princeton University Press, 1990.

Julian E. Hochberg, *Perception*, second edition. Englewood Cliffs, NJ: Prentice Hall, 1978.

Stephen M. Kosslyn, "Mental Imagery." In Dan Osherson, Stephen M. Kosslyn, and John M. Hollerbach, *Visual Cognition and Action: An Invitation to Cognitive Science*, Vol. 2, 73–97. Cambridge, MA: MIT Press, 1990.

David Marr, *Vision*. San Francisco: Freeman, 1982.

Steven Pinker, "Visual Cognition: An Introduction." In Steven Pinker, ed., *Visual Cognition*, 1–63. Cambridge, MA: MIT Press, 1985.

Infant vision

Elizabeth Spelke, "Origins of Visual Knowledge." In Dan Osherson *et al.*, *Visual Cognition and Action* (see Kosslyn reference above), 99–127.

Face recognition

Susan Carey, "A Case Study: Face Recognition." In Edward Walker, ed., *Explorations in the Biology of Language*, 175–201. Cambridge, MA: MIT Press, 1979.

Ideals

Max Wertheimer, "Laws of Organization in Perceptual Forms." In Willis D. Ellis, ed., *A Source Book of Gestalt Psychology*, 71–88. London: Routledge & Kegan Paul, 1938.

Chapter 14

The unconsciousness and innateness of thought

Daniel C. Dennett, *Consciousness Explained*. New York: Little, Brown, 1991.

Ray Jackendoff, *Consciousness and the Computational Mind*, Chapter 14. Cambridge, MA,: MIT Press, 1987.

John Macnamara, *Names for Things*. Cambridge, MA: MIT Press, 1982.

Massimo Piattelli-Palmerini, ed., *Language and Learning: The Debate between Jean Piaget and Noam Chomsky*. Cambridge, MA: Harvard University Press, 1980. [The quotation from Jerry Fodor comes from his "Reply to Putnam" in this volume, p. 333.]

The Whorf Hypothesis

John B. Carroll, ed., *Language, Thought, and Reality: Selected Writings of Benjamin Lee Whorf*. Cambridge, MA: MIT Press, 1956.

Ekkehart Malotki, *Hopi Time: A Linguistic Analysis of the Temporal Concepts in the Hopi Language*. Berlin: Mouton, 1983. [The case against Whorf.]

Geoffrey Pullum, "The Great Eskimo Vocabulary Hoax." In his *The Great Eskimo Vocabulary Hoax and Other Irreverent Essays on the Study of Language*, 159–71. Chicago: University of Chicago Press, 1991.

The figure–ground distinction in language

Leonard Talmy, "How Language Structures Space." In H. Pick and L. Acredolo, eds, *Spatial Orientation: Theory, Research, and Application*. New York: Plenum, 1983. [The source of the "next-to" example.]

The same organization in spatial and nonspatial domains

Jeffrey Gruber, *Studies in Lexical Relations*. Doctoral dissertation, MIT, 1965. Published as part of *Lexical Structures in Syntax and Semantics*. Amsterdam: North-Holland, 1976.

Ray Jackendoff, *Semantics and Cognition*, Chapter 10. Cambridge, MA: MIT Press, 1983.

Ray Jackendoff and David Aaron, Review of George Lakoff and Mark Turner, *More Than Cool Reason: A Guide to Poetic Metaphor*. *Language* 67 (1991), 320–38. [A reexamination of the metaphor analysis of Lakoff and associates.]

George Lakoff and Mark Johnson, *Metaphors We Live By*. Chicago: University of Chicago Press, 1980. [A somewhat different interpretation of similar facts in terms of metaphor.]

The pitfalls of definitions

Ray Jackendoff, *Semantics and Cognition*, Chapter 8.

George Lakoff, *Women, Fire, and Dangerous Things*. Chicago: University of Chicago Press, 1987.

Ludwig Wittgenstein, *Philosophical Investigations*. Oxford: Blackwell, 1953. [The original statement of the problem.]

Legal issues arising from difficulties with definitions

Lawrence Solan, *The Language of Judges*. Chicago, University of Chicago Press, 1993.

Chapter 15

Older work on evolution of human culture

Robert Ardrey, *The Territorial Imperative*. New York: Atheneum, 1966.

Konrad Lorenz, *On Aggression*. London. Methuen, 1966.

Desmond Morris, *The Naked Ape*. New York: McGraw-Hill, 1967.

More recent work on psychology of human culture

Jerome H. Barkow, Leda Cosmides, and John Tooby, eds, *The Adapted Mind: Evolutionary Psychology and the Generation of Culture*. New York: Oxford University Press, 1992. [See especially Chapter 1, "The Psychological Foundations of Culture," by John Tooby and Leda Cosmides.]

Donald Brown, *Human Universals*. New York: McGraw-Hill, 1991.

Jared Diamond, *The Third Chimpanzee*. New York: HarperCollins Publishers, 1992.

Irenäus Eibl-Eibesfeldt, *Human Ethology*. New York: Aldine de Gruyter, 1989.

Alan Page Fiske, *Structures of Social Life: The Four Elementary Forms of Human Relations*. New York: Free Press, 1991.

Ray Jackendoff, *Languages of the Mind*, Chapter 4, "Is There a Faculty of Social Cognition?" Cambridge, MA: MIT Press, 1992.

Biological bases of human nature

Carl N. Degler, *In Search of Human Nature*. Oxford: Oxford University Press, 1991.

Stephen Jay Gould, "The Nonscience of Human Nature." In his *Ever Since Darwin: Reflections in Natural History*, 237–42. New York: W.W. Norton, 1977. [A case against sociobiology.]

R.C. Lewontin, "The Evolution of Cognition." In Dan Osherson and Edward E. Smith, *Thinking: An Invitation to Cognitive Science*, Vol. 3, 229–46. Cambridge, MA: MIT Press, 1990. [Another case against it.]

Charles Lumsden and E.O. Wilson, *Genes, Mind, and Culture*. Cambridge, MA: Harvard University Press, 1981.

E.O. Wilson, *Sociobiology: The New Synthesis*. Cambridge, MA: Harvard University Press, 1975.

E.O. Wilson, *On Human Nature*. Cambridge, MA: Harvard University Press, 1978.

Universals of facial expression

Paul Ekman, ed., *Emotion in the Human Face*, second edition. Cambridge: Cambridge University Press, 1982.

See also Eibl-Eibesfeldt, *Human Ethology*, cited above in this chapter.

Brain specializations for face and voice recognition and visual and auditory emotional recognition

Nancy L. Etcoff, "Asymmetries in Recognition of Emotion." (see references for Chapter 5)

Primate social organization

Dorothy L. Cheney and Robert M. Seyfarth, *How Monkeys See the World*. Chicago: University of Chicago Press, 1990.

David A. Hamburg and Elizabeth R. McCown, eds, *The Great Apes*. Menlo Park, CA: The Benjamin/Cummings Publishing Company, 1979.

Barbara B. Smuts, Dorothy L. Cheney, Robert M. Seyfarth, Richard W. Wrangham, and Thomas Struhsaker, eds, *Primate Societies*. Chicago: University of Chicago Press, 1986.

Jane van Lawick-Goodall, *In the Shadow of Man*. New York: Dell, 1971.

Index

abortion, 201
abstract domains of thought, 194–7
adjective, 68, 69, 71
  see also parts of speech
adults, difficulty in learning second
  language, 124
aesthetic pleasure, 170
agrammatism, 146
Aitchison, J., 102
Alzheimer's disease, 148
ambiguity
  phonological, 56
  syntactic, 48, 72–3
  visual, 47, 175–6
American Sign Language, 83–98
  acquisition by children, 122–4
  Argument for Innate Knowledge,
    95–6
  Argument for Mental Grammar,
    95
  articulation, analogy to vocal
    articulation, 89
  basic facts, 83–6
  brain-damage aphasias, 151–2
  elements of grammatical
    organization, 86–95
  facial expression, 94–5
  historical development, 84–6
  iconic signs, 88, 89–90
  negative sentence, 94
  Paradox of Language
    Acquisition, 96
  questions, 89, 94
  rhythmic structure similarity to
    spoken language, 89
  signs that differ only in hand
    motion, 88

signs that differ only in
    handshape, 87
signs that differ only in location,
    87
syntactic structure, 89, 94–5
third-person pronouns, 90, 186
verb forms, 90–4
anomic aphasics, 147
apes, teaching language to, 135–9
Arabic, 94
Argument for Construction of
    Experience, 161–4
  conceptual structure, 197
  music, 170
  social organization, 209, 211–12
  vision, 177, 179
Argument for Innate Knowledge,
    21–35
  American Sign Language, 95–6
  conceptual structure, 189–90
  genetically determined language
    specialization of brain,
    26–32
  social organization, 209
  social perception specializations
    of brain, 210
  vision, 177, 179
Argument for Mental Grammar,
    8–20
  American Sign Language, 95
  communicative situation, 8–10
  conceptual structure, 188–9
  music, 167
  social organization, 208–9
  vision, 177, 179
  see also mental grammar
ASL, see American Sign Language

Baker, E., 106–7
Bellugi, U., 108–10
Bickerton, D., 131
birds, learning songs, 119–20
blindsight, 143
body language, 210, 211
brain,
    auditory signals, 63–4
    corpus callosum, 143
    electrical stimulation, 142
    functions and identification of
        various areas, 142
    genetic influences, 29–30, 142
    hemispheric lateralization in
        brain, 143–4, 146–7, 153–5
    information flow of combined
        speaker–hearer, analogy with
        that in VCR–antenna–TV,
        42–3
    and language, 26–32, 141–55
    language perception and
        production, modularity
        hypothesis, 50–2
    left hemisphere areas relevant to
        language, 143, 147
    localization studies, 143–4
    neurotransmitters, 144–5
    right hemisphere and musical
        perception, 169
    social perception, 210–12
    storage of words, meanings and
        patterns, 10–15
    variation and plasticity, 152–5
    unconscious grammatical
        principles, 10–15
brain damage,
    aphasia in ASL, 151–2
    language deficits, 146–51
    left hemisphere removal, 154
British Sign Language, 84
Broca, P., 146
Broca's aphasia, 146, 149–50, 151

Carroll, L., *Jabberwocky*, 16
CAT scans, 142, 143
causation, 198–9
"Chelsea", 122, 124
children,
    babbling, 102
    consonant articulation, 105

distinction between names and
        common nouns, 106–7
    English past tense, 110
    environmental influence, 204
    first words, 103
    grammatical correction, 22, 104
    knowledge that indefinite article
        signals common noun,
        106–7
    learning not the result of
        teaching, 22–5, 80, 104,
        129, 133, 209
    learning second language, 21,
        103–4, 117
    negative sentences, 109–10
    syntactic understanding, 106
    visual understanding, 178–9
    wh-questions, 108–9
    word order, 103
    words and meanings, 21–2, 190
    see also language acquisition
Chomsky, N., ix, 6, 26, 77
communication, use of word in
        book, 10
communicative situation, 8–10,
        39–40, 161–2
computer analysis of language, 26
concepts,
    imprecise cases, 198–207
        defrosting, 198–9, 200
        killing, 199–201
conceptual organization,
    abstract domains of thought,
        194–7
    spatial relations between objects,
        191–4
conceptual structure,
    Argument for Construction of
        Experience, 197
    Argument for Innate Knowledge,
        189–90
    Argument for Mental Grammar,
        188–9
    innate parts, 190–1
    use of term, 188
conduction aphasics, 147
Creole, 132–5
critical period, 117–20, 124–5,
        130, 135, 153

culture,
  capacity compared with
    language, 204–8
  evolution of innate knowledge,
    207
  see also social organization
Curtiss, S., 120

deep dyslexia, 148
developmentally dysphasic children,
  see specific language
  impairment
dominance, social, 213–14
dopamine, 145

EEG, 142
emotional tone, 63, 210
Eskimo language, 185
expletive infixation, 23–4

face recognition, 210
facial expressions, 211
Filipino languages, 131
fingerspelling, 83
Finnish, 186
Fodor, J., 191
Fouts, R., 136
free market, 220–1
French, 22, 62, 69, 72, 81
French Sign Language, 84–5
Freud, 18–19
Fromkin, V., 120
functionalism, 44–50

Gardner, A. & B., 136
Genetic Hypothesis, 30–1, 33
genetic impairment of language
  acquisition, 113–17
"Genie", 120–1, 123, 124
German, 62, 70
Goldin-Meadow, S., 127–30
Golinkoff, R., 106
Gopnik, M., 113
grammar, *see* mental grammar
grammatical patterns, learning by
  children, 22, 29, 105–11
grammaticality judgments, 45–50
group membership, 212–13,
  215–18
  codes of conduct, 215
  common territory, 217

group uniformity, 216–17
hostility to non-members, 216
identity of members, 216
Gruber, J., 194–5

Hayes, K., 136
hearing speech, 55, 56
Hebrew, 185
hemispheric lateralization in brain,
  143–4, 146–7, 153–5
Hirsh-Pasek, K., 106
Home Sign, 126–30
human experience, effect of
  language understanding and
  speech, 4
human nature,
  description, 218–19
  need for beauty, 219, 221
  need for dignity and self-esteem,
    221
Hungarian, 81, 93

imprinting, 119
incest taboo, 212
inflection,
  rule of, 116
  where verbal communication
    withheld in early years, 122
innate knowledge, *see* Argument
  for Innate Knowledge
intelligence, difference with ability
  to learn language, 116–17
intuition, 187

Jakobson, R., 57
Japanese, 69, 72, 81, 131
Japanese Sign Language, 84
Johnson, J., 124

Katz, N., 106–7
kinship, 212
Klima, E., 108–10
Korean, 76, 81

landmarks, use of large immovable
  objects, 194
language,
  acquisition, 35, 102–11
  basic stages, 102–4
  character of, 21–6
  critical period, 117–20

language (*continued*)
　　verbal communication
　　　withheld in early years,
　　　120–2
　　genetic impairment, 113–17
　　second language, 103–4, 117,
　　　212
　　sentence production, 107–11
　　see also children
bilinguals, 21, 187
and the brain, 141–55
brain variation and plasticity,
　　152–5
comparison with culture capacity,
　　204–8
computer analysis, 26
conversion between thought and
　　sound, 39–44
　　phonological structure, 41–2
　　syntactic structure, 41–2
creation, 130–5
deficits due to brain damage,
　　146–51
information flow in spoken and
　　signed language, 97
perception and production, 50–2
prerequisites, 5
relation to thought, 4, 184–203
relationship with meaning,
　　184–203
rules stored in memory, 14
teaching to apes, 135–9
translation, 185–6
use of word in book, 10
variation, 205
Lenneberg, E., 118
linguistic experiment,
　　description, 46
　　example, 48
linguistics, meaning in book, xi
location of objects, 194
long-distance dependencies, 49, 81
　　constraints, 77–80
　　description, 78

Macnamara, J., 106–7
Manual English, 83–4
marriage, 209
Martha's Vineyard Sign, 84, 85

mental functioning, determining by
　　brain structure, 30
mental grammar, 206
　　compared with grammar, 17
　　construction by child, 24, 25
　　definition, 14
　　experiments to explore
　　　properties, 45, 48–50
　　notion of, 15–20
　　parceling between innate and
　　　learned parts, 34
　　rule of, 45–6
　　unconsciousness, 18–19
　　vision, 171
　　where verbal communication
　　　withheld in early years, 122
　　see also Argument for Mental
　　　Grammar
Michel, C., 84
mind, parts not accessible to
　　consciousness, 18–19
MRI scans, 142, 143
Müller-Lyer illusion, 46, 47
music, 165–71
　　Argument for Construction of
　　　Experience, 170
　　emotional content, 170–1
　　patterns, 166–8
　　reasons for existence, 170
　　twelve-tone, 168
　　Universal Musical Grammar,
　　　169–70
musical grammar, description, 167

names, distinction from common
　　nouns by children, 106–7
Necker cube, 47
negative sentences, acquisition by
　　children, 109–10
Newport, E., 123, 124
noun phrase, 66, 81
nouns, 67
　　inability to occur with direct
　　　object, 75
　　Universal Grammar, 81
　　see also parts of speech

Paradox of Language Acquisition,
　　26–31, 61–2, 190
　　American Sign Language, 96
Parkinson's disease, 145

parts of speech,
  not definable in terms of
    meaning, 68–9
  see also nouns; prepositions;
    syntactic structure; verbs
past tense, 70, 110, 115
Patterson, F., 136
personal relationships, innate, 214
PET scans, 142
phonological structure, 41–2,
    53–65
  definition, 55
  speech sounds, 57–61
pidgin language, 130–5
plurals, 58–60, 61–2, 108, 115
pointing gestures, 127
possession, 197
preposition, 22–3, 67, 68, 71
  see also parts of speech
pronoun, unpronounced, 77
psycholinguists, definition, 49

questions, 69–70, 76–8
  signal by intonation, 95

reading, 25, 139, 147–8
reading/writing system and
    speaking/hearing system,
    psychological distinction, 44
recursion, 74
rhyming words, 189
Rumbaugh, D. 136

Savage-Rumbaugh, S., 136
second-person pronoun, 186
sentence construction,
  evidence of use of rules in
    children, 107–11
  genetic impairment of language
    acquisition, 115
  see also syntactic structure
sentences, meaning of, 188
sign language,
  teaching to apes, 136–7
  see also American Sign Language
Skinner, B.F., *Verbal Behavior*, ix
social organization,
  Argument for Construction of
    Experience, 209, 211–12
  Argument for Innate Knowledge,
    209

Argument for Mental Grammar,
    208–9
  see also culture
social perception, brain
    specializations, 210–12
social understanding,
  basis of, 212–14
  dominance, 213–14
  empathy, 217–18
  group membership, 212–13
spatial relations between objects,
    191–4
specific language impairment,
    113–16
speech sound production, 54
speech sounds,
  distinctive features, 57–8
  internal structure, 57–61
  variations in acoustic signals, 63
spoken language,
  experience constructed by
    hearer's mental grammar,
    161–4
  relationship to written language,
    44
Stokoe, W., 86
Supalla, T., 123
syllables, counting and use by
    children, 25
syntactic patterns, examples in
    English, 70–3
syntactic structure, 41–2, 66–82
  American Sign Language, 89,
    94–5
  distinction from meaning, 68–70,
    185–6
  distinction from phonological
    structure, 66–7
  Universal Grammar, 80–2
  see also parts of speech

Talmy, L., 194
Terrace, H., 136
third-person pronouns, American
    Sign Language, 90
time concepts, 197
Trubetzkoy, N., 57
Turner's Syndrome, 116

unconscious patterns, acquiring
    unconsciously, 25

Universal Grammar, 28, 164, 205
  description, 159–60
  exclusivity to humans, 138
  inflectional endings, 116
  sign languages, 96–7
  syntactic structure, 80–2
Universal Musical Grammar,
  169–70

verb phrase, 68, 71–2, 81
verbs, 205
  American Sign Language, 90–4
  Universal Grammar, 81
  see also parts of speech
Victor, Wild Boy of Aveyron, 120
vision, 171–83
  Argument for Construction of
    Experience, 177, 179
  Argument for Innate Knowledge,
    177, 179
  Argument for Mental Grammar,
    177, 179
  Contour Principle, 176
  illusions, 46–8, 173–7
  impossible figures, 176
  pattern of one object partly
    occluding another, 173–4
visual images, inadequacy as vehicle
  of thought, 187–8
visual perception, innate, 178
visual understanding, 172, 177
  conforming to ideal forms,
    180–3
    examples showing tolerance of
      deviation, 180–2
    using A's and H's, 180–1
  infants, 178–9

vocabulary acquisition, 102–3, 121,
  122
  apes, 137–8
  without early verbal
    communication, 122
vocal tract, 54
voice recognition, 63–4, 210
vowel sounds, variation of
  frequencies used, 63

Weir, R., 102
Wernicke, K., 146, 148–9
Wernicke's aphasia, 146–7, 148,
  150, 151
wh-questions, 76–7
  American Sign Language, 89
  children learning to form, 108–9
wh-words, 76–7, 81, 205
  movement to beginning of
    sentence, 77–8
Whorf, B.L., 186
Whorf Hypothesis, 186
wild children, 120
Williams Syndrome, 116–17
word boundaries, 56–7
word order, 70
  children, 103
  comparisons of different
    languages, 69–70, 71–2
  Creole, 132
  pidgin language, 131
  where verbal communication
    withheld in early years, 122
words,
  children learning by parental
    instruction, 21–2
  meanings, 189, 190, 202–3
  see also vocabulary acquisition